GYPSY EMPIRE

www.transworldbooks.c
www.transworldireland

GYPSY EMPIRE

Uncovering the Hidden World
of Ireland's Travellers

Eamon Dillon

TRANSWORLD IRELAND

TRANSWORLD IRELAND
An imprint of The Random House Group Limited
20 Vauxhall Bridge Road, London SW1V 2SA
www.transworldbooks.co.uk

GYPSY EMPIRE
A TRANSWORLD IRELAND BOOK: 9781848271692
First published in 2013 by Transworld Ireland,
a division of Transworld Publishers

Addresses for Random House Group Ltd companies outside the UK
can be found at: www.randomhouse.co.uk
The Random House Group Ltd Reg. No. 954009

The Random House Group Limited supports the Forest Stewardship Council® (FSC®),
the leading international forest-certification organisation. Our books carrying the FSC
label are printed on FSC®-certified paper. FSC is the only forest-certification scheme
supported by the leading environmental organisations, including Greenpeace. Our
paper procurement policy can be found at www.randomhouse.co.uk/environment

Typeset in 11/13pt Plantin Light by
Kestrel Data, Exeter, Devon.
Printed and bound by
CPI Group (UK) Ltd, Croydon, CR0 4YY.

2 4 6 8 10 9 7 5 3 1

Contents

THE TRAVELLER TRADERS

Introduction

Irish Travellers are a bright light burning furiously. They constitute a young community in Ireland, where more than half their people are under the age of twenty. Their average age is twenty-two compared to thirty-six in the wider society, according to Ireland's Central Statistics Office.

The origins of Irish Travellers are unclear. It is sometimes argued that they are the descendants of nomadic artisans and entertainers from as far back as the fifth century, and that the clans each stayed within the boundaries of one of the seven kingdoms of ancient Ireland, taking their names, such as Ward or McDonagh, from the reigning monarch.

They are a distinct social group, separate from the majority of Irish society. The last census in Ireland suggested that there are thirty thousand people in Ireland who regard themselves as Irish Travellers. There is a similar number living in the UK. In the UK they are recognized as a separate ethnicity, and they are now claiming a similar status in Ireland. As a community, their population is much the same size as that of a town such as Tralee in Ireland or Cleethorpes in England – not very big. It is estimated that there are another thirty thousand Travellers in the United States, made up of both recent arrivals and those descended from immigrants who arrived in the nineteenth and early twentieth centuries.

Many Travellers speak their own dialect or 'gammon' which, to an outsider, is as indecipherable as any exotic language. There is debate about whether it is a true language with its own grammar and structure, or is merely a verlan, or an argot, based on English and using coded or corrupted words from English, Gaelic and Latin. Irish Travellers are a separate entity from Roma Gypsies and from the English Traveller community, but the term 'Gypsy' is often applied to Irish Travellers – as it is to the Sinti people in Germany or the Kale from the Iberian peninsula. In their own language Irish Travellers refer to themselves as *Pavee*.

A key feature of Irish Traveller life is the longing to be nomadic. Different families have different approaches to being on the road. Some may spend extended periods, lasting several years, constantly moving between camp-sites across dozens of countries, while others may never leave their home, be it a caravan or a house. This aspect of Traveller life is often expressed through their love of horses and their attachment to the piebald and skewbald ponies used to race their sulkies on Sunday mornings.

In contrast to the wider community, many but not all Traveller families prefer to live in close proximity to members of their own extended clan. This applies to both those who spend their time travelling and those who prefer a more sedentary lifestyle. This clannishness is one of those aspects of Traveller life that can provoke fear and anger among their neighbours in the wider community.

Irish Travellers have remained marginalized from the rest of society. This is due in part to the conscious choice of Travellers to remain separate, but also because state policies in Ireland and the UK have failed to come up with any strategies for better integration.

This failure to find common ground is most obvious when it comes to accommodation for Travellers. Large-scale halting sites developed without permission can flare up into major sources of controversy, as evidenced by the row over Dale Farm in Essex that culminated in the enforced clearance of the site in 2011. In Ireland, houses bought for Traveller families have been burned down to prevent them moving in, while specifically built accommodation has been destroyed in the course of inter-Traveller feuds.

Any Irish journalist working a crime beat will at some point end up reporting on Irish Travellers. This is not because Travellers are any more naturally predisposed to committing crime or falling victim to it than any other section of society, but because many of them live on the margins of society, where those kinds of bad things happen. If a town of the same population were generating as many crime stories for the media, it would raise the question: 'What the hell is going on?'

The Irish Prison Service doesn't keep count of the number of Irish Travellers who are incarcerated. In an effort to obtain this information I recently spoke to contacts in the jail system. That day, when the prison population was around 3,500, my sources came back with approximate figures totalling 340, suggesting around 9 per cent of prisoners were Travellers. To put that into perspective, if the number of Traveller prisoners was in proportion to their size in the wider population, then there should have been just twenty-one in prison that day. Even if my estimated figure had been twice the actual number it would still have been way out of synch. If it was a town, the Irish Traveller community would need to have its own jail the size of Castlerea Prison in Roscommon, which is one of Ireland's eleven closed institutions for people in custody.

In Ireland bail can only be refused to accused people who

are likely to pose a threat to witnesses or to run away at the first opportunity. Those who don't have a fixed address are caught under the second requirement. People who ascribe to a nomadic lifestyle such as Irish Travellers, even if they do have a permanent address, are likely to be denied bail on the same grounds – which may explain their over-representation in the prison system. Notwithstanding this mitigating factor, the only conclusion to be drawn from my unscientific research is that Irish Travellers appear more likely than most to be put in jail.

Another explanation is that crime is endemic within their community. There is no doubt that the Irish Traveller community has its problems. According to the National Traveller Suicide Awareness Project, the suicide rate among Travellers is six times higher than in the general population. Life expectancy is also much lower. The statistics don't exist, but I'm sure, from speaking to members of the community, that Irish Travellers are also over-represented in fatal road accidents. But there is also a serious criminal element within the community, which is involved in full-scale organized crime. These individuals hold a disproportionate sway over other Travellers, who don't entirely trust the wider society. The deep-seated reasons for such a high rate of criminal activity are best explored by qualified sociologists.

Many of the individuals most widely known among the Irish Travellers as being involved in sharp business practice and outright criminality were written about in my book *The Outsiders: Exposing the Secretive World of Ireland's Travellers*. Since that book was published in 2006 some of these colourful characters have featured in other mainstream media. As a result the wider community has become increasingly aware of the existence of Irish Travellers as a distinct and separate community both in Ireland and the UK. The documentary *Knuckle* won praise at the Sundance Film Festival in Utah, where it was shown in 2011. It featured bare-knuckle fighter James Quinn-McDonagh and his brother Mikey. The filmmakers were given unprecedented access and produced a stylish movie that provided an insight into Irish Travellers, delivering it to a wide audience. Around the same time Channel 4's *Big Fat Gypsy Weddings* became a huge ratings hit. Six million people watched one episode of the reality TV show, which followed young Gypsy and Traveller girls as they prepared for their weddings. That, in turn, introduced bare-knuckle fighter Paddy Doherty to a television audience that went on to vote him the winner of *Celebrity Big Brother*. The sudden and successful appearances of Travellers and Gypsies on mainstream television touched on the wider community's huge and somewhat contradictory curiosity about this nomadic people, who cling to their traditions in the face of hostility.

Gypsy Empire provides a snapshot of Irish Travellers under three main headings, none of which were dealt with by those TV shows. Firstly, it deals with feud violence between clans and the horrific brutality meted out to people who are sometimes closely related to each other. In a small community such violence has reverberations that can span decades, ensuring that the cycle can erupt again in subsequent generations. As the stories of the killings of Michael Faulkner, Charlie McDonagh or John Mongan will show, such dreadful attacks have a devastating effect on everyone involved. The level of animosity between extended clans can materially affect where people can live, go to the shops or even where they can park their car. These incidents usually result in a brief upsurge in media interest in Irish Travellers and the reasons why such attacks take place. Such interest rarely lasts too long.

Secondly, the book takes the reader into the world of the bare-knuckle boxers. These are the elite among the hard men of the community. They are willing to risk their dearly held personal pride and honour to make public challenges against equally determined and proud men. Like the feuding, the shock waves from a disputed bout can spill over into the rest of the Traveller community. The disputes behind the fights are never brought to a resolution even when a clear winner emerges. To some extent it is among the bare-knuckle boxers that the integration with wider society is at its most successful. Dan Rooney, now a born-again Christian, was lionized in his native Crossmaglen and by Traveller and 'country people' alike. Members of the clans who put a large store in boxing have produced notable Olympic-level amateur fighters as well as an impressive cohort of professional boxers. In the ring, fighters such as Tyson Fury, Michael Armstrong and Willie Casey are judged solely on what they can do with their fists.

Thirdly, *Gypsy Empire* explores the world of the Traveller traders, some of whom are multimillionaires. More than anyone else, the Traveller traders confound the stereotype of scruffy scrap dealers, scraping a living on the edge of society. While some operate in the legitimate world, dealing in garden furniture, antiques and household items, others have turned illicit trading and rogue building work into an art form. Irish Travellers appear to have cornered the global market in supplying antique rhino horns to the traditional Chinese medical market. Skilled salesmen can effortlessly sell tarmac deals to unsuspecting householders in dozens of languages in a multimillion black-market industry. Their influence has extended to the four corners of the world, and regardless of the enterprise or scheme each one shows a remarkable ingenuity. Five years after I wrote about a Traveller teenager jailed for organized tobacco-smuggling in Belgium, he was jailed again in the United States for rhino-horn smuggling.

This book hasn't been written to bolster anyone's prejudices towards Irish Travellers. Nomads haven't felt welcome since the Mongol warriors of the thirteenth century cut swathes through the serried ranks of European soldiers. But that can hardly be the origin of the irrational response that many normally right-thinking people can have when it comes to Irish Travellers. Travellers are blamed for widespread criminality and grotesque antisocial behaviour and are seen as responsible for creating the straitened circumstances in which many of their families live. If anything, by separating individuals from the collective, *Gypsy Empire* opens up the idea that Irish Travellers, like everyone else, are ordinary and extraordinary people too. *Gypsy Empire* provides a snapshot of those Travellers who have a high profile within and without their community.

There is no such thing as a typical Traveller, and to a large extent *Gypsy Empire* is all about the atypical characters. Over the years of writing for the *Sunday World*, I focused on people who would have preferred to stay in the shadows. They included dealers in stolen antiques, bank-robbers and drug-dealers. There were also sinister figures who forced protection money from other Travellers and the highly organised ram-raider gangs who carried out a prolific number of robberies. There were multilingual con-artists who travelled the highways and byways of Europe. They also did deals in Asia, China and the United States. There were likeable rogues and unstable psychopaths, along with foolish youngsters led unwittingly into deep, deep trouble. I have met Irish Travellers who have lavished money on ornate properties and spent more than the average worker's annual salary on a wedding for their teenage daughter. There are those who have reached the heights of Olympic athleticism, and others who have turned welfare dependency into a profitable, illicit business. Their resourcefulness and ingenuity has allowed Irish Travellers to set up deals and scams all over the world.

Such stories don't tally with the narrative regularly presented in the media of a community oppressed by prejudice and imprisoned by poverty. Neither do they reflect the reality of those families who are mired in straitened circumstances. The truth is not black and white. There are rich and poor as well as the noble and the criminal among Travellers, just as there are in the wider society.

THE FEUDS

1

Kingdom of Fear

In modern western societies the blood-feud is largely a thing of the past. Destructive and wasteful, feuds between rival factions are limited to organized criminal gangs, whose leaders derive their power from their reputation. Vendettas are all about protecting the family honour and saving face against slurs, insults and physical attacks. Such feuds are alive and well in many parts of the world where societies are based on tribal and clan networks. For a clan in the wilds of Pakistan's north-west frontier or among the deserts of southern Yemen, to slip down the hierarchy is to court disaster and even annihilation in a world where central governments have no writ. Simple disputes, if handled badly by clan elders, can develop into long-standing inter-generational feuds that rumble on years after the initial conflict has been forgotten.

This sense of remoteness and distance from the machinery of the state that deals with personal disputes is shared by many Irish Travellers. Their natural instinct seems to be to sort out a dispute among themselves rather than resorting to a third party to find or impose a solution. When there's a wild and impulsive response to a problem, violence can quickly get out of hand. In tight-knit Traveller clans news of an act of violence or even a public threat is quickly transmitted throughout the extended family, sometimes in an exaggerated tone or an embellished version that serves to stoke tensions. It is a Pandora's box of emotion that once opened is very difficult to shut again. The voices of reason, usually from the women, are too weak and easily ignored. The shocking level of violence used, the overkill, in many cases is in itself a form of communication, as if it's not just enough to murder a bitter rival. Retribution has to be bloody, savage and a warning to others.

Such killings have been shown to be premeditated, yet they are executed in an impulsive fashion, the attackers often making no attempt to hide their identities from witnesses. The message seems to be that there is no point in killing a person for family honour if no one knows who did it. Quite often there is little interest in finding a solution to a feud – as if the dispute itself is as important as a clan leader's reputation. Only when the heavy hand of the state gets involved, and jail sentences are being handed down or allowed to hang over the heads of those participating in feud violence, is a peaceful alternative found.

In 2004 there was one such feud-related killing in County Kerry that left the wider community as well as Travellers horrified. It was the brutal slaying of a man in front of his young son and neighbours.

On Ireland's south-west coast, County Kerry's picturesque mountains, lakes and bays have made it a natural tourist destination. The people who live there are rightly proud of their home and refer to it as 'the Kingdom'. Over the years there have been additions made to Kerry's natural attractions to help the tourist trade. Created in the 1950s, the Rose of Tralee has been a boon for the industry in the north County Kerry town. The hotels are always booked out and the final stages of the competition are televised live on the national broadcaster, RTÉ.

At the official event in the Dome, the men in black-tie suits and the women in their ballgowns are dolled up for what was once Ireland's most glamorous television event. Outside, the rest of the revellers and the various hangers-on get stuck into the beer. Just as the Dome is always full, so too are the pubs. There are outdoor events and music and plenty of booze. Sometimes the beer-fuelled boisterous crowd can get a little out of hand. The Croppy Boy statue in the town's main thoroughfare has, at times, been the target of tanked-up festival-goers looking for an elevated vantage point. The festival goes on for the week, and the annual horse-racing festival then takes over, ensuring as many people as possible give the hospitality trade a boost before the summer season finally comes to a close.

It wouldn't have been unusual to have seen Michael Faulkner walking back to his home in Tralee at Mitchel's Crescent after enjoying the atmosphere and a couple of pints. It was a Monday night, just after 11.15 p.m., at the start of the week-long festival. A father of six, the 43-year-old Traveller had no background in criminality and would have been largely unknown to the wider community. However, he wasn't a man to back down from an argument, especially if he had been drinking. A little tired perhaps, Faulkner rested against the bonnet of a car near his house where he was seen by his son Patrick, then aged eleven. Unworried, the young lad ran home where he poured himself a bowl of breakfast cereal and waited for his father to follow him to the house. He went back outside to check on his dad's progress. Young Patrick then witnessed one of the most brutal killings in the feuds that exist between Ireland's Traveller clans.

A van drew up close to Faulkner and from it jumped Michael McCarthy, a much younger man. Armed with a slash hook, he went to attack Faulkner who, despite the booze, was able to fend off the initial onslaught and forced

McCarthy to drop the weapon. He then picked it up and smashed the windscreen of McCarthy's van. The older man seemed to have got the advantage, but two other men with McCarthy intervened and Faulkner was felled to the ground. McCarthy picked up the slash hook and began to hack at and stab Faulkner as he lay prone. Faulkner suffered horrific injuries, with part of his jaw being severed, and deep abdominal wounds. The youngster raised the alarm as the attackers drove away from the scene. Not long afterwards Faulkner was declared dead in the nearby regional hospital. Within a few hours McCarthy, who had made no attempt to disguise himself, was arrested by Gardaí.

It soon emerged that there had been a festering feud between some members of the Faulkner and McCarthy families. It also included individuals from the O'Brien, Coffey and Quilligan families who were also related to the rival factions. The latest round of violence had its origins in a row at a wedding more than twelve years previously. In the lead-up to Michael Faulkner's murder there had been more than half a dozen violent incidents in the County Kerry towns of Tralee and Killarney between members of these two extended families. One of Michael's brothers had taken things seriously enough to have sent two sons to live in Cork to avoid being caught up in the tit-for-tat violence. Yet despite the skirmishes, the level of violence used against Michael Faulkner was a huge shock to both Travellers and the wider community. There had been nothing in the previous incidents to suggest that the feud could escalate so quickly to such a lethal level. Judging by Michael Faulkner's own relaxed attitude to his safety it wasn't something he had envisaged either.

In the immediate aftermath of the murder feelings ran high. Michael was brought back to his native Knocknaheeny in Cork for burial after an emotional funeral. There were at least four hundred friends and relatives at the ceremony who had travelled from all over Ireland to show their respects. Chief among them were Michael's wife Nora and their children. At St Mary's on the Hill Church one man in tears and clearly angry began shouting during the Mass: 'The dirty tramps, the bastards, they used everything they had on him.' Other relatives calmed him down, but later there were distressing scenes as family members clutched at Michael Faulkner's white casket before it was lowered into the ground in St Catherine's Cemetery in Kilcully on the northern outskirts of Cork city.

During the Mass Father Damian O'Mahony appealed to the mourners for reflection and restraint, reminding them that enough heartbreak had already been caused by this man's death:

> There are so many emotions here today, and sometimes
> emotion can get the better of us and we may do something
> or say something that is totally out of character, and that
> can lead to even more pain and more suffering and more
> misery. And that's the last thing anyone would want to
> happen – there's enough heartache, enough suffering,
> enough tears in this church to last a lifetime.

At first, it seemed the priest's wise words fell on deaf ears. Michael's brother John refused to call for an end to the long-simmering feud which had cost Michael his life. He told the *Sunday World* just days later:

> This is far from over. They think they are going to get
> away with the murder, but they won't. I've told the Gardaí
> I've called for a truce for the next two or three weeks,
> but after that I don't know what will happen. There are
> long, dark, winter nights ahead. I don't drink or smoke
> so I wasn't out with Michael as he walked home. I was in

watching the Rose of Tralee. It scares me when I think of all them drinking and having fun while my brother lay dying on the road.

He claimed that three years previously Michael had been the target of another murder attempt, and that another family member had suffered a bad beating but had been too frightened to report it to the Gardaí:

> But Michael's murder has changed how we feel. We are angry about this and something is going to happen, I know that. The guards are doing the best they can but, Jesus, they murdered him. They even taunted him hours before he was killed, saying, 'You're dead, you bastard, you bad breed.' I want to see what happens during the truce. These people, these animals, knew Michael was drunk and they were waiting on him. They're the worst you could ever meet. I've been hoping for peace for years but it never happens and now I think it may be too late.

Fears of retaliation, however, were to prove unfounded. The killing had left family members distraught, but willing to let the Gardaí do their job and build a case against the killers. In the event, Michael McCarthy was charged with the murder in a case that went to trial nearly two years after the fatal attack. The week-long hearing at the Central Criminal Court sitting in Cork heard a pathologist's details of the injuries Michael Faulkner had received. Even the detached clinical atmosphere of a courtroom couldn't disguise the visceral brutality which had left Faulkner to die on the street. He had suffered two serious injuries to the jaw, one of which completely severed a section of his jawbone, with three teeth attached. He had also been stabbed in the back. A wound to his abdomen had left his guts literally hanging out. Pathologist Margaret Bolster told the court he had died from asphyxia relating to 'a mechanical interference with breathing'. He had died after choking on his own blood.

The trial heard eyewitness evidence from his son Patrick, then a thin young boy. Recalling the incident, Patrick said: 'I saw Michael McCarthy at the back of the van – he went and pulled out a slash hook in his right hand and threw it at my father on his left-hand side. My father caught it and he took it off him – my father caught it with both hands.' Patrick described how his father had hit the front window of the van with the slash hook, but that another man had come up behind him: 'He hit him with something to the side of the jaw – my dad fell back on his back. Michael McCarthy hit him two to three times with the slash hook. It fell out of my father's hands.' There was a poignancy to the testimony given by Patrick through a video link to the court. No child should have to witness a parent's brutal murder and then face a cross-examination of what they recall having seen.

In doing their job, McCarthy's defence team tried to persuade the jury that the Faulkner family members who had witnessed the attack had rehearsed their stories. Michael Faulkner's niece Amanda had been babysitting at a nearby house when the attack took place. 'I was throwing something into the bin and I heard Michael saying, "Help, help,"' she said. During her cross-examination she said she had seen McCarthy hit her uncle, 'into the stomach – he had a slash hook. I was two doors down – I had a clear view. He was on the ground. The blood was everywhere.' She also said that she had clearly seen McCarthy drive away in his wine-coloured van: 'He was wearing a white T-shirt and my uncle was in a black jacket, blue shirt and blue jeans.'

'I have to say to you that you are very, very wrong –

you didn't see Michael McCarthy behaving like that,' suggested defence barrister Anthony Sammon.

She replied simply: 'I did.'

Michael Faulkner's brother John also said he had seen the accused man attack his brother. 'I saw my brother on the ground. I saw Michael McCarthy driving a slash hook through my brother. After it he put the slash hook into the van and drove off in the Ballymullen direction.' The defence again suggested that his testimony might not be true, but he stuck to his guns: 'There are no lies – that's the man who killed my brother.' He explained that on that night he had been about to have a cup of tea in his own house after breaking up a row between Michael and another man, unrelated to the McCarthy family. He said he gave the other man a lift away from Mitchel's Crescent because he felt that his brother was 'in his face'.

Questioned about the veracity of his evidence John Faulkner replied from the witness box: 'You accused my daughter of telling lies yesterday. That is the man who murdered my brother.' He pointed at McCarthy. He explained that there had been tension between the two families for fifteen or sixteen years. 'They are the people who do the physical. We don't do the physical. My brothers, sisters and sons had to leave Kerry over these people,' he said in his evidence. He added that things had happened between the families and they were unlikely to stop. Asked if he was simply repeating a statement which he had learned off by heart John Faulkner said:

By heart? Two years I seen that man in my eyes killing my brother with my nephew beside him. My brother down on the ground and this man, the pure force of the slash hook. Why didn't he break his legs and arms? I seen him the same as I am looking at him now.

He also said that he had seen McCarthy throw a slash hook into the van after the attack. Forensic scientists later gave evidence of discovering flesh stuck to a black mat in McCarthy's van which DNA analysis established as being that of Michael Faulkner.

In the event, McCarthy admitted a charge of assault and the state dropped the murder prosecution. The court heard that, while the initial confrontation was between Michael McCarthy and Michael Faulkner, two other men became involved in the fracas and one of them might have inflicted the fatal wound. McCarthy's defence lawyer told Judge Paul Carney that his client had made a plea for both families to end the 'futile' feud. On behalf of McCarthy, it was said that the feud had begun in England years ago, though no one could remember the precise cause, and that this lay behind the confrontation which had cost Michael Faulkner his life. 'Michael McCarthy was just nine or ten years of age when all of this started,' his lawyer said. The court also heard that Michael McCarthy had himself been attacked by a member of the Faulkner family when he was just seventeen, which had left him with bad scarring to his arms and hands.

In jailing McCarthy for six years, Judge Paul Carney said that the case was no longer a murder and that that was reflected in the sentence. He said that the assault on Michael Faulkner was 'most vicious in character', and that anyone who armed themselves with a slash hook to commit an assault on another person would have to face the full consequences.

Yet despite the apology delivered through Michael McCarthy's counsel there was little sign of the tragedy helping either side to back down from the feud. Reckless violence had brought the two clans to this point. At no stage did the protagonists seem to have taken stock or reflected on the self-destructive nature of their interaction. Neither did they seem to have the ability to put it behind them. As he was led away by jailers to serve his sentence McCarthy was verbally abused by members of the Faulkner clan. He hissed back at them: 'Fuck yiz.'

He wasn't the only one sentenced as a result of the court case. During the court proceedings Gardaí had to maintain a heavy security presence to keep the rival clan members apart. Tensions were high at Cork Circuit Court throughout the six-day trial. One morning, as the judge waited to hear evidence, John Faulkner, a young relative of the victim (and who shared a name with the victim's brother), lashed out and kicked Patrick McCarthy, the accused man's father, in the head. 'I will kill you,' he threatened, before Garda officers were able to restrain him. Another relative, Charles Faulkner, also made threats and tried to get at members of the McCarthy family. The judge and jury both witnessed the sudden fracas.

The two attackers were immediately remanded in custody by Judge Carney after being arrested by Gardaí on duty in the court. Later they were brought back in front of the judge for a brief hearing in which the Gardaí gave evidence of the incident. Judge Carney told the men that they would be prosecuted for contempt. 'I have unlimited powers of fine and imprisonment – this is an extremely serious matter,' he said, remanding the two men back into custody until the following week. Carney took a hard-line view of the courtroom fracas, and when they appeared before him again he said that their conduct struck at the very root of a criminal trial. 'This has nothing to do with disrespect to the court and it has nothing to do with the dignity of the court. This is all about protecting the integrity of a criminal trial,' he said.

John Faulkner, then aged twenty-three, with over sixty previous convictions, was jailed for four months, while Charles Faulkner, aged twenty-seven at the time, with over forty previous convictions, was sentenced to one month in prison. The relative youth of these men who had tried to take the law into their own hands underlines how feuding cuts across the generations. It's no wonder that young Traveller men can notch up a long list of previous convictions when they are literally born into feuds not of their making. It is bred into their psyche, and even as children they will have witnessed atrocious acts of self-perpetuating violence. This wouldn't be the last time the bitter enmity between the clans in County Kerry would erupt during courtroom proceedings.

Two years after McCarthy was sent down to do his jail time, the constant threat of violence still hung over various Traveller clans in County Kerry. Traveller organizations such as the Irish Traveller Movement tried to mediate, and local politicians raised the issue at meetings and through the media. It was claimed that residents living in Mitchel's Crescent were frightened of being caught up in the violence and wanted to get out of the area. For Traveller families who had nothing to do with the feud things were even worse. Simply because of their family name or through marriage they were identified as being part of one faction or the other. Some women needed Garda escorts simply to bring kids to school or to do their shopping. Other families felt they had to abandon their houses and move to unauthorized halting sites to find respite from the ongoing threats and intimidation.

One of those badly affected was Michael Faulkner's son Patrick, who had witnessed the terrible slaying of his father in 2004. His cousin Michael O'Brien explained how teenager Patrick was still the target of abuse and physical attacks, while his own children were also singled out by some members of the McCarthy family. O'Brien claimed that his own son, then aged just nine, was punched and kicked by a nineteen-year-old and told that his father would be castrated. He told the author in an interview with the *Sunday World*:

> I've tried to go the right way on this and reported
> things to the guards. My uncle wrote to the Garda
> Commissioner and made loads of complaints to the
> guards before he was killed. If they're not brought up
> the steps of the court it won't stop. I'm going to the law
> for three years and I am getting no law.

The vicious nature of the verbal threats as well as the indiscriminate violence against children provide an insight into the apparently intractable nature of the feud. O'Brien said his family had been targeted because he was the oldest male member of the family who had stuck it out living in Tralee. The nature of the attacks also had the potential to inspire revenge actions, which would keep the spiral of violence spinning. 'If I had got hold of him, I would have done something that would have put me in prison. I don't want that to happen,' said O'Brien of the teenager alleged to have assaulted his young son. He went on:

> I don't fear for myself, it's for my kids. They are trying to
> get at me through others. We did nothing and we are the
> ones getting attacked. It's not all the McCarthys, it's just
> a minority. They want the whole town for themselves. I
> want my wife and family to be able to stay in Tralee.

He expressed the fear that the Gardaí were reluctant to get involved in cases between Travellers even where there was independent evidence and eyewitnesses to the incidents. 'It's like 1980s England where the police didn't care about black-on-black violence. They just say it's between Travellers,' he claimed.

In reality the Gardaí had been very busy in Tralee and

north Kerry as members of the feuding families continued to target one another. Public Order Units were called out in May 2009 and deployed in the town after information emerged that a large number of weapons including hatchets and knives had been bought locally. The following month scuffles broke out at Rath Cemetery, spilling out on to the busy main road for a while. Then in July 2009 Gardaí from as far away as Cork had to be drafted into the town again to maintain order between the feuding sides. Fighting lasted for at least nine hours and spilled out into the grounds of Tralee General Hospital, where those injured had sought treatment. A mob of over two dozen masked men attacked a house in Tralee in October as the large-scale disturbances rumbled on. It took a huge effort on the part of state agencies to impose law and order on these two Traveller clans determined to attack one another. It was as if nothing had been learned from the tragedy of Michael Faulkner's death.

In November 2009 a Public Order Unit kitted out in riot gear sat in a bus close to the courthouse in Tralee. The building itself was lined with uniformed officers. Everyone was searched and checked as they entered. Even inside the lobby, visitors had to walk through two lines of officers to get into the courtroom. Inside, more officers stood around, filling the aisle which ran down the middle of the seating area for members of the public. Every doorway and possible flashpoint was closely guarded. A total of thirty-two men were charged with a wide variety of offences. With people from both sides now sharing space in a relatively small room, the officers on duty had their hands full keeping a lid on the hotheads ready and waiting to battle each other.

A court hearing the previous month had had to be adjourned as fighting had broken out on the street outside. A group of Gardaí managed to separate the two sides after a fracas between up to thirty people broke out. Traffic was blocked while the sides squared up to each other until the Gardaí restored order. Officers inside the court were also able to keep the rival factions apart before any fighting erupted. It later emerged at another court hearing that the fighting began when members of the Coffey clan drove by and began shouting abuse at Quilligan clan members who had congregated on the steps of the courthouse. (The Quilligans would have been seen as siding with the McCarthys against the O'Brien and the Faulkner clan.) They in turn charged down the steps in pursuit of those who had been taunting them. This time the Gardaí had mounted a large and expensive operation to ensure that the administration of justice could go ahead.

The accused men were outnumbered by Gardaí by two to one but even that didn't stop incidents forcing Gardaí to make arrests in front of the judge. Stressed and obviously angry, one of the defendants clashed with one of the officers. He tried to leave the courtroom to go for a cigarette but told a sergeant to, 'Fuck off', when ordered to sit back down. Within the hour the same officer was giving evidence of arrest, charge and caution in relation to the incident as the man was charged with abusive behaviour. Later in the day he was jailed for eight months for making threats to slit the throat of a Martin Quilligan and for public affray.

The day-long hearings illustrated the difficulties faced by the criminal justice system when dozens of Traveller men decide to engage in feud violence with one another. The shared surnames and the chaotic nature of the offences added to the difficulty the Gardaí had when trying to quell Traveller factions determined to attack each other. Among those charged and appearing in court that day were three different Francie O'Briens, three Jimmy Quilligans and two Patrick McCarthys. Dozens of weapons were brought in by Gardaí in evidence bags. They included chair-legs, slash hooks, pitchforks, hurleys, golf clubs, iron bars, samurai swords and knives, as well as five shotguns and two handguns which had been seized over the previous year.

The atmosphere remained tense throughout the day. During the lunch break one of the factions, which included members of the O'Brien and Coffey families, was held back while the Quilligans were allowed to leave. They were led down the street by Patrick 'The Punk' Quilligan as they marched together en masse. During the afternoon session there were some interruptions as shouting broke out in the corridor outside the courtroom. Those who stood up in the public gallery were ordered to sit down again as Judge James O'Connor continued to work methodically through the various charge sheets. One man got four months for a mob attack on a house, while another got five months for an opportunistic attack carried out in revenge. By the end of the day eighteen men had been jailed for taking part in the long series of tit-for-tat attacks.

The large-scale faction-fights in 2009 were the most visible manifestations of the intractable vendettas that can lurk beneath the surface of Traveller society. The various court hearings provided an insight into how such a feud can feed on itself, providing new fuel for the fire with every incident and every witness statement made in court. The young teenagers and children who have been caught up in mob attacks and who have been the target of violence grow up with the pressure of defending their family's honour. In the years since Michael Faulkner's brutal death feud violence has remained a constant presence in the lives of many Traveller families. Despite the efforts of mediators and individuals from both sides the potential for further incidents still remains.

2

Cut Down in London Town

Charlie 'Soldier' McDonagh is remembered by his family as a big, gentle giant. He was idolized by his wife Kathleen and their seven children. Despite the moniker 'Soldier', inherited from his father, he was a world apart from the image of a bare-knuckle brawler – and the wretched violence that dogs the Irish Traveller community. The nickname came from the fact that members of his family had served in the Irish Defence Forces.

In a photograph taken at his daughter Nell Louise's first Holy Communion, Charlie poses for the cameras. He stands head and shoulders above the priest, a broad smile stretched across his clean-shaven face. With dark brown hair and strong features he cuts a handsome figure as he enjoys the family's day out. Kathleen holds their baby girl in her arms and with her right hand clutches the hand of their youngest boy. The event is an important landmark for young Irish Traveller families, who are not shy about being religious. Christenings, communions, weddings and funerals complete the full circle of life as organized by the Roman Catholic Church. Their oldest daughter Geraldine is already dressed up to grab the eye of a potential suitor. No doubt she already had plans in her head of how her wedding dress would look as her father gave her away. It is a proud moment for the family, living the Irish Traveller lifestyle in southern England.

Many members of the extended McDonagh family lived close by in Middlesex. Among them were Charlie's parents, Bernard and Geraldine, as well as some of his brothers and sisters. Once a Traveller clan are together they feel at home wherever they find themselves. Charlie McDonagh got by on social welfare and some of the off-the-books trading that is part and parcel of Traveller existence. His love for life was evident to all as he frequently belted out songs on the pub karaoke machine. Life in the sprawling western suburbs and satellites of London was no bed of roses, but things could have been worse.

For Kathleen and the children, however, things did become much worse on 5 March 2007. The night before another Irish Traveller living in the English capital had been attacked with a slash hook. Sitting in the Blues Bar in West Drayton, Brian Lawrence was unprepared for a sudden and violent onslaught. Without any warning, he was set upon by men wielding an array of makeshift weapons in a replay of the violent attacks which have claimed the lives of more than twenty Travellers over the last two decades. A slash hook was swung towards his head. Instinctively, Lawrence put his hand up to deflect the blow and the blade cut through his fingers. The damage done, the assailants ran from the pub and disappeared. The injuries were serious. Later, as his fearful and furious family gathered around his hospital bed, the surgeons were not sure if his hand could be saved.

Brian Lawrence pleaded for everyone to stay calm and not to seek revenge for the grisly assault. But his plea went unheeded. A large group of men, all close relations of Lawrence, set about getting back at those they believed responsible for the attack. The slash-hook attacker was known to them as being a relation of Charlie McDonagh.

They went off in search of blood. It was Old Testament time – an eye for an eye, blood for blood.

In fact, Charlie had no part in the attack on Brian Lawrence at the Blues Bar. No doubt he had heard about it, but it had nothing to do with him. As far as he was concerned it was business as usual, and that meant one of his regular trips to the pub. His family always knew where to find him. There was no malice or bravado about Charlie, and he had no idea that he could be the target of a group of young Travellers bent on exacting revenge. Unfortunately, in the tight world of Irish Travellers, just as his family knew where he would be, it was easy for anyone else to track him down. Like Brian Lawrence the night before, he was completely unprepared for the vengeful gang now searching for a target.

Charlie was as usual in the Great Western pub on Dawley Road with his wife Kathleen. Without warning, fourteen men, including members of the Lawrence clan, their faces masked, barged into the pub carrying axes, hatchets and samurai swords. They had travelled in convoy from the western suburbs of London, making the trek across the city to satiate their lust for vengeance. Charlie didn't have a chance. Before any stunned customers or Charlie's family could react, the mob of attackers singled out their prey. In front of his shocked family and pub regulars, they descended on him in a frenzy of hacking and stabbing, a visceral tribal assault. A hatchet blow struck him squarely in the face and a samurai sword was thrust into his chest. The attackers, bent on murder, inflicted deep wounds in what was a relentlessly savage attack, horrifying and inflicted without mercy. It was vicious, swift and lethal, lasting forty-seven seconds, all of which was chillingly captured on the pub's CCTV.

Charlie was left lying on the pub floor in a pool of his own blood. One of the weapons was still protruding from his body. His father Bernard compared the attack to a scene from the Discovery Channel in which a pack of wolves chase down and tear their prey apart. In the immediate aftermath a distraught Kathleen held her dying husband in her arms. The carnage Charlie's wife witnessed that day, and the memory of cradling her dying husband, will be with her for life.

As usual, in such attacks by Travellers on their own, the victims knew who was behind it. Even though the attackers had worn masks or covered their faces, the McDonagh family were able to identify them by their voices and clothing. The attackers even used each other's names and nicknames during the assault. It wasn't a tough job for the police to work out the identities of those involved. As well as cooperation from the shocked members of the McDonagh family they also had the camera footage, which captured the entire attack. The samurai sword was recovered at the scene and two brand-new hatchets were also found by police, which they hoped would yield forensic evidence.

The first to be arrested was William 'The Godfather' Lawrence, then aged just twenty-three. The day after the killing officers collared their man as he was due to board a flight to Dublin at Stansted Airport. Cousins Michael 'Fish' Lawrence (twenty-five) and Bernard 'Spike' Lawrence (twenty-two) were next as the investigating officers sought to track down as many of the mob as they could. The intense police investigation saw officers use DNA forensics to match up the sequence of events as recorded on the pub's security cameras. On 22 March, seventeen days after the brutal killing, the three cousins all appeared in court where they were charged with the murder of Charlie McDonagh. They spoke only to confirm their names and were remanded in custody.

It was three weeks before the funeral of Charlie

McDonagh could take place after the police finally released his body to his family. In the space of just a few months from Nell Louise's communion day, the family returned to the Immaculate Heart of Mary Church in Botwell Lane, but this time it was to bury Charlie. Hundreds of people lined the streets of Hayes, testament to the shock felt by the wider community at the brutal murder, as well as to the friendly nature of Charlie. Friends and family laid flowers outside the pub where he had died, which remained closed for the day of the funeral. Charlie was then brought to his final resting place at West Drayton Cemetery, where his heartbroken wife Kathleen became a frequent visitor.

Meanwhile, as the investigation progressed over the following months, cops were able to link William Lawrence with DNA evidence to the samurai sword found at the scene. The McDonagh family then had to steel themselves for the prospect of reliving the horrific attack in the sterile environs of a court. When the case came to trial at the Old Bailey, in March 2008, it was a fraught and tense affair as relatives from both sides of the divide packed into the courtroom. Extra police officers were on guard to prevent any outbreak of violence as emotions ran high among the Traveller families. The brutal nature of the killing was laid bare during the hearing. Kathleen listened as the prosecution explained in dry legal tones exactly how Charlie had been smashed in the face with a hatchet and how the samurai sword driven through his chest had most likely killed him.

William 'The Godfather' Lawrence didn't deny he was at the pub when Soldier McDonagh was cut down. But his defence took some believing. He maintained that he had gone to Dawley Road for a fist fight and just happened to pick up the sword for protection when he found it on the floor of the Great Western. The prosecution claimed that William Lawrence, then living at Upton Park, east London, carried out the vicious revenge attack in retaliation for the stabbing of Brian Lawrence by a relative of Charlie's. Witnesses from the McDonagh family said in court that they had heard him threaten at the hospital: 'Someone's going to die for this.'

Charlie McDonagh's family weren't happy with the attack being characterized as a feud between two Traveller families. They denied there had been a previous history of bad blood between the two clans and that the violence had originated with the attack on Brian Lawrence on 4 March 2007. When the three guilty verdicts were delivered at the Old Bailey there was chaos in the public gallery. Angry scenes erupted as about a hundred members of the killers' family screamed insults from the public gallery above Court 1. Members of Charlie's clan shouted back furiously – one man climbing on to the bench at the side of the court in a bid to reach those taunting his family. Members of the McDonagh clan were eventually led out of court, with the Lawrence cousins yelling at them as they were taken away to jail.

Judge Peter Rook hadn't been impressed by the three men's attempt to play down their part in the vicious hacking to death of Charlie McDonagh. At the sentence hearing just a year after McDonagh's death, he told the convicted men: 'This was a premeditated and well-planned attack. While Brian Lawrence didn't wish you to take the law into your own hands, you did, and by doing so you have let down your whole community. You took it upon yourselves to plan an execution. This was not spontaneous violence.' William 'The Godfather' Lawrence was convicted of murder and sentenced to life with a minimum term of twenty-two years. Cousins Bernard 'Spike' Lawrence and Michael 'Fish' Lawrence were ordered to serve at least eighteen years before parole was considered.

As the trial and sentence hearing came to a close there

was a brief insight into the self-perpetuating nature of inter-Traveller violence. One of Charlie's distraught young sons standing in the Old Bailey's public gallery shouted: 'They are fucking murdering bastards. They murdered my da.' Once again, the murder of a Traveller was having a profound effect on a young boy, who would struggle not to react to his wider family's need for revenge. Outside court, Detective Inspector Alan Baxter, who had led the police investigation, said: 'The men were described in court as "vigilantes", a description that is not without foundation.' They had taken part in a posse that had gone seeking redress for the attack on Brian Lawrence and exacted revenge on an innocent man.

The end of the court case didn't bring any closure for Charlie's widow. Nearly two years later Kathleen picked up the phone and spoke to the author at the *Sunday World* office in Dublin. She feared that the other eleven men involved had got away with their part in her husband's savage killing. In a low, shaky voice that betrayed her deep grief she spoke about how the murderous incident had destroyed her happy life and left her in an unending nightmare of personal despair:

> I don't want anyone to think I've forgotten about this. I cannot understand how these men can still be free for the brutal murder that I watched, as my husband died before my eyes. Nearly two years on and I am still watching my husband die every night when I close my eyes and try to sleep. There is an empty space in our lives where Charlie should be, he just lives in our hearts. The children still ask every day when is their daddy coming home? In my heart I will never forgive the cruel thing these men have done to destroy such a perfect life, because Charlie was such a kind and good husband and father, always happy, always laughing, never got into rows or arguments with anyone.

We used to go out every weekend, twice a week, now I never go out because I can never hear him laughing or speaking. It is sad to go anywhere. When everybody goes out, I sit at home crying, asking why my husband was murdered. I feel so lonely.

The case remains open according to Middlesex Police, who are still looking for a number of men in connection with the pub murder. A large group of the Lawrence clan moved back to Ireland shortly after the incident, presumably to avoid any potential fallout, revenge attacks or further police investigation. Some members of the group, relatives of those jailed for McDonagh's murder, have been involved in violent crime in Ireland. These include unreported attacks – aimed at extorting cash – on other members of the Travelling community.

Charlie's murder shows how feud violence, while sometimes well planned and clearly premeditated, can result in impulsively executed attacks. A snap decision can cause a festering grudge to escalate lethally. The ensuing actions, whether harmless threats or cruel killings, inevitably lead to another round of bad blood, the wrenching apart of families and the polarization of groups within an extended family. In the intense, closed world of the Irish Traveller, every violent action has ramifications that ripple for longer and more destructively than in the wider community. The personal cost and emotional toll on individuals can be huge and difficult to cope with. What Kathleen didn't say, in her quiet dignified way, was that as a Traveller widow she would be very unlikely ever to remarry. She would be left in the care of her husband's family to bring up her seven kids without their father. Conservative Traveller mores dictate that a widow, regardless of her age, should remain in mourning. For the widows, the tragedy never ends.

3

No Soothing Words

The deaths of Charlie McDonagh and Michael Faulkner have a lot in common. They were both fathers murdered in front of members of their families by multiple attackers. Neither man appeared to be worried that they could be the target of a lethal attack, and as a result their assailants knew where to find them. Neither were regarded as being prominent protagonists in any of the violence. They were singled out because of their family name or because the opportunity had presented itself. Both men would have known their attackers, and yet the level of violence used and the injuries sustained were truly horrific. They were both hacked to death by people wielding bladed weapons. While some Travellers were prosecuted and convicted for their part in the murderous assaults, others got away without sanction. The seeds of future trouble were sown at the moment of each murder.

Another common theme was the raw grief and emotion displayed by the close relatives of both Faulkner and McDonagh in the aftermath, at the funerals and interviews. Court hearings also became potential flashpoints as the authorities went about dealing with matters through the criminal justice system. It doesn't bode well for the ability of younger members of the clans to resist being sucked into future vendettas. Calmer heads struggle to prevail, so inter-Traveller feuds tend to erupt suddenly without much warning. By any standards these murders could be classified as hate crimes, committed by people unconcerned by the fact that their actions have the effect of tearing apart their own community.

At first glance, the murder of Tom Ward, a 23-year-old father of one, appeared to fit into the same category. His wife Cliona was expecting their second child when he was killed on 13 August 2007 near the family home at Joe McDonnell Drive in Cranmore, Sligo. He and his brother Charlie had a reputation for nuisance crime around the city, while his mother, Brigid, and his father, Tom Ward, had also notched up their share of District Court convictions over time. The young Traveller, who boxed in the ring with Ballina Boxing Club, had also represented Ireland in the Four Nations Amateur Championship. He worked hard at his fitness and as a keen runner was a regular figure pounding out the yards on Sligo racecourse.

The night he died, Tom had been out with relatives and Cliona, whom he had dropped back to the house. Suddenly, he was set upon by a group of men who tried to drag him from his Ford Transit van. In a bid to protect himself from his attackers, he managed to crawl under the vehicle. However, at least one of the assailants persevered with the assault and landed a single blow, most likely with a hatchet, to the back of Tom Ward's head. Awoken by the fracas, neighbours emerged to the sound of screams, shouts and women weeping as a car sped out of the estate into the night. Tom's family cradled him until the ambulance arrived and he was rushed to Sligo General. Nearly five hours after the attack he succumbed to the serious head injury he had suffered and was declared dead. His family were beside themselves with grief.

A Garda forensic team spent the rest of that Monday

at the scene examining the place where Ward had been fatally injured. As they wrapped up their work, taking away the tent protecting the spot where the young man had lain, his father fell to his knees. He reached out and touched the pool of congealed blood that had come from his stricken son and daubed his own cheeks. It was a visceral display of grief from Ward senior, who had to be helped away from the scene, barely able to walk. There was an agonizing three-day wait before the Gardaí were able to release Ward's body to his grieving family. His brother Charlie spoke to a reporter:

> We won't get over this at all. That's the truth. We just
> wish this never happened. He was a very dedicated runner
> and boxer. He never caused trouble or any bother. He was
> always out running. If he missed a day it would annoy
> him. He was always in good humour when he had his
> running done. God love him, it's an awful thing.

When Tom senior was later able to speak he said he wanted to see justice for his son. 'I hope the guards solve this. All I want from them is to see justice done. I just want peace and to get these people off our backs. I cannot get my head round it at all. They organized it and just came and done it.' As far as the Wards were concerned there was no doubt as to who was responsible for the killing, and there was a danger of reprisals.

Four days after the murder, Father Steve Walsh said at the young man's removal service that too much blood had already been spilled. He told the three hundred mourners that the nature of the 'cowardly act' meant that the family had to wait before they could grieve over his body. He was not oblivious to the concern that some form of retaliation could take place while emotions ran high. The priest urged the men of the family to stay cool and calm,

in this difficult situation and in the face of great
provocation, not just for themselves but for the sake
of their children and families. Too many women have
been widowed, too many children have been orphaned,
too many fathers have had to carry fine sons to their
graves and too many mothers have had to look into their
children's coffins, God's creation disfigured by violent
death.

Hundreds of people, including many from the wider community, attended the funeral the next morning in Sligo. Well before the ceremony had started the Gardaí were on the scene near St Anne's Church, prepared for any trouble, yet keeping a low profile. A neighbour, who was asked to speak on behalf of the family during the funeral Mass, paid tribute to Tom as 'a lovely lad, who was very respectable, and who loved his family'. She told how she had spoken to Tom about angels less than two hours before his death that Monday, and how he had taken an angel that was in her car and blessed his face with it and then kissed it. 'The angels have wrapped their arms around him now,' she said.

There were floral tributes around the coffin that included a representation of a boxing ring, a Transit van and a pint of Guinness, along with numerous ones spelling out Tom's name. After Mass the casket was carried by Tom's brothers and cousins, the cortège led by Tom senior, head bowed, who walked slowly ahead holding a framed picture of his tragic son as they made their way past the family home. From there the coffin was driven by hearse to the graveyard at Ballymote, some miles outside of the city.

Years before, in 1999, Patrick 'Deuce' Ward was shot and killed at the graveyard during a funeral in a feud-related attack, as detailed in *The Outsiders*. This time the Gardaí weren't taking any chances. There was tight security imposed as officers searched vans and vehicles for weapons. A mile from the graveyard, the hearse came to a halt and the casket was transferred to a glass-sided carriage pulled by two horses adorned with large black plumes. Such spectacular visual expressions of grief are an important mark of respect among many Traveller clans. Family and friends later lingered for hours at the grave singing ballads and taking turns to help fill the grave, as is traditional among the wider community in many parts of Ireland.

Members of another Traveller clan were blamed for involvement in Tom Ward's death. But there was considerable speculation in some media and among Travellers that a number of factors might have been involved. Two years previously, in April 2005, another young Traveller from Sligo town, Hughie McGinley, had been shot dead in what still appears to be an unconnected killing. Gardaí at the time said they had a definite line of inquiry but were also keeping an open mind.

Charlie Ward was of the opinion that he too could be the target of violent attacks. In October, two months after his brother's death, he appeared in court on a shoplifting charge. Charlie pleaded with the judge in a bid to avoid a jail sentence, saying that he feared that a spell in prison would be tantamount to a death sentence. 'Prison would not be good for me and I will put my head forward for the future and keep the family together,' he promised in court. Even though the judge was not impressed that he had used his young son in the theft by stuffing flip-flops up his jumper, Charlie was allowed to walk free with a suspended one-month sentence.

By November 2007, fifteen people had been arrested and questioned by officers investigating Tom's killing. It would be another year and half before the Gardaí were in a position to send a file to the Director of Public Prosecutions as a result of their investigation. It had been a long painstaking job. In January 2011, when the local authority removed a memorial the family had erected at the murder scene, Tom senior used the occasion to highlight in the *Sligo Champion* newspaper how he felt that so far his son's killers had gotten away with murder. Later, in June 2011, a young Traveller from County Mayo became the first person charged in connection with the murder, accused of withholding information.

The fact that no one has been brought to account for the killing of Tom Ward has troubled members of his family. The very mention of her dead son's name at one boozy funeral gathering four years later was enough to send Brigid into a rage. She was in Claremorris, County Mayo, in the west of Ireland, with her husband Tom on 7 October 2011. Her son Charlie was also there. After the funeral of a man named Patrick Collins they had gathered at a house where a Traveller couple lived. Arguments between other people had already broken out, and at 8 p.m. local Gardaí were called to separate two groups of people. In the meantime Brigid had taken exception to something said about her dead son by the householder, Patrick McDonagh. A shouting match ensued between Tom and Brigid Ward and Patrick McDonagh and his wife.

An entirely sober Charlie had been sitting in the corner minding his own business. It would later be said in court that he had stayed off the drink because one of his children was sick and he needed to get back home to Sligo. But his mother, who was in her late sixties, wasn't happy to let go the perceived slight of Tom junior's name. She riled up Charlie and slapped him across the face, demanding that he do something about the situation. In a moment of temper, Charlie pulled a knife from his pocket and slashed McDonagh across the abdomen. The Gardaí arrived back at the house as Charlie left in his own car. The officers were greeted by a scene of pandemonium. McDonagh was shouting that he had been stabbed, and Brigid Ward's top had been pulled off. The two couples were separated by the Gardaí, which helped to calm the situation. McDonagh needed several stitches to his stomach. He wasn't entirely cooperative with the ambulance staff on his way to hospital and was later convicted for his role in the disorder. The two couples were each bound to keep the peace for a year at a sitting of Castlebar District Court.

Charlie, on the other hand, now aged thirty-two, was jailed for eighteen months for the knife attack, which was carried out in front of several people, including children. Judge Keenan Johnson noted that Charlie, who had thirty-five previous convictions, had brought a serious weapon to a funeral. The judge also urged both sides to engage in mediation and do something to 'stop the feuding' and prevent further incidents which might be unfortunate for members of the public and the Gardaí.

Charlie's lunge at Patrick McDonagh ended with one man needing stitches and the other spending time in prison. It could easily have resulted in a death. While Tom Ward's killers have so far managed to evade justice, it is possible that very little premeditation went into their attack. Just as Charlie, his ears hot with his mother's taunts, lashed out with a knife, so too Tom's killers may simply have been reacting to circumstances or to an opportunity that presented itself. Very often, an act of violence which occurs on the spur of the moment can have enduring effects. If Charlie had been drunk, or if he had caught McDonagh on the wrong part of his body, there could have been another fatality. Perhaps if the hatchet had connected with Tom Ward's shoulder instead of his head he would be alive today. On such tiny slivers of fate rest so many Travellers' lives.

4

Circles of Hate

Finding Irish Traveller families a place to live is a task loaded with incendiary baggage, sometimes in the literal sense of the word. Over the last decade, millions of euros' worth of public housing stock has gone up in smoke. Few people, if they are honest, are comfortable at the prospect of a halting site being set up near their home or business. Members of the wider community are not the only ones worried by the arrival of new Traveller neighbours. The truth is that no one wants troublemakers or a criminalized family moving in next door. Extended Traveller families would prefer it if only their own relatives lived in proximity to them. For local authorities trying to juggle priority cases on a housing waiting list, the problems posed in finding a home for a Traveller family beset by feud violence are numerous. Even a plan to build and allocate accommodation itself can cause friction between individuals who feel they are competing with each other to get in.

A prime example is a purpose-built scheme at Dunsink Lane in Finglas, County Dublin. Bill Shelley Park was the ideal design, with each of the eight units built with houses, sheds and enough yard space to accommodate caravans and horseboxes. The families allocated the units by Dublin Corporation were decent people who wanted to do well for their children. Yet they became the focus of a campaign of violent intimidation by members of their own community, who were envious of the houses and wanted the properties for themselves. Eventually, the housing units were all left vacant as the families moved out. The only exception was the unit into which Anthony 'The Mole' McDonagh had moved. He was a violent criminal, whose horrific attacks on other Travellers were highlighted in *The Outsiders*. McDonagh had moved in just as those behind the intimidation thought they had completed the job. However, The Mole's presence was enough to put them off wanting to live there despite all their previous efforts. Sick and ailing after being shot in a gangland assassination attempt, The Mole and his immediate family are the only residents of the estate, which cost €2.4 million to build.

Kilbarry halting site in Ballybeg, Waterford, doesn't look like much to the passing motorist. Just a dozen houses are set back from the road, surrounded by fallow greenfield sites and shuttered with steel security fencing. Like Bill Shelley Park, it is a purpose-built development designed to cater for the accommodation needs of local Travellers. In the summer of 2007 there were dozens more caravans parked close by on unauthorized camps and along the recently built link road. It was the scene of the sort of haphazard Traveller life that springs to the minds of most people living in the wider community. The previous summer there had been early rumblings of discontent between members of various families, which had resulted in at least one incident where a shot was fired. By August 2007 tensions had built to a head. A five-bedroom house, newly built by the local authority in the area but earmarked for a Traveller family, was burned out. Following that arson attack a number of illegally parked caravans on the nearby link road also went up in flames.

A few days later, in the early morning hours, there

were pitched battles between different factions of men at Kilbarry. One man suffered a gunshot wound to his leg while two others were injured with bladed weapons, most likely slash hooks. Gardaí had to mount a large operation to prevent further trouble, and carried out several searches on caravans and properties in the area. Over the following days relatives of the families involved began returning from the UK and other parts of Ireland in a show of strength as more trouble threatened to break out. By Irish Traveller standards this was all-out war.

Things remained tense as summer ended and autumn began. In October many of the youngsters from the wider community, as well as Travellers, were out drinking in the fields and watching the fires burn to celebrate Hallowe'en. The annual outdoor mayhem provided the spark for the feud to flare up again. A man from one faction accidentally stumbled into a gang from the other side at a bonfire on the outskirts of Waterford city. He was attacked without mercy and received knife and slash wounds to his head and his legs. He was found by Gardaí who had been alerted, lying on the ground close to where he had been assaulted. In apparent retaliation just a few hours later, a car loaded with young men was driven at high speed into another halting site at nearby Old Kilmeaden Road, where it was used to ram a number of caravans. A sixteen-year-old Traveller, who was heavily pregnant, was run over as she tried to flee from her trailer. Hours after being admitted to Waterford Regional Hospital, she gave birth to a baby boy. In the same hospital the man who had been attacked was in a critical condition.

But even then, the hotheads among the clans hadn't finished. Two vacant houses at Kilbarry halting site were also burned down. In a single night the violence had risen to an even greater level and no one could feel safe. Attacks were sudden and reckless, and just as the young mother-to-be discovered, anyone could find themselves standing in the path of disaster. For a couple of weeks, the people involved in the feud violence bided their time, yet tension remained bubbling under the surface. Two months later, in the same area, Gardaí had to intervene as Traveller men began gathering in anticipation of another pitched battle after a fight between two individuals threatened to reignite the violence. Armed officers set up checkpoints and searched vehicles to enforce the peace.

The next flashpoint came in April 2008 when 22-year-old John Delaney, the man accused of running over the teenage mother-to-be and ramming caravans, appeared in court. Rival groups of young men from the Delaney and the Reilly families shouted threats and taunted each other outside the grounds of the court, which had been effectively sealed off by a force of twenty Gardaí. When the court sitting eventually took place John Delaney took the stand. The father-of-two had lived all his life in Waterford at the Kilbarry and Bilberry halting sites. A convicted criminal with an alcohol problem, he pleaded guilty to reckless endangerment and assault causing harm to the sixteen-year-old pregnant girl. It came out in court that his younger brother, Michael Delaney, had been the victim of the brutal attack at the bonfire who had been left with serious injuries. In fact, John had been brought home by the Gardaí after the shocking incident.

A picture of the bedlam created that night was painted in court by the prosecution team. There were nine people crammed into the silver Primera car when Delaney drove it on to the Reilly campsite. He did handbrake turns at speed and rammed caravans even though he knew families were sleeping inside. He drove so fast that he took the door off a tractor as well as running over the girl. His defence lawyer pointed out that there had also been two other cars on the site being driven at speed by members of the opposing faction, and that vehicles had been deliberately crashed into each other. The Gardaí had been quick to reach the scene and had seen several people running away. Delaney had been arrested later, but had denied being involved when questioned. He had tried to claim that he had been at the hospital where his brother was undergoing emergency surgery. However, two security guards working at the site had seen who was driving the car, and the prosecution eventually had fourteen separate witnesses who were able to identify Delaney as having been behind the wheel. When the case came to court he made a guilty plea.

Despite his relatively young age, however, it appeared that John Delaney had taken a significant part in the feud violence. A Garda witness told how Delaney had been part of a mob armed with machetes and golf clubs that had marched on a Waterford house on New Year's Day 2007. They were forced to stop by the Gardaí. He also had a criminal record with convictions for drug possession, criminal damage, dangerous driving and burglary. As well as all that, Delaney had been on bail on a burglary charge at the time when he ran over the young woman.

The details of what had happened to the sixteen-year-old victim were heard in the court. Just a few hours after being hit by the car, her baby was delivered by Caesarean section. She also suffered a compound fracture of her leg and was later transferred from Waterford Regional Hospital to Cork University Hospital where she underwent a total of five operations. Her treatment was still ongoing at the time of the trial almost six months after the incident. The baby boy was delivered without any complication, but he was ill in hospital at the time of the hearing. The young mum exercised her right to give evidence and told the court that her leg had been very seriously damaged and that she was still in pain. The treatment included cosmetic surgery on her leg and skin grafts taken from her hip. She said that she faced further operations and was still attending hospital for dressings of her wound. She explained that she was unable to go for a walk with her baby. 'I do not know why this happened to me. He's in hospital all the time, he's been like that since he was born. My life is ruined, I can't bring my baby outside, I can't go shopping,' she said in her statement.

In his evidence, John Delaney apologized to the girl and said he was 'more than sorry' for what happened and that he had never meant to hurt her. Gripping a religious pendant around his neck, he said: 'I'll swear by this relic that I'm very sorry, that was never meant for her.' He said he was willing to serve his time in prison and wanted no more trouble. There was a serious feud between the two families but his part in it was over. Delaney's defence counsel told the court that he had left school at fifteen and had worked on and off with his father dealing in horses and scrap metal. While in prison he had attended a project to learn to read and write along with AA meetings, and taken woodwork and pottery classes. If Delaney had not pleaded guilty, it was pointed out, there would have been a lengthy trial with sixteen witnesses being cross-examined, which would not have been helpful with regard to the ongoing feud. The lawyer said that the two families had been waiting to see how Delaney would plead. It had been wrong for Delaney to have taken the law into his own hands, but his lawyer said that his apology was genuine and he would not be joining battle again.

Judge Olive Buttimer told the accused man he was extremely lucky that he did not kill the girl that night and that he was not before a higher court, facing a more serious charge. She said that she did not accept that a feud was an excuse for knocking down a pregnant woman or driving recklessly when children were present. However, she accepted his apology and remorse. Imposing a sentence of five years' imprisonment, the judge suspended the last two years. 'Let that be an end to the feud,' she said. Unfortunately, events would prove the judge's hopes to be somewhat optimistic.

Despite the serious injuries sustained by Michael Delaney and the sixteen-year-old girl, there was no sign of any common sense being applied to the feud. Just two months later, in June 2008, violence flared again outside Waterford city, where a number of people were injured in a large-scale clash. Several were injured, including one man who was treated for a gunshot wound and another badly hurt with a slash hook. Christopher Stokes, a victim of one assault, was left in a critical condition in hospital. That incident was then followed by a number of petrol-bomb attacks on properties in Waterford thought to belong to family members of the rival clans. In fact, many of the houses targeted were the homes of people who had nothing to do with the feud.

Gardaí were forced to mount another large operation to quell the feuding and carried out searches of various locations around the city. Within a week fourteen people had been arrested, and two sawn-off shotguns found, along with thirty-seven petrol bombs prepared and ready for use. A collection of slash hooks, machetes, pickaxe handles, swords and knives were also confiscated. Eight people were charged with various criminal offences, including four men accused of the brutal attack on Christopher Stokes. The court appearances of the various different defendants were marked by a large Garda presence around the courthouse to stop any trouble from developing. However, despite the high-profile policing operation, the reckless attacks continued. In one incident, a car drove into a cul-de-sac known as Nash's Boreen where a number of rifle shots were fired at two houses. This time no one was injured and the hooded gang abandoned their car and fled on foot.

An uneasy calm settled for a few weeks, but in August 2008 another incident suggested that the level of violence the protagonists were prepared to use had been ratcheted up even higher. On 12 August, shots were fired through the kitchen window of a Waterford house, but no one was home at the time. Two days later, however, a fourteen-year-old boy was hit with a shotgun blast which left him with fifty pellet wounds to his body. He had been standing at the door of a house in Ardmore Terrace, Ballybeg, when the gunman had walked across a green area and fired a shot from about thirty metres away. The shooter had calmly left in a waiting car, which the Gardaí later found burned out.

The next month yet another teenager suffered the consequences of feud violence in which they had no part. This time it was a sixteen-year-old girl who became a victim of the reckless combatants. In her pyjamas, she had gone to close the gates at Bilberry halting site late in the evening. Like the teenage boy she was hit in the abdomen by pellets from a single shotgun blast. The shooter, described as being dressed in a white tracksuit, escaped and later the suspected getaway car was found burned out to destroy any forensic evidence. Her injuries were not life-threatening but her bowel was damaged by the shotgun blast. A week later a man from the Stokes family was charged with the attack on her.

From the summer of 2007 to the summer of 2008 Travellers and neighbours from the wider community in Waterford had been living under intolerable pressure, unsure of where and when the next round of violence might suddenly explode. During the second summer of tit-for-tat attacks, fourteen houses were damaged by arson and six families forced from their homes. In August, a meeting of the Waterford Joint Policing Committee heard from Garda Superintendent Chris Delaney, who explained that

€400,000 had been spent on overtime for officers drafted in to deal with the feud violence. When the latest round of attacks had begun in July 2008, a total of forty-seven people had been arrested.

There had been a lull in the violence for almost two weeks when the superintendent delivered his report. Two days later there was another escalation. A pipe bomb was found near a house in Waterford and the army's bomb-disposal unit were drafted in to carry out a controlled explosion to make it safe. Another crude home-made bomb was used in an attack in November, when it was thrown into the Bilberry halting site. Although it exploded, no damage or injuries were caused. The next month there was a sickening attack on horses belonging to Traveller families. Three horses were mutilated in two separate incidents, in which each had a leg almost hacked off. One four-year-old animal had to be put down. The next day another two were badly injured in a similar fashion in what was suspected as a revenge attack. The same week there were two more shootings and a petrol bomb was thrown. At this stage the Gardaí had logged 148 incidents related to the feud. It was a bad end to 2008.

By now the level of violence, with shotguns, rifles and pipe bombs being used, was akin to sectarian conflict of the type seen in Northern Ireland. Early in 2009 it was reported in the *Waterford News and Star* that the warring families had called a truce ending the ongoing litany of attacks. Christopher Stokes said:

> It's been going on since July, over a bare-knuckle fight, and the Travellers have come to an agreement that there will never be a bare-knuckle fight in Waterford again. It's gone on too much. People have been hurt, houses burnt, horses were killed. It has to end before someone is killed and it's not fair on the people of Waterford either.

Four men from the Mongan, Stokes, Reilly and Quilligan families posed together for a photograph in a public show of reconciliation. 'It was ridiculous, it had to be stopped. This is very important to us. We can get back to some normality in the town. Every one of us is sick of it and terrified,' said James Reilly.

The truce apparently held for the first half of 2009 until a horrific assault on William Burke, a Traveller in his twenties. Two masked men entered his home at Ferrybank on the outskirts of Waterford at 2.30 a.m. and set on him with a machete. He suffered severe cuts to his hand and arms as he tried to defend himself, and also lacerations to his legs. Later, he was transferred to Cork University Hospital amid fears that he could lose his hand as a result of his wounds. There appeared to be no immediate retaliation in the wake of this incident, although in August a shotgun was fired at a halting site in Dungarvan, County Waterford. A young man received facial injuries, but was discharged soon afterwards from hospital. The attack on Burke and the shooting incident appeared to be random and isolated incidents. If they were connected with the feud then no one was saying.

There was, however, worse to come. William Stokes, a 48-year-old father of four, had lived in Tipperary town for more than twenty years. He was originally from Waterford, so some of his relations would have been caught up in the feuding. He had not been involved in the ongoing aggravation and had quietly got on with his life well away from the chaos. On 18 December 2009, he was going about his business in the town. Beside him in his van was his fourteen-year-old son. He stopped outside the Supervalu supermarket on the town's Bridge Street. It was 6 p.m., a time when people drop in to buy their groceries and their Lotto tickets for the weekend. There was nothing out of the ordinary to suggest that Willie Stokes had much to worry about. Two men suddenly approached the van and without warning stabbed him a number of times. He managed to fend off the attackers long enough to start the van and drive off. But the vehicle came to a stop at the junction with Main Street. Willie had been fatally wounded. He was later declared dead at the scene by medics.

It was a shocking event that left people in Tipperary stunned. No one had a bad word to say about Stokes or his family. Less than a week later the town came to a standstill for his funeral. Archdeacon Matthew McGrath commented at the funeral that the large crowd of mourners was an indication of the esteem in which the dead man had been held. 'It is bad for all of us that this should have happened in our midst. The silence around the town now is saddening, to have such a funeral during Christmas week when the Prince of Peace appears,' he said. In the days after the killing fourteen people were arrested by the investigating Gardaí. It appeared that Willie Stokes was targeted simply because he was related to other figures involved in the feud. After dozens of attacks, several badly injured victims and burned-out properties, the feud had finally claimed its first fatality. Despite the major Garda investigation into the killing so far no one has been charged, except for one individual who had withheld information.

There were other days of reckoning approaching as the criminal justice system continued its work. More than thirty people had been charged with various offences since the start of the feud in 2007. By the end of 2010 one of those trials was that of Simon Quilligan. He had been charged with taking part in the bonfire attack on Michael Delaney, which had also led to the incident in which the young mum-to-be had been run down. By now there was the standard Garda security operation around the court-house in Waterford to ensure trouble wouldn't kick off as Quilligan was brought to trial. For four days Garda units tried to keep the peace as the prosecution witnesses took the stand.

The court heard how it had been a confused and chaotic scene when Michael Delaney had been set upon by a group of attackers. Delaney himself admitted he had been drinking and the previous night had taken ecstasy tablets. There were also a lot of inconsistencies between what the various witnesses said they had seen that Hallowe'en night in 2007. Some said there had been twenty aggressors while others insisted there had just been six. One woman testified that she had been threatened and did not want to get involved.

At least there was no argument about the medical evidence. Delaney had suffered multiple stab wounds. A doctor gave evidence that there were signs of secondary surgery from an old gunshot wound to the knee. Delaney had had to undergo a number of operations on his leg, while his bowel had been perforated in five places from a stab wound to his abdomen. Whoever had attacked him meant business.

Such were the inconsistencies in the testimony that Quilligan's defence made an application to have the case dismissed. Judge Tom Teehan said that 'reluctantly' he had to withdraw the case from the jury. He said that while there was no doubt Delaney had been attacked, and it would be naïve not to think someone from the opposing side had carried it out, it would still be unsafe to convict anyone. He did, however, say it was in his power to bind Quilligan to be of good behaviour for ten years. The judge also commented that the most honest witness before him was the young woman who had told him she was frightened about giving her evidence. 'If Simon Quilligan is found to have interfered with a witness or in any way with the course of justice that is a very serious matter and issues will follow,' the judge warned.

The consequences of reckless feuding came home to

roost for Simon Quilligan and other members of his family within a few short weeks. He had been living in Galway city to escape the ongoing violence in his native Waterford, where he had been based on the Kilbarry site. His was not the only family to have moved from the city. While the dispersal of various families may have cut down on the number of violent incidents, it also had the effect of spreading the feud across the country.

After midnight on 6 January 2011 at least four masked men pulled up outside Quilligan's house at Cluain Ard, Galway. They smashed in the front window and then threw in petrol bombs. Simon had left his daughter, Joan, with his sister Ann and her family to go to the funeral of 22-year-old P.J. Harper in Dundalk, his wife's first cousin. (P.J. and his friend Susan Larrigan, aged seventeen, had died in a horrific car accident on the M1 in the early hours on 1 January, when his BMW had careered off the road and sliced through a wooden fence.) Whether or not the attackers had known Simon Quilligan would be away at the funeral, and whether or not they intended to kill those inside, hasn't been established. The fact is that the occupants of the house had a very lucky escape.

A few days after the event, Quilligan's sister Ann, and their mother, recalled the close brush with death Ann and members of her family had. The conversation took place at a hostel in Galway city where they were being temporarily accommodated. Still in considerable pain from her injuries and with her left leg in plaster, she recounted what had happened. Ann was the only one awake at the time, just after midnight. She heard the window being smashed and looked out in time to see the firebombs being thrown in. She explained:

I was upstairs, I went to get the kids out of the house.
My father was in the next bedroom to me. He was asleep

in bed. He'd had a few drinks, he'd been drinking that night. My other brother James, he has a disability, he was upstairs too. The other two boys were there as well. My father took them downstairs.

Within a few minutes the petrol-fuelled fire had begun sending choking black smoke upstairs. Time was running out for Ann and her eighteen-month-old niece, Joan. In a panic she phoned her mother, Mary, who had been staying at a nearby halting site.

'She was screaming for help, she was on the phone to me, telling me she was trapped in the house,' recalled Mary.

Despite the chaos, it began to dawn on Ann that her only way out would be to jump from a window with the toddler in her arms. She said:

I went to the stairs twice, I couldn't get down the stairs with the smoke, I had to take the window. There was no other way out. It happened so quick. I sat on the edge of the window. I put Joan on my lap and I just leaped off the window. I landed on my back on the side, that's how I got the injuries, but she was fine.

Ann suffered a cracked backbone, broken ribs and a shattered ankle, but eighteen-month-old Joan was miraculously unscathed:

She was left home the following day, she was kept in for smoke. She got the all-clear that night. If they had done it at four in the morning we'd all be dead, no one would have been awake to hear them. There was no chance of anyone getting out.

Just how close the arson attack had come to being a terrible tragedy wasn't lost on either of the women.

'Only for Ann they would have burned to death. She was the one who set off the alarm shouting and roaring at them to get up. There were four innocent children in bed that night. They didn't know what was going on,' said Mary. The family's possessions went up in flames with the house, including the kids' Christmas presents, their clothes, mementos and photographs: 'Everything was destroyed by smoke. There's nothing left. The house is only all black, that's all there's left.'

Not for the first time, women had borne the brunt of the violence in a senseless feud. The arson attack raised the prospect of more revenge attacks being carried out. The people being blamed were members of another Traveller family, originally from the south-east of Ireland, who had moved to a location in the midlands. A male relative who had been hanging back as the women recounted the story eventually came forward and quietly said: 'There will be revenge over this. If they target our children, we'll target theirs.' His threatening comment neatly encapsulated the constant spiral of violence that some individuals find themselves locked into.

A single individual can have a powerful and sinister effect within a feuding clan. While some tire of the violence and the intolerable stress it imposes on families, others appear to thrive on the chaos or else cannot allow matters to come to rest. In Waterford there were a number of people who were key in stoking up trouble and fanning the flames of hatred among Travelling people. But one man in particular, Patrick 'Rubber Óg' O'Reilly, has a track record that charts his own malign influence on the people around him. Years ago he had been convicted for his part in a melee at a halting site in Cork. During this incident he pointed a shotgun at a member of the Gardaí who, despite being hopelessly outnumbered, had intervened in a bid to stop the trouble. At a court sitting in 2003 Rubber Óg was jailed for five years. He also had a significant role to play in what became one of the most notorious incidents of feud violence that occurred between the clans originating from Waterford.

In March 2011, the usual early Sunday-morning horse fair was taking place at Smithfield Market. The mart and exchange had its roots in medieval Dublin, which allowed traders to ply their wares on the fourth Sunday of every month. Over the years it had gained a somewhat notorious reputation for shady dealing and also for the unregulated buying and selling of horses. By 2011, the Gardaí and inspectors from the Dublin Society for the Prevention of Cruelty to Animals were in regular attendance. The dealers and customers, often young teenagers from the outskirts of the city, had become more conscious of their animals' welfare. The improved marshalling of the event had tamed the wild streak for which it had garnered a name. But that came to a spectacular end in a sudden and terrifying burst of unexpected violence.

With thousands of people in the cobbled square, along with hundreds of animals, it was already a restive scene that morning in March. There was some consternation, then, when a group of men armed with weapons began approaching another group. That became outright panic when shots rang out, sending market-goers scurrying for cover in every direction while others struggled to keep panicked animals under control. One young man was hit with a machete, leaving him with a gory, gaping wound to his upper arm. As he was attended to by Gardaí and then paramedics a vivid red bloody rivulet ran across the pavement.

It later emerged that the victim was a Traveller named Wesley McDonagh who had already proven himself to be a promising young boxer. Also injured in the attack were two other men from the Traveller community, John McInerney and Gerard Donoghue. A revolver was also found hidden nearby by Gardaí shortly afterwards. They were quickly on the trail of the attackers and the prime suspect was Patrick 'Rubber Óg' O'Reilly. He was soon arrested and charged in connection with the attack. The pandemonium sparked by the violence played into the hands of those who wanted to be rid of the ancient but boisterous city market. There were calls at Dublin City Council to pass legislation that would outlaw it.

Rubber Óg had been in jail on remand for a year and half when his case came to trial in October 2012. He pleaded guilty to violent disorder. It emerged in court that he had been photographed carrying a stick during the melee along with a group of men, one of whom was also armed with a machete and another with a home-made shotgun. He was given four years. Six weeks later the man carrying the shotgun appeared in court. He was Rubber Óg's nineteen-year-old son, Daniel O'Reilly. Led by his father and other men, young O'Reilly had knelt and fired his weapon from a range of just four metres as they approached McInerney and Donoghue. The home-made shotgun was effectively two pipes welded together. One man suffered thirty pellet wounds while the other was hit nine times. Both wounded men were able to identify their assailants and the Gardaí were able to use forensic evidence to link Daniel O'Reilly to the shotgun and a cartridge found at the scene. He pleaded guilty to violent affray and possessing a weapon.

His defence lawyer pointed the finger at his father as being the senior man involved in the attack. He explained how Daniel had been under the malign influence of his father, a man who had seventy-five previous convictions. A family friend gave evidence that he had been approached by Daniel's grandfather to help get Daniel away from Tallaght in Dublin where he had been living with his father. 'This would not have happened were it not for his father,' he said. He had taken the youngster in and had helped find him a job. There was also evidence of how the teenager became involved with the Midlands Traveller Conflict Mediation Initiative and that 'matters had calmed down'.

Daniel O'Reilly's defence lawyer put forward an argument that Daniel's father 'had not guided him in the way you would expect a father to' and that people around him were encouraging him to fire the weapon. He added that young O'Reilly was committed to leaving 'all this behind him' and had hoped to get married, get a job and stay out of prison. Judge Martin Nolan accepted that the teenager had tried to reform while in custody and was confident he would continue that way if he managed to stay away from his father. He imposed a sentence of five and a half years.

The trial highlighted how Rubber Óg's malign influence and violent nature had been a significant factor in a long history of trouble. In no way, however, was the feud all his fault. Even while he was in jail and as the mediators did their work, there was more aggression. One teenage mother endured an attack on her car in County Laois as she went to see relatives. An assailant with a slash hook broke the windows, showering her baby son with glass. 'I'll kill your husband,' he shouted, before breaking off the assault.

The feuding among the Traveller clans in Waterford ticked every box when it came to the factors that make such vendettas so intractable. First, Rubber Óg's influence over his teenage son went as far as to push him into carrying out a shooting in a public place in front of hundreds of potential witnesses. Their relationship is an extreme example of feuds being passed from one generation to the next. Second, no one seemed able to exert an influence to broker a lasting truce. Various mediation initiatives were started, while mediators from the Department of Justice had discussions with members of the Traveller clans. Senior Garda officers also tried to get influential figures among the clans to listen to sense. Finally, the criminal justice system, at great cost, had varying degrees of success when it came to dealing with the feud participants.

In the event, the final cost to the taxpayers is most likely to be measured in the millions, adding together the cost of policing, the court trials, medical costs and damage to council-owned property. Spread over four years, the feud had a greater physical and emotional cost for those Travellers who had to live in considerable fear because of it. One innocent man lost his life in an attack witnessed by his teenage son, others suffered disabling injuries, and dozens of properties were destroyed in arson attacks. It was an episode made all the more tragic by the ultimately pointless character of the feud.

5

'I Can't Hit a Stop Button'

From the outside it can appear as if Traveller feuds erupt with sudden and furious violence, without any prior warning. Such attacks, while seemingly random at first, are usually the culmination of long-held grudges. The incidents at Smithfield Market were a perfect example. Thanks to the gory photographs and the public nature of the assaults during the horse fair there was a brief media focus on the affair. But the connection with the Waterford feud would not have been widely known at the time. The element of the feud being passed from one generation to the next only came out in the Garda investigation, which exposed Rubber Óg's influence over his son. It also demonstrated that in the tightly knit Irish Traveller world people that are at the very periphery of a feud can quickly become the new epicentre, be that as aggressor or victim. It was an unfortunate lesson that one young Traveller family were to find out.

Many Travellers marry at a young age compared to the wider community. In that regard John Mongan and his wife Julia were no different. Their first baby, Shannon, came along in 1998 when John was nineteen years of age. Their second girl, Naomi, was born four years later. A family portrait taken when Naomi was still a baby showed a fresh-faced young couple. In an open-neck check shirt John posed, looking intently at the camera, square-jawed, not entirely relaxed, but his little daughter looked perfectly at home resting on his left arm. Shannon sat in Julia's lap, who was every bit the proud young mum with her toddler daughter.

However, they later suffered the tragedy of Shannon's death due to complications of Down's syndrome. It was a heavy burden of grief for such a young couple to bear and they never forgot it. One of eleven children born to Martin and Margaret Mongan, John was a dutiful son, husband and father. He made regular visits to his mother, buying her gifts and giving her money to treat herself. The young couple were blessed with another child, Patrick Lee, born in 2004. Living in a red-bricked terraced house on Fallswater Street, just off the Falls Road in Belfast, they had a happy family life.

By 2007 Julia was expecting again. Everyone in the extended family was happy for them. John was delighted with the news and even more excited when he learned he was to be the father of another baby boy. He still hadn't forgotten little Shannon and had saved hard to buy two guardian angel statues for her grave in Dundalk, County Louth.

Yet despite the apparently happy family life, young John Mongan was part of a Traveller clan that had been caught up in a dangerous feud. Such feuds can often remain latent, but suddenly flare into dangerous violence from the tiniest spark. His father, Martin, became embroiled in a conflict with a member of the Maughan clan in Belfast. One of the Maughan men suffered a bad beating which left him with a fractured neck. Martin was blamed for that attack and it's claimed he was shot and injured as a result. A member of the Maughan clan, Brian, was convicted and jailed for sixteen years for the attempted murder. According to members of Maughan's family the conviction was a miscarriage of justice and Martin Mongan's eyewitness evidence was given out of spite.

In June 2002 Mary Maughan, who was living at a caravan site at Nutts Corner, a few miles outside Belfast, came under attack from three masked men armed with a slash hook and baseball bats. Her husband was forced to flee across fields as the men battered the caravan and broke up their vehicle. John Mongan and two others were later charged with aggravated burglary and making threats to kill after they were identified by Mary Maughan. In September 2002, however, the trial judge in the case at Antrim Crown Court directed that the charges be dropped amid a number of inconsistencies, and they were all acquitted. Despite the case against him being thrown out, John remained a potential target for attacks by vengeful members of the Maughan clan.

In February 2007 a cousin of John Mongan's was at a wedding in Ireland. There was an exchange of words with an older member of the Stokes clan, many of whom live in Derry. It wasn't a big row but the older man demanded satisfaction and challenged the younger to a fist fight. He was somewhat surprised, however, when he was bested by the Mongan man. It should have ended there and then: a minor argument sorted by a fight to clear the air from which a winner emerged. But it didn't. The older of the two fighters wasn't happy to have been beaten and he wasn't prepared to let the matter lie. It stirred a growing tension between the Stokes and Mongan clans, and a festering bitterness that John Mongan's family would claim he had nothing to do with.

A year later, John and Julia were almost prepared for the latest addition to their family. On Wednesday night, 6 February 2008, Naomi and Patrick Lee, then aged six and four, were fast asleep. Heavily pregnant, Julia was in bed too. John was by her side in the bedroom of their Belfast home. Sometimes Patrick Lee would seek out the comfort of his parents' bed but that night he was in his own. In the early hours after midnight the front door of their home was smashed in. Groggy and still half asleep, Julia woke to see a hatchet being smashed through their bedroom door. The pair jumped out of the bed and tried to shove it up against the door, but it was too late. The man wielding the hatchet hit John hard with the implement. Wounded, he fell to the floor. Julia screamed and begged the attackers to stop. Instead, with a number of bladed implements including the hatchet and a sword they stabbed and hacked at the prone body of John Mongan. Awoken by the clamour, Naomi watched in terror as her father was brutally assaulted. Despite being pregnant Julia tried to shield her badly injured husband with her own body. During the chaotic attack she suffered a severe cut when hit in the back with one of the weapons.

The assailants left nonchalantly, walking straight out the front door, according to one eyewitness. They damaged John's jeep before getting into their own four-wheel-drive vehicle, and left Fallswater Street to the echoes of Julia's terrified inconsolable screams. When the police arrived at the house it was a scene of bloody chaos. Julia, covered in blood, was screaming over and over: 'Please don't die, John, please don't die.' He was rushed by ambulance to the Accident and Emergency Unit at the Royal Victoria Hospital, where he was later declared dead. Shortly afterwards, a hysterical Julia was taken to the maternity unit.

Outside the Traveller community there was some speculation that members of the Maughan clan were behind the killing. After all, the 'bad blood' that existed between the families had been well aired in various court hearings. Instead, the attack had come from an entirely different quarter, and it was quickly claimed among

Travellers that the wrong man had been targeted. The Mongans would later say that members of the Stokes clan had passed on a message to them shortly after the attack claiming that that was the case. The message, whether it was true or not, was of no comfort to Julia or John's distraught family. Just over two days later, on Saturday 9 February, Julia gave birth to a baby boy. He was immediately named John in memory of his recently slain father, who had yet to be buried.

John's own parents, Margaret and Martin, claimed they knew who had been behind the shocking murder. In an interview with *Sunday World* journalist Paula Mackin, a distraught Margaret said:

> We know who did this and we want them brought to justice. What they did to my son I'll never be able to forgive, the death they gave him is just too horrible for words. We know who murdered our son, we know who did this, and I would just like to ask them why? They never had a fight with my son, he was innocent in all of this, they killed the wrong man.
>
> I spoke to him the night before he was murdered and he told me he would be up the next day with a big surprise for me. That's what my John was like, he was very generous, he was always doing things for me, giving me money and telling me to treat myself. I never expected the surprise to be this. My life has been destroyed by his death. My life and the life of my family will never be the same again. I should have been celebrating my birthday. Instead I am arranging a funeral. Julia threw herself on top of John to help him, she tried to save him, that's how she got hit. The people who did this should be charged with her attempted murder and the attempted murder of the baby she was carrying.

Martin Mongan said:

> They meant to kill my son that night, why else would you
> break into someone's house with machetes and baseball
> bats as they lay sleeping in bed? I am devastated by this,
> totally devastated. I can't stop thinking about what it must
> have been like for him to die like that. I can't put how I
> am feeling into words.

Despite his own background with feud violence Martin
publicly declared that he did not want to see any retaliation
carried out in his son's name. 'We don't want any more
violence. We want to see justice for our son, but we want to
see that happen through the courts,' he said.

Police in Northern Ireland were able to move quickly and
seven people were arrested within days of the murderous
onslaught.

A week after the attack, and when baby John was just
four days old, John Mongan was laid to rest. At the Church
of the Nativity in Poleglass, Belfast, several hundred
Travellers paid their respects. From the pulpit Father
Eugene Lewis repeated the family's desire to see no acts of
revenge being carried out:

> All of you brothers and sisters and relatives and friends
> of our murdered brother John, what kind of world do you
> want John junior to grow up in? Do you want a world of
> continuing family feuding, hatred and violence? If you
> do, you are destroying the lives and the future of all your
> children.

In a prepared statement released at the time of the funeral
the family said of the dead man:

John was a husband, a loving father of four children,
a son, a brother to ten siblings and a loving uncle. We
would like to inform the public that John was not involved
in any feud. He did not deserve to die, but especially
not in such a horrific manner in front of his pregnant wife
and children. We as a family do not want any revenge
to be carried out in John's memory. We do not want any
other family to go through what our family has suffered
over this past couple of weeks. All we want for John is that
those who murdered him be brought to justice through
the legal system.

These were earnest pleas for peace from the Mongan family and the priest. The callous and savage murder in front of a child easily had the potential to provoke an equally destructive reaction from an enraged member of the clan bent on vengeance.

However, the Police Service of Northern Ireland (PSNI) apparently had plenty to go on. After their initial seven arrests they went on to compile a twelve-thousand-page file for the Director of Public Prosecutions. It included statements from a hundred witnesses who could be called on to give evidence. Charges were brought against three people: Christopher and Edward Stokes, both first cousins of Julia Mongan, along with a teenage nephew who was just fifteen at the time of the attack.

Despite the pleas for peace there were still rumblings of violence. A year later in February 2009 Julia's mother, Bridget Mongan, had her flat targeted in a gun attack. By then it would have been clear that John's widow was to be the star witness in any prosecution. Bridget, and Bridget's granddaughter Louise Ward, were lucky to escape without injury in this incident, when shots were fired through the front window of their flat on Suffolk Road in west Belfast. As well as being John's mother-in-law, Bridget was also related to the accused men. Being closely related, however, doesn't offer any immunity from violence when feuding breaks out between individual clan members. There's no middle ground when the battle lines are drawn. People are forced to choose sides, and failure to choose might as well be a declaration of hostile intent.

The trial against the three accused men opened in October 2009 at Belfast Crown Court. A strong security presence was to be a feature throughout, with a real threat that violence between members of the opposing families could break out. The prosecution counsel, Gordon Kerr, outlined the case to the jury, explaining how four men had burst through the sleeping couple's bedroom door. He said that DNA evidence would link Edward Stokes to the scene and that a mobile phone belonging to Christopher Stokes showed that he had travelled from his home in Derry to the Mongans' home in Belfast. The unnamed teenager could be linked to an Isuzu Trooper used by the men, which was found burned out near Kesh, in County Fermanagh, a few hours after the killing.

The case was heard against a backdrop of tension. On the street outside the courthouse, police had to intervene when members of the opposing clans clashed. The PSNI maintained tight security throughout the rest of the trial, both in court and in the area outside the court building. It was a mirror of scenes that the Gardaí had dealt with in Waterford and Tralee.

For the case to succeed, Julia would have to take the stand and give evidence against her cousins, the men accused of killing her husband. She then had to go through the tough task of being cross-examined by the defence lawyers. It wasn't easy, and she spent days in the box as the defence lawyers did their job and tried to sow seeds of doubt in the minds of the jury. She described in court the horrific attack which had left her husband dead, and said that the men:

'were enjoying every minute of it while they were killing my husband'. The teenager, she testified, was 'grinning' during the attack. She had only been two feet away when her husband was 'getting battered, brutally battered in front of me'. Julia said that at one point when she turned around: 'I saw my little girl standing there while the attack was continuing on her daddy.'

Under cross-examination, she admitted that when questioned early in the investigation she had lied to the police by claiming that the men had been wearing balaclavas. Julia explained she did so because she hadn't realized her husband was dead: 'I wasn't sure what John would want me to say – I didn't want him getting any more trouble from that family. He was petrified of them.' She told the defence lawyer that John 'wasn't one for getting anyone charged with anything that they had done to him'. It was put to her that she had named the three accused men only after she had spoken to her brother-in-law and her father. 'I seen the three faces of the three people I know in front of me beating my husband. I wasn't thinking about improving the case. I'm telling the truth. It's up to you to believe it.' Julia did admit that there had been 'bad blood' between her husband and the Stokes clan but said, 'No matter who he fell out with he didn't deserve to be killed in front of me and my child.'

With a defence lawyer for each of the three accused men, Julia spent four gruelling days being grilled over her testimony and her recollection of the murderous assault. One lawyer asked her if she had been making up her version of events as she went along. He suggested that her claim that she had sustained her injury by being hit with a sword was a new detail which hadn't emerged until three months after the attack. 'That's what he hit me with and I blanked it out, it only came back to me afterwards,' she replied. In response to another query she said: 'I didn't make it up.

They killed John. What happened there, can you explain that?' A neighbour who lived across the street also gave evidence which supported Julia's version of events.

Julia's testimony was also backed up by the evidence of Police Constable Sarah McGrath, who arrived on the scene at Fallswater Street that night. She described the bloody, chaotic scene and finding a heavily pregnant Julia Mongan, hysterical, covered in blood. Constable McGrath had asked Julia if she recognized any of the killers. 'She stated that yes, she did. She recognized two males to be Christy Stokes and a teenager, both from Derry. She stated that she recognized them by their voices and she had known them all her life,' Constable McGrath told the court.

There was also some gruesome evidence from pathologist Dr Peter Ingram who said that John Mongan was hit up to forty times by two bladed weapons. He said the attackers had continued to slice and stab John even after he was dead. Dr Ingram said that the main cause of death was a wound which had sliced through an artery, causing 'torrential bleeding' which would have caused 'rapid, but not immediate death'. Asked how many weapons were used he said: 'At the very least, two.'

Another critical piece in the jigsaw of evidence against the accused men was the record of Christopher Stokes's mobile-phone use. A telecommunications expert was able to determine which phone masts connected his mobile phone when it was used to make calls. The expert said that the records put the phone in the area of Fallswater Street near the time John Mongan was fatally attacked. The phone was then used close to the area where the men's Isuzu jeep was found burned out near Kesh, on the other side of Northern Ireland, later that morning at 4 a.m. A bloodstain on Edward Stokes's shirt matched the DNA of the slain man, while forensics also linked the teenager to the Isuzu jeep.

The defence team did their best to highlight inconsistencies in the evidence, particularly between the testimony given by Julia and in her statements to police. But prosecuting counsel Gordon Kerr, in his summing-up of the prosecution case to the jury, pointed out that all the forensic and circumstantial evidence pointed to the same men named by Julia in her testimony. He also stressed the fact that none of them had taken the witness box when they had the opportunity to give an explanation for the evidence against them. The ferocity of the attack and the type of weapons used, he argued, left little doubt over the intention to kill John Mongan rather than just to give him a beating.

On the other hand, the defence team told the jury that everything hinged on whether or not they believed Julia Mongan. The counsel for Christopher Stokes said that her evidence was 'toxic' with 'fatal weaknesses', adding that she was a 'proven liar'. 'You have been lied to time and time again in this case, and it's a very, very big ask to ask you to walk in and convict a man of murder and be confident for the rest of your life that you have done the right thing,' said the lawyer.

The following week, on 16 December 2009, there were emotional scenes as the jury returned guilty verdicts in the cases of Edward and Christopher Stokes. Members of the Mongan family in the public gallery jumped in the air, clapped and cheered when they heard the verdicts returned. The trial judge had to ask them to stay quiet several times while they were kept separated from the members of the Stokes clan by a dozen police officers and court staff. It took a further nine hours of deliberation before the jury were able to deliver a guilty verdict in the case of the teenager. All three were given life sentences. Edward stuck two fingers up at the Mongan family, while Christopher told them: 'I'll do me time, but he'll never be back.'

Despite the sentences, no one was really happy. The losses suffered couldn't be undone. The stress and tension of the trial for both sides meant that an entirely new layer of animosity had settled over the pre-existing turmoil. The Mongans suspected or felt they knew that other people may have been involved in the murder of John Mongan, and may have helped those who carried out the gruesome deed. On the other hand, the belief persisted among the relatives of the convicted men that, as the defence claimed, Julia had singled out those members of the Stokes clan who she hated the most, and the police had made the evidence fit her testimony.

No one on either side was backing down. The month after the verdicts were handed down Julia spoke again to the *Sunday World*, and in a candid and sometimes emotional interview spoke about what had happened that night and the subsequent turmoil she had experienced.

Nobody deserves what happened to John, to be killed in the way he was. To do that to someone is almost unbelievable because any normal person wouldn't be able to do it. To hurt someone in the way they hurt John you have to have no heart, no conscience and no guilt. You are not a human being, you are pure evil. John was asleep when they came, I wasn't, so I got up when I heard the front door coming in. John jumped up too, but I think he was in shock, he didn't say anything, he just stood there. I pulled the bed in front of the door to try and stop them getting to us but it was only a wee iron bed, it was nothing compared to the weapons they had. The axe came through the door, it came over my shoulder, the next thing I knew they were at John. They never said a word, they just kept attacking John, there was blood everywhere. I was begging and pleading with them to stop, I begged and begged them to leave him alone but they wouldn't.

Julia's poignant and eloquent description of the killing and its aftermath give some insight into the devastating personal grief she suffered. She had been as physically vulnerable that night as she had been emotionally vulnerable during the trial under cross-examination.

> I tried to stop them, the next thing I remember is my daughter Naomi appearing, she was screaming and crying too, it was awful. She tried to stop them, too, but all I could do then was to try and calm her, reassure her everything was going to be all right, she was hysterical, shaking and crying. She kept asking me what they were hitting her daddy for. The sad thing is that at that time I really did believe John would have been all right. I regret every day that I never stood in front of John, that I never stopped them killing him.

The aftermath was a scene of carnage in her family home which she likened to a horror movie as she struggled to understand that her husband was actually dead.

> The blood was everywhere within seconds after they left. There was a pool of blood coming from John. It was like the seashore, waves and waves of blood coming out towards me. I had to walk into it to get to John to help him, but there was nothing I could do. It was like a film you regret watching, one that keeps coming back to haunt you, all the details and the images, but for me I can't hit a stop button. I remember screaming and screaming, 'Please, John, don't die.' I remember begging the paramedics to take him to hospital. I begged and begged them but he was already dead. When they told me he had died I remember thinking they had got it wrong, that it couldn't be John, that it could never happen to us or to him. He had survived so much in the past. He was shot,

stabbed and suffered from severe depression at times but he always fought back, he always survived.

The real sting in the tail was the knowledge that such an atrocity could have been committed by members of her own extended clan.

Knowing it was caused by people who are supposed to be family makes it worse. Christy and John were friends, how could they have done it to him? No words can describe how I feel, what they did to me that night and what they did to my children. I am so angry at his killers, I will never forget what they did to John and to his family and I will never ever forgive. They had no right to take John away, only God has the right to make that decision, nobody else. Why did they destroy my husband and the lives of my family?

The young mother and widow pointed directly to the suffering caused, not only to her own family but to the killers' as well:

There has been so much pain and suffering because of this, not just for me but for their family too, and it was for nothing. If there was a reason for it or if John had of been a threat to them then I might be able to try to understand on some level, but there was no reason.

Of course, within two days of the killing, life had moved on, as Julia had given birth to their baby boy. Initially named John, she later christened him Sean, the Gaelic version of the name.

It should have been one of the happiest moments of my life, but I honestly remember nothing of my Sean's birth.

I was numb with pain, I was in shock because of what I had seen happen to John, it was like an out-of-body experience. I spent the entire time waiting for John to walk in and be with me, but he wouldn't come. I couldn't understand it, I just couldn't accept he was dead, not my John. The first time I saw him was at the chapel of rest, after I gave birth to Sean. It was so strange, I remember looking at him in his coffin and thinking, 'So it's true, it's not a nightmare.' I was on medication, so I kept thinking there was some mistake, that it wasn't real, because there was no way my John would have left me and our children, he lived for us, especially the kids.

Even with the convicted killers in jail, the ordeal continued, as all three men appealed their convictions. The prospect of another hearing and even a retrial loomed large. At the same time it was claimed that members of the Mongan clan were getting death threats. The potential for more violence was ever-present.

Life wasn't easy, either, for those members of the Stokes family who were behind bars in Maghaberry Prison, County Antrim. In September 2011, Edward's wife was caught by prison staff as she attempted to pass cannabis to her husband during a visit. She had smuggled the stash into the visitor's centre, then dropped it into a paper cup as she sat opposite her husband. Officers pounced just as he was about to put the cup to his lips. At Craigavon Crown Court she was given a six-month sentence, suspended for eighteen months after the judge took her family background into account.

There was some good news for the Stokes clan when the teenager had his conviction quashed and a retrial ordered. However, there was no such luck for Christopher and Edward, whose sentences were upheld by the appeal court. Struggling with being locked up with no chance of

THE FEUDS

Above: Michael Faulkner, slain near his Tralee home.

Above: Charlie McDonagh in happier times, before his brutal slaying.

Tom Ward leading the funeral procession and carrying a picture of his son Tom Ward Jr.

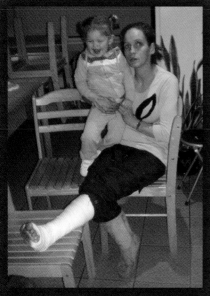

Top left: Ann Quilligan and her niece Joan.

Bottom left: Julia Mongan, widow of feud victim John Mongan, who was hacked to death at their Belfast home.

Below: The brothers of John Mongan celebrate as they leave the High Court in Belfast after hearing that both Christy and Edward Stokes' appeals had failed.

Above: The scene of panic after shots rang out at Smithfield Market.

Top right: Wesley McDonagh is treated after suffering a horrific arm injury during the infamous Smithfield market attack.

Bottom right: Christopher 'Ditsy' Nevin appears at Mullingar District Court.

Below: The scene at Dalton Park as members of the Nevin clan face off against the McDonaghs.

THE FIGHTERS

Above: Ainey McGinley and Dan Rooney slug it out at Crossmaglen in 1990.

Top left: Dan Rooney, the preacher.

Bottom left: Barney 'The Gorilla' McGinley.

Above: Paddy 'Jaws' Ward fighting Barney 'The Gorilla' McGinley in 2008 with Big Joe Joyce and Paddy Doherty acting as fair-play men.

Right: Big Joe Joyce with a framed copy of a *Sunday World* article about his 1989 'Fists of Fury' fight with Anthony O'Donnell.

FISTS OF FURY!

Big Joe punches his way to 'King of the Travellers'

Right: James Quinn McDonagh, star of *Knuckle*, now retired from bare-knuckle fighting.

Below: Boxer Tyson Fury poses with *Celebrity Big Brother* winner, Paddy Doherty.

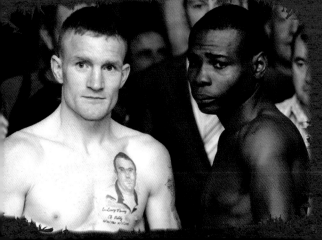

Left: Willie 'Big Bang' Casey prior to his title fight with Guillermo Rigondeaux.

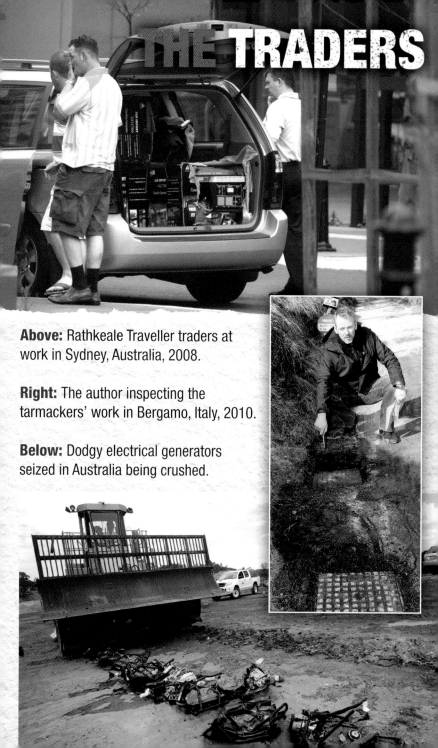

THE TRADERS

Above: Rathkeale Traveller traders at work in Sydney, Australia, 2008.

Right: The author inspecting the tarmackers' work in Bergamo, Italy, 2010.

Below: Dodgy electrical generators seized in Australia being crushed.

Top left: A rhino horn which Traveller traders claimed to have acquired.

Top right: Tommy Connors, family boss jailed for enslaving his workforce.

Above: The high-rollers back in Rathkeale for Christmas.

parole for twenty-two years, Christopher suffered severe depression, not helped by his addiction to prescription medication. In June 2012 he was found hanging in his cell.

There were further developments later that year. First, new evidence uncovered by the police resulted in a murder charge being brought against a fourth man. Then, in November 2012, the teenager was acquitted at his retrial. When the jury returned the not-guilty verdict he punched the air. 'Yes! Thank you, thank you. Thank you for proving my innocence,' he shouted to them. Some members of the Mongan clan who were in the public gallery yelled their own abuse at the man, now aged nineteen. He turned back to the jury and said: 'That's what you have to deal with.' As police officers kept the families apart, the teenager was taken from the building under guard to begin his life again as a free man.

Like their counterparts south of the border, the police and the judiciary found that Traveller feud-related crimes could be difficult and complex to prosecute. The fierce family loyalty among some Travellers can give rise to concerns that any testimony delivered may be tailored to serve the best interests of the family. Julia, in her own evidence, admitted that even at the height of her panic immediately after John's death, and solely to avoid further trouble, she had told police that his attackers wore balaclavas. It had taken a considerable police effort, as shown by the twelve thousand pages delivered to the DPP, even to bring the case to court. Forensic evidence was meticulously gathered and eventually shown to be vital in securing the convictions. Despite the weight of the police investigation, there were still attempts to frighten Julia away from going to court by attacking her mother's house. The battle lines, when they were drawn in this case, cut across family ties and relations. It was a case of: 'You're with us or you're against us.'

The reactions from some of the family members suggest that the court convictions, rather than drawing a line under events, will serve as the next staging post in the feud. Julia also expressed in moving terms how the effects of such pointless and horrible acts of violence can ripple out, like her husband's blood, to impact on the lives of so many other people. The young widow is not the only one who would have wished for a stop button.

6

Mullingar Mayhem

Until the meteoric rise to global fame of singer Niall Horan from the boy band One Direction, it was an old-school crooner, Joe Dolan, who was by far the most famous son of Mullingar, a market town in the Irish midlands. His shows were legendary across the country and were attended by thousands of devoted fans prepared to travel almost anywhere for 'a Joe show'. A statue of the performer stands today in the town square and people regularly pay their respects at his grave in a local cemetery. There are other famous Mullingar natives, such as Olympic silver medallist John Joe Nevin and his Irish boxing team colleague John Joe Joyce.

Several Traveller families in the town are well integrated, holding on to their Traveller identity yet still working in regular jobs, playing sports and mixing with their neighbours. Brigid Myers's home is in Grange Crescent, Mullingar, an estate in the town where Traveller families and those from the wider community live together. Her corner house, which she shared with her husband and children, is a modest dwelling. She and her husband Ned lived there for twenty years. One of her sons, Patrick, who was an accomplished licensed boxer, was cajoled into taking part in an organized bare-knuckle fight on the shores of

Lough Ennell in 2004. When he was bitten on the chest by his opponent the fight came to a chaotic end.

It had nothing to do with the Myers family, but as a result the Nevin and the McGinley clans became entangled in a dangerous feud that culminated in a paramilitary-style attack on two couples as they drove to a wedding. Their car was rammed just outside Longford town before a gunman opened fire with a shotgun. The assailants then smashed up the car with slash hooks, leaving two men injured at the scene. The incident caused terror, and for two years there were more clashes between the clans. It seems that from 2004 there had been constant outbreaks of violence between rival members of different Traveller gangs for a variety of reasons. Disputes over bare-knuckle fights and the payment of bets placed on the bouts have regularly been cited as two of the causes.

Trouble had been rumbling away for weeks between various Travellers in Mullingar over the summer of 2006. Homes had been singled out for vandalism, and vehicles full of men driven by rivals' homes to intimidate the occupants. When one of Ned and Brigid Myers's youngsters got into a primary-school playground spat with another Traveller, they didn't get overly worried. After all, it was a minor thing and kids will be kids. The first hint of further trouble came when a bottle was thrown through the window of their house on a Wednesday evening in September 2006. Ned recalled how he then saw members of the wider Nevin clan start to gather in a nearby estate. His house on Grange Crescent is separated from the next estate by a gently sloping green area. 'I saw the vans going up the road and I knew they were gathering for something. I could see a crowd of them up the road,' he said. Brigid had been at the kitchen sink, and through the broken window she saw a group of men armed with different implements.

Ned immediately knew that if the Gardaí were to take

any complaint seriously then he needed to get evidence. He told Brigid to find the video camera. 'I didn't even think of the video, my husband roared at me to get the video on. There were women and men with billhooks, and hatchets, golf sticks, rocks, everything they could lay their hands on,' said Brigid. The shaky film clip that she took provided a taste of the pure terror inspired by a mob attack. It showed a group of at least two dozen people armed with an assortment of weapons charging down the slope to the Myerses' house. The younger children had been moved to the relative safety of the shed while Ned and his older sons met the mob at the wall of the property. From upstairs, a panicked Brigid did her best to film the attack. Rocks and a metal bar can be heard slamming into the house and on to the ground. One man is seen wielding a fire axe while others brandish sticks and long-handled slash hooks. The scene is almost medieval. From the top of the slope a group of women scream abuse and shout that they want the Myers family to leave their home of twenty years. It is a disturbing video and it must have been a terrifying experience for Brigid. 'My two hands were shaking, my knees were jelly. My children were outside at the time. I didn't know were they in the shed or outside? I had to stop filming,' she said.

Brigid also told of the devastating emotional effect which the threat of such violence can have on a family. She said many other Traveller families were living in 'fear, fear, fear' because of such ongoing violence and intimidation. 'People need to know what's going on among Travellers. There's people who can't go to sleep at night. They can't go down to the shops. It's all about the big families bullying the small ones,' she said. A year later the Myerses' house was attacked again by members of the Nevin clan. This time the case went to court after the Gardaí were able to bring charges against twenty individuals.

The Myers family were not the only people being targeted by feud-style attacks and violence in Mullingar and other towns across the Irish midlands. For years members of the Nevin and the Quinn-McDonagh clans had been sniping at one another. Both are large clans containing plenty of people who have no interest in getting tangled up in never-ending arguments. As we've seen in previous chapters, it only takes a handful on either side niggling away to ensure that the potential for more serious violence is a constant worry.

Thomas 'Knock-out' Nevin fancied his chances at beating Martin McDonagh in an arranged bare-knuckle bout known as a 'fair fight' that would end the simmering dispute between various members of the two extended clans. (After a bare-fist bout the well-known bare-knuckle fighter James Quinn-McDonagh had made a comment about the Nevins which had had the effect of feeding the animosity between people on both sides.) On a summer's day in 2008 Nevin and McDonagh met in Navan, where a few dozen spectators were allowed to watch. It was a grudge match, as are most bare-knuckle fights. The two men got down to business with both weaving and swapping punches. As the fight wore on, neither man seemed to gain the upper hand. McDonagh had a height and reach advantage but Nevin kept cagily going forward. Then after several minutes Nevin went in for a body blow but was slow in getting out of the way as McDonagh countered and connected cleanly to his jaw. Nevin swayed unsteadily on his feet for a few moments, clearly concussed, before staggering backwards and falling to the ground. Despite shouts that he was beaten he got back shakily to his feet and initially turned in the wrong direction to fight. When he was facing the right way, McDonagh had little difficulty in finishing off the fighter, who was clearly out on his feet. Nevin landed on his back and for a few brief seconds was entirely stretched out. Minutes after the fight had ended, Nevin regained his senses and insisted that the bout continue. Obviously, he had been knocked out, but he had no memory of it and felt he had been cheated out of his chance for glory.

What happened in the wake of that fight made headlines across Ireland. Some members of the Nevin clan felt that a triumphant reaction by some of the McDonaghs was unnecessarily rubbing salt into the wound. It was as if family honour had been slighted, and the hotheads in the clans wanted satisfaction. Calls were made to cousins and brothers from all over Ireland and the UK that they were needed in Mullingar. Many, though not all, heeded the clarion and made the journey to play their part in defending their family name.

Chief among those who seemed to have no compunction about stirring up trouble was Christy 'Ditsy' Nevin. Then in his mid-fifties, he had a long reputation as a bare-knuckle fighter. It no doubt rankled that years before, when he had challenged and then lost to one of the Quinn-McDonaghs, he had in effect launched the younger man's successful fighting career. Living in Traveller-specific accommodation in Mullingar, the elder Nevin had amassed more than fifty convictions, many for public-order offences and violence.

As groups of rival Travellers began to gather in the Dalton Park estate in the town, where members of both sides lived, there was an expectation that fighting would break out. A number of Gardaí appeared on the scene in a bid to keep a lid on the simmering tensions. But more and more Traveller men continued to arrive in the area, parking up close to their relatives' homes in a show of strength. Among those who turned up were Ditsy's old nemeses, James Quinn-McDonagh and his brother Mikey.

All it needed was a spark to light the tinder and in

that regard Ditsy didn't disappoint. He broke from the ranks on his side, dropped his trousers and *Braveheart*-style taunted his rivals with a display of his bare buttocks. Before the two groups could charge into one another, a small group of Garda officers got in front of one gang of men who were ready to escalate the confrontation. Without protective equipment, riot gear or helmets the Gardaí stood between the opposing mobs, pushing back anyone attempting to make a sally into the ranks of the enemy. They couldn't, however, stop the rain of missiles that each side threw at the other over their heads. Rocks clattered off walls, windows and cars as both sides brandished slash hooks, iron bars and other weapons at each other. Some of the men wore balaclavas but most were clearly identifiable.

The exchanges continued for well over an hour. In one video clip taken at the scene a woman wheeled a shopping trolley laden with rocks and bricks to the combatants. She returned a second time with the trolley to resupply the rioters. As more Gardaí arrived in the area the situation began to quieten down. A small number of people were arrested at Dalton Park. It was quickly dubbed the Dalton Park riot and thanks to the ubiquitous YouTube clip, as well as the presence of photographers, it became a headline news story nationally.

There were more clashes between rivals at Mullingar hospital where the injured had gone to seek treatment. More and more Garda units were drafted into the area, and even the Air Support Unit put a chopper in the air to assist their colleagues on the ground. Checkpoints were put in place, and a group of Traveller men were arrested elsewhere in the town when various weapons were found in their car. The difference between the Dalton Park disturbance and the spectacular violence in Waterford is that Dalton Park had been captured on video and posted on the internet. It couldn't easily be ignored.

Among the early arrests was Christy 'Ditsy' Nevin, who appeared in court just two days later, on 31 July. Superintendent John Gantly, a former head of the Emergency Response Unit, told the hearing that the Traveller was one of the key instigators of the violence and had obstructed any attempts to broker a peace deal between the clans. The Garda wanted Ditsy to be kept in jail.

An insight into Ditsy's frame of mind came the following year in a bizarre video clip which was sent to the family of Big Joe Joyce in an exchange between some of the younger members of the two families. It was a reply from Ditsy to a comment made by Big Joe in a video which had been sent to the Nevins. Ditsy began his part of the video message in a relatively calm tone and said, 'I want no fight off anyone, I'm not able to fight.' Almost straight away, however, he switched into a confrontational tone and told his rival: 'I'm fighting you on Sunday because you sent for me. You'll never beat me, you dirty big hairy arse.' Then he stripped off his black vest and his face became contorted with anger. His face reddened and his neck muscles tensed as he flexed his arms and shoulders. In a sudden rage he waved his fists and shouted: 'Come on, Joe, come on. I thought I'd never get the day.' Such fury and intensity would definitely be inflammatory in a tense crowd. It was this quality that the superintendent had identified in the District Court when he had said that he wanted the senior Nevin man kept in custody. Ditsy was one of eight men charged in the first court sitting in connection with the Dalton Park incident.

More arrests continued in the days and weeks following the Dalton Park riot as charges were laid against some of the estimated two hundred people involved. At the same time efforts were being made by organizations such as Navan Travellers Workshop, along with Superintendent Gantly and his colleague Superintendent Michael Devine, to broker a truce. Eventually an agreement was made between the warring parties, although there were concerns that those involved in the negotiations might have trouble selling it back to the various hotheads. There was always the danger that some people might be unable to resist meting out casual violence if the opportunity presented itself. With so many people living close together and in some cases intermarried, the chances of a sudden reignition were always high.

An unfortunate aspect of the mayhem and feuding violence was that it came at a time when there was a great opportunity to showcase some sporting talent from the Traveller community. Two boxers, both from Mullingar, John Joe Joyce and John Joe Nevin, were fighting for Ireland in the Olympic Games in Beijing in August 2008. They were widely supported, as people remembered the goodwill towards Francis Barrett in the 1996 Games, the first Traveller to represent Ireland at the Olympics. Instead, the feud violence over the summer fuelled the ongoing prejudice towards Travellers held by many people in the wider community. The sight of unarmed Gardaí without even a protective helmet trying to hold back Traveller clans intent on fighting each other didn't go down well. As the Gardaí continued to do their job, arresting and charging people involved in the riot, the feuding continued despite initial hopes that the truce would hold. It was low-level violence, stuff that didn't make the national news headlines, but it had a terrible effect on those being targeted. Some Travellers were forced to give up jobs because it would have made them easy targets for attacks. Others parked their vehicles a distance away from their own homes after cars and vans were burned out. There were also reports that young Traveller girls had been threatened with rape. It caused the 'fear, fear, fear' that Brigid Myers had referred to and added to intolerable social pressures on families trying to keep away from the trouble. The fact that the feuding in Waterford was at its height added to the sense that the Irish Traveller community was beset by anarchic violence.

One Nevin woman, married to a member of the McDonagh clan, spoke at the time of how her life had been affected. There had been a petrol-bomb attack on her house, while her son's car and house had also been damaged. 'I don't get any sleep. They are threatening me all the time. I'm expecting to be burned out. I'm afraid. I'm afraid for my boys. It's gone out of hand,' she said. Protective grilles were put over the windows, adding to her sense of 'being caged in'.

In that same month of August 2008, there was another arson strike on a different house in which a Nevin family lived. Their kitchen window was smashed in and then petrol was poured through and set alight. 'If my husband didn't wake up, all seven of us would have burned to death. It was the most terrifying experience of my life. What sort of animals would do that with a baby sleeping? They have no mercy,' one of the victims said.

At a bail hearing for four people in October some of the evidence given by an investigating Garda provided more insight into the implacable nature of the feud, where neither side was willing or able to back down. Sergeant Roger Nicholson explained that he had been investigating the riot at Dalton Park on 29 July and was opposing a bail application on the grounds that more trouble was likely to break out. The application was being made in front of Judge John Neilan, who has made a number of remarks concerning Travellers that have sparked controversy. Some of those comments came while dealing with the after-math of the feud violence in Mullingar. On this occasion the judge opted for a geological metaphor: 'It is like a volcano, no sooner has one side of the volcano been con-tained than it erupts in another part of the landscape.' The sergeant, going with the metaphor, said the situation was beginning to erupt again, with a lot of people who were not previously involved now being dragged into it. He said that in some cases it was brother against sister, adding that 'by and large, there is not a lot of sense to it'.

There were other men before the court that day over charges that stemmed from incidents that had occurred as far back as 2006. Inspector Jarlath Folan said that 'a considerable amount' of time and Garda resources had been committed to the investigation, with efforts at mediation attempted by the Gardaí proving unsuccessful. He also said there had been several confrontations between the warring Travellers since 2006, and reported that even the night before the court hearing, thirty members of one family and eight of another had been involved in a clash.

When bail conditions were eventually set down, they included curfews between 8 p.m. and 8 a.m., with various individuals banned from entering certain estates around the town. The judge even ordered that the address of one defendant not be published to avoid the family living there being targeted in revenge attacks.

Even before the criminal justice system could get down to the business of sorting out all the charges in the aftermath of the Dalton Park riot there were still other matters before the court. The second attack on the Myers home in 2007 had resulted in twenty people being charged and prosecuted. Some of those in front of the court on that account had been charged in connection with the events in July 2008 as well. The hearings overlapped, and this had the potential to kick things off again.

The case was heard in November 2008, when both Ned and Brigid Myers took to the witness stand to give evidence of the mob attack on their home at Grange Crescent. Ned Myers told how he saw Christy 'Ditsy' Nevin approach his house. According to Ned, Ditsy and his sons were part of a much larger group of forty or fifty people who were armed with billhooks, baseball bats, stones and hatchets. Ned had run back into his house where he told Brigid and his children to get upstairs: 'I was afraid of my life.' When the mob reached the house they began to smash up the three cars outside and throw stones at the windows. Ned explained that he was related to a number of those who took part in the attack. 'I have no difficulties at all with these people, these people have difficulties with everybody,' he said in court. Asked if he could be mistaken in his identification, Ned replied: 'I know all of these people because I am living me whole life in Mullingar.'

Brigid then took her turn in the witness box, where at times she struggled to keep her emotions in check. 'I heard the children roaring that there's a crowd of Nevins coming. I roared to them to put a table again the back door,' she said. The crowd were shouting, 'Come out, ye dirt ye, come out ye Myers bastards,' according to Brigid. She saw some of those accused 'breaking the car with a billhook' while others were throwing rocks at the house. 'If a bull or an elephant got a clout of one of them rocks I'd say they'd never rise again,' she said. Describing the chaos and mayhem Brigid gave evidence of people running in all directions while rocks were coming through the window 'like you wouldn't know what' during the attack, which lasted no more than four or five minutes. 'I know these people all my life, some are first and second cousins to me I'm ashamed to say it,' she explained.

She said that her and her husband's decision to give evidence and go through with the criminal prosecution was motivated by the desire to see justice being done and had nothing to do with making insurance claims. Her ten-year-old daughter, who had locked herself in the bathroom during the attack, hadn't slept in her own room since. Brigid said that the group of individuals who had threatened her were 'going from one innocent family to another, burning and breaking'.

A solicitor for the defendants made an application for the dismissal of all charges, claiming the 'evidence of the prosecution is unreliable' due to the large numbers of individuals involved. One woman then gave evidence that her accused husband had been elsewhere at the time. Judge David Anderson accepted the evidence and the case against the man was dropped. At this point the case took an unconventional turn when the judge said that he would attempt to be fair to the remaining defendants by organizing a line-up. He called Ned and Brigid Myers to the top of the courtroom and told them to tell him if anyone called up hadn't been involved in the attack on their house. Each defendant was then summoned by name and date of birth and stood along two walls of the courtroom. Neither Myers made any indication to the court as the men were called forward.

The twenty defendants were found guilty by the judge. He then imposed the maximum sentence of three months in jail on seventeen of them for the charge of threatening and abusive behaviour. Three others who had been charged with criminal damage were jailed for twelve months. Judge Anderson said that 'the behaviour of these people has gone beyond the boundaries'. He described it as an extraordinary case and said ordinary people in Ireland would not tolerate such behaviour. He applauded the Myers family, who had 'shown remarkable courage in coming to court to testify' about the incident. After the hearing Gardaí had to organize a bus to transfer all twenty men to prison.

The unusual courtroom identity parade and even the transport arrangements again served to highlight how Traveller feuding violence requires a different approach from the Gardaí and the courts. Just as Gardaí had to mount security operations in Waterford and Tralee around court hearings, so too did their colleagues in Mullingar. The grounds of the court and even the approach streets can be flashpoints when defendants from rival clans – along with family, friends and witnesses – arrive at the same time. Quite often prosecution cases are used by members of rival clans to bargain with each other and to find ways to have criminal charges dropped. With the Dalton Park riot, however, there were plenty of independent and reliable witnesses in the form of the Gardaí at the scene. With sixty-four people eventually being charged, though, the proceedings had to be carefully managed. Special court dates were set up to ensure that things went as peacefully as the circumstances would allow. The procedure was fraught with difficulties and conducted under the eye of an intrigued and watchful media.

Judge Gerard Haughton, who had dealt with one of the first court hearings, clearly understood that these were no ordinary public-order charges. Eleven men, including Christy 'Ditsy' Nevin, were brought before him eight days after the Dalton Park riot. He granted bail, but did so under strict conditions. He set out ten bail conditions that the defendants had to obey, including staying away from certain addresses, not gathering in groups of more than three, staying out of pubs and not trying to contact anyone from the opposing side. They also had to sign on at the local Garda station, with members of the rival clans doing so on different days so that they could avoid each other.

He made the men wait in court while their bail bonds, normally posted to defendants, were prepared. Each man was made to initial the pages so that there could be no misunderstanding about exactly what was required. The judge told the Gardaí that, if needed, he was available any time for a special sitting of the court. He warned that he would find it difficult to re-release anyone if they breached their bail conditions. The various arrests and bail conditions had the immediate effect of preventing any major conflagration, even if low-level attacks continued sporadically.

At a subsequent hearing, Judge John Neilan also recognized the unusual circumstances surrounding the case, as well as the need to impose bail conditions to prevent further incidents. The judge expressed his concern that the ongoing litany of attacks could lead to a terrible tragedy:

> There seems to be an intent in respect of all these families to continue feuding over the most trivial of issues, without any regard for public safety and welfare. It seems to be the main focus of these particular families who have nothing else to do. The tragic reality of this is someone's house is going to be torched some night and four or five people will be burned to death, or a car will be hijacked and its occupants will be butchered to pieces. It would appear to me that these people have absolutely nothing to do in life but engage in this conduct.

By February 2009, after months of investigation by the Gardaí, the Director of Public Prosecutions gave the green light to go ahead with the prosecutions of another forty-six people in connection with the Dalton Park riot. In a carefully planned operation ten separate Garda units made the early-morning arrests on 8 February. The next day, those being charged all appeared in court, including one pregnant woman. There was a heavy security presence around the courthouse, where the Dog Unit was on hand along with the Public Order Unit. The Air Support Unit was also back in the skies overhead.

The defendants included twenty-three members of the

Nevin family, eight McDonaghs and nine Dinnegans who had been on the side of the McDonaghs. The sheer number of defendants made for a long session, and at times tempers frayed. One of the Dinnegans complained that he had been badly treated by the Gardaí, who had failed to take his diabetes into account. He claimed: 'They wouldn't give me any food.' When told he should complain to Mullingar Garda Station or to the Garda Ombudsman he replied: 'I have me rights.' The exchange ended when Judge Neilan said that if he continued he would be remanded in custody. Another man was held in contempt of court after swearing at the judge. Told to complain at Mullingar Garda Station, he said: 'I have been doing that for the last three years and I'm getting the deaf ear every fucking time.'

At the end of the court session Christy 'Ditsy' Nevin reacted to news cameras outside the courthouse by dancing an Irish-style jig. When the judge learned of this at a subsequent hearing he wasn't impressed and revoked Ditsy's bail. 'He is not going to treat this court with the contempt he showed in the courtyard after he was given bail,' the judge said. He added that as one of the older men Ditsy should be setting an example for the youngsters in his community instead of inciting them to commit further acts of violence.

Two weeks later it was the turn of one member of the Nevin clan to lose his cool with the same judge, calling him 'a prick' during proceedings. The man, then aged twenty-two, had been brought to court after breaking his bail conditions by getting rowdy in Longford town. When approached by Gardaí he had dropped his trousers and exposed himself to them. The Gardaí found details of a Credit Union account in his name when he was arrested, which showed he had €100,000 in an account. The judge then set his new bail bond at that amount and said he wanted to send out the message that breaking bail conditions would result in more than just a slap on the wrist. 'If I don't move to attract the highest price, then the community involved will say, "It doesn't cost that much, we'll have another day out."' The young man was less than impressed, and shouted: 'If I murdered all of Mullingar I wouldn't get that.'

In the meantime, Ditsy had again failed to stay out of trouble after going to the bother of getting bail again. The Dalton Park riot had resulted in high levels of attention from the Gardaí. In April 2009 two officers from the Criminal Assets Bureau called to Ditsy's home in Mullingar to deliver a tax demand. He didn't take it too well. In May he was charged with making threats to kill the officers and was back in court again. Evidence was given that Ditsy had emerged from a caravan, bare-chested and swinging his belt in his hand. He had told the officers to 'get off the site' or he would shoot them and shoot himself, pointing his fingers to his head. He had continued to shout abuse and threatened that he'd get three nearby men to beat them up. He apologized in court and said the threats were 'a slip of a word' and that he had nothing against the two officers.

By December, the cases were finally ready for the Circuit Court session in Mullingar. The number of defendants had grown to sixty-four, and it was a long day as the indictments were read out. Everyone pleaded guilty to the charge of violent affray even though it could attract a maximum sentence of ten years. The presiding judge was Anthony Kennedy, who remanded all the defendants until the following sitting in February 2010, warning them to stick to their bail conditions. When the day of reckoning came, there was another big security operation launched by the Gardaí to prevent more violence breaking out.

As the prosecution case was reviewed, the court was told that the riot had begun because a member of the Nevin family had not paid a debt owed to the Dinnegan family. This stemmed from a bet staked on the bare-knuckle fight between Thomas 'Knock-out' Nevin and Martin McDonagh. Prosecuting counsel John Hayden said that the families had been unable to reach a compromise, with the heads of the opposing factions being unwilling to back down. The families had then decided to settle the issue with a thirty-minute fight, using rocks and weapons that included swords, baseball bats and pitchforks. Judge Kennedy said the evidence was indicative of the criminality and lawlessness that had terrorized the local community. Christy 'Ditsy' Nevin and Anthony Dinnegan, however, said that a truce had since been reached and promised there would be no more trouble.

Each of the defendants was then called forward and sentenced to jail, ranging from six months to four years. Tensions rose until, at the end, Judge Kennedy finally indicated that he would suspend all the prison terms on condition that everyone sentenced stayed out of trouble. There was a collective sigh of relief on both sides as they realized they wouldn't be going to jail that day. 'Thanks be to God and His blessed mother that no one is going to prison, and it will learn people to respect and get on with one another, that's the most important thing, and it's a good thing,' said Dinnegan on behalf of his family outside the court. As for Ditsy, he too appeared to have come around to the idea of a truce. He commented to reporters: 'There won't be any more of that in Mullingar ever again. I don't think there'll be any more trouble.'

If Ditsy's words prove to be wrong, then it won't have been the first time a Traveller has promised peace only to see the feud flare up somewhere else. The enmity that builds up in the course of a feud can take a long time to dissipate. Relationships within clans can be poisoned, especially if one faction is seen to have failed to provide the requisite support to another. The passion that can drive a vendetta is an unfortunate corruption of the intense family pride that should work as a positive factor in favour of young Travellers. Being part of a Traveller clan provides a network of contacts that could spread across the world. The feuds described in this book highlight the remoteness Travellers feel from wider society. That sense of being apart makes it far harder for the police or judiciary to get to grips with the hard core of perpetrators who insist on continuing a destructive vendetta. The knock-on effect is to concentrate even more power and influence into the hands of the thugs among Travellers. It also feeds into a negative perception of Travellers by the wider community, who are frightened and perplexed by feud-related violence.

Among Travellers, feuding leaves many families living in fear and worried about doing simple things, such as bringing children to school or going to buy groceries. It also contributes to Travellers' negative self-perception, which has to be a factor in the tragically high rate of suicide in the community. Feuds can develop into downward spirals of violence that benefit a handful, who appear to take personal pride and pleasure in making others miserable.

THE FIGHTERS

7

Fighting for Jesus

Bare-knuckle boxing, some would say, is the purest form of pugilism. But it was not always the preserve of Travellers. Until gloves were introduced, it was how the sportsmen of the nineteenth century made their names. It was a brutal sport in which boxers were 'adopted' by rich gentlemen in the manner of racehorses, to fight when required for their master's amusement or pride. The best were physically brutish men, whose knuckles were so scarred and calloused they could punch the bark off trees without injury. The sport had evolved from the tradition of duelling, indulged in by the upper crust. The higher echelons of Irish society in the eighteenth century were enthusiastic duellists when it came to settling conflicts. Among the lower classes, a bout of fisticuffs might be employed as a form of dispute resolution between neighbours. It's probably no accident that that practice survived in Ireland through Irish Travellers as a poor man's way to settle disputes over matters of honour. Afterwards the combatants would shake hands and the argument would be at an end, at least in theory.

The tradition of a staged, formal bout between two men, in which their seconds arbitrate on the rules and procedures, still exists among modern Irish Travellers.

Irish Traveller bare-knuckle contests are genuine. Each fighter brings a fair-play man and these have the task of refereeing the fight and the responsibility of declaring the winner. The contest continues until a fighter is knocked out or 'gives best', in other words he concedes the bout. A fighter is disqualified if he hits an opponent who is not on his feet or if he bites his rival. Kicks, headbutts or the use of the elbow are similarly regarded as 'dirty fighting', with the miscreant deemed to having lost the contest by default.

As a method of settling disputes, bare-knuckle boxing often causes more trouble than it solves. After a fight, arguments may begin to surface over whether the fair-play men called a result too quickly or some kind of underhand trick tipped the balance unfairly against the loser. Such arguments can even be the spark to ignite a fully fledged round of feud violence. While bare-knuckle fights may have once been a form of dispute resolution, they are now all about being the big dog on the block. A Traveller in England, sick of hearing how a distant cousin in Ireland 'is the best of the fighting men', might issue a challenge. There may have been an underlying source of friction between the families in the past, but now it's about being recognized for fighting ability. Among the Traveller men who regard themselves as bare-knuckle fighters, reputation is everything. While there may be considerable sums of money gambled on the outcome, it's more about the bragging rights than the cash.

Winning is important, but that can't happen until a challenge is accepted. Issuing a challenge to an established fighter has become an art form. The favourite method now is to post a message on YouTube which the entire world can see, adding to the pressure to take up the gauntlet and fight. But it still takes word of mouth and chit-chat among the Traveller men to force a fighter out of his comfort zone and make him take on a mouthy new arrival to protect his precious reputation. Many of the video clips posted on the internet by challengers are thick with hyperbole and colourful insults and to outsiders come across as deeply insulting. In reality such videos are closer to the 'trash talk' employed by professional boxers keen to hype up audiences and the media ahead of a matchup. As the much-loved British heavyweight boxer Frank Bruno said: 'Boxing is just show business with blood.'

One bare-knuckle fighter certainly knew how to hold the crowd's attention. Even in his sixties Dan Rooney is a physically imposing man. There is no mistaking the intensity when he takes an offered hand and grips it in his maw. His steely-blue, unblinking gaze adds to the sense of deep strength. It's no doubt part of the reason why Rooney is adored by so many Travellers. His legend as a fighter has, for the most part, survived the decades since his retirement, although some claims still surface about who really won what fight. The power of that legend now comes as much from his commitment to God as it once did from his prowess as a bare-fist fighter when younger.

With his silver-grey hair brushed back from his sallow face, Rooney looks like a country gent. Dressed in a pristine sports jacket and an open-neck shirt with neatly pressed chinos, he exudes a steely confidence. Over his eyes and upper lip faint scars hint at the violence in his past. There is nothing else to suggest that he was once a man who would take up position at the centre of a heaving crowd to fight an opponent with his bare fists. He has since changed himself from a rock of physical strength to one of spirituality, whose purpose on earth is to convert unbelievers. There is a slow, deliberate sense of him assessing whoever talks to him. But when he speaks, his words are urgent, almost plaintive, and entirely about the need to let Jesus into your heart. The power and passion his opponents once faced have now been harnessed by Dan Rooney the preacher. His higher calling is genuine and unswerving.

There was a time when Dan Rooney had a different cross to bear. He had a reputation to defend and he did it with his fists. He was the man other fighting men wanted to take on. If a Traveller was handy with his fists then he needed to challenge Dan Rooney if he was to prove himself above all other Travellers. Ainey McGinley was once one of those young Travellers who wanted to test his mettle against the legend. In the summer of 1990 he arrived in Crossmaglen, South Armagh, with the intention of fighting Rooney in the town square. In the days before YouTube a challenger would have to go looking for the man he wanted to fight. Ainey spent three days waiting in Rooney's home town, where he told all and sundry he was going to beat their hero. The whole event was captured on video.

As the challenger, McGinley had no choice except to sit tight until the man with the reputation arrived to put his status on the line. Thousands of people, not just Travellers, had gathered to see the encounter in Crossmaglen. Spectators had travelled from all over Ireland and the UK to witness the bare-knuckle legend in action. Dozens of young people were seen on the video sitting on a roof to catch a glimpse of the fight. Children, adults, old-age pensioners, Traveller and country people had all mingled together, waiting for the spectacle to start. Among them were many people who were clearly adoring fans of Rooney.

Ainey was not one of them. At one point he stood on a concrete and wire-mesh security structure with his arms aloft, winding up his crowd of supporters. He spoke dismissively of Rooney, who had previously announced his retirement. 'I've come to bate him anyway. Any time that's good for Dan is good for me,' he told the crowd.

All the time Rooney played it cool. He kept McGinley waiting as he returned home from London. In the town square, crash barriers were linked together in a bid to keep the crowd under control. Eventually news came through that Rooney had arrived and the fight was about to take place. Ainey McGinley emerged from the crowd and immediately went into a huddle with the fair-play men. He quickly found some space and began rolling his shoulders and shadow-boxing to warm up. When Rooney finally appeared the pair were made to shake hands twice by the fair-play men, who were anxious that they be seen to do their jobs. Rooney then took off his blue shirt and dropped it to the ground without even looking to see if anyone had been ready to take it for him. It was a swaggering display of arrogance from Rooney, who was doing his best to psych out the challenger.

Straight away the fighters went at it as the self-appointed marshals struggled to keep the crowd from closing in on the two men. Their fighting styles couldn't have been more different. They both fought in orthodox stance, leading with the left fist, but Ainey bobbed and danced like a ring fighter. He leaned slightly forward, with his hands high in defence and his chin close to his chest. Rooney fought in a straight-backed style, with his fists carried in front of him almost in the style of sepia-pictured Victorian pugilists. His movements were minimal compared to McGinley's. His long-armed hammer blows emerged with surprising speed. McGinley opened with the first flurry of punches, but Rooney quickly got the range of the challenger. His left jab connected with McGinley's face and one haymaker from his right just missed the target. But the crowd had begun to close in and the overexcited marshals made things worse. It looked as if an all-out riot was on the brink of breaking out.

Yet the fighters kept their concentration and ignored the surrounding chaos even as it threatened to engulf them. At one point they were standing toe to toe, literally trading punches, with Rooney's height advantage working in his favour. As they broke apart, McGinley waved his arms for the crowd to move back just before the two locked into another furious exchange of heavy punches. They both absorbed blows, any one of which would have knocked out most normal people. Leaving aside the brutal nature of the exchange, it was an exciting contest. The cameraman recording the fight was swamped as the crowd surged forward to get even closer, some of them screaming at the top of their lungs. The pair continued to slug it out in a space that had shrunk from the size of the town square to a narrow heaving hole no bigger than the average sitting room.

The final exchange of punches was obscured from the camera by the bodies of the men jostling for a better view. Soon afterwards Ainey McGinley was hoisted on his supporters' shoulders and raised his arms in victory. His face was bloodied but he looked convinced that he had won the match. Rooney was then filmed urging McGinley to return to continue the fight. His right eye was badly bruised and almost swollen shut after presumably being caught with a hard punch by the challenger. Then it was Rooney's turn to be celebrated as the victor. One of the fair-play men, another Ainey McGinley from Longford, said that both men had claimed victory, but cut himself off to shout at an off-camera partisan to 'shut his mouth'.

The next day a relaxed Dan Rooney rested on an ordinary sitting-room sofa. A pair of aviator sunglasses covered his bruised eye while a cousin conducted an interview on video camera in the style of a sports documentary. Rooney appeared as a fighting Traveller at the height of his powers, the epitome of hard-man cool and the subject of open adulation by those who surrounded him. Asked how he had won the fight, he replied with a grin: 'The other fellah, running away, if he'd stayed it would have went a lot better for me. If he says he's not finished why didn't he stay and finish his battle after all his talking and mouthing? He didn't do much talking when the fight was over.' The video has long been a sought-after cult classic among young Travellers and bare-knuckle fight fans.

A dispute over who won the fight is standard fare when two fighters are evenly matched. Sometimes a well-known fighter who doesn't want to lose face will look for a 'technicality' to void the fight. There could be a suggestion of a bite or that a punch was landed when a fighter was down. It is part of the continuous spiral of bare-knuckle fighting. The boxers can't afford to admit defeat and will deny it happened even when they have been cleanly knocked out in front of everyone. Every possible excuse is proffered to explain how a fighter somehow came to be laid low. It ranges from 'I was sick' to having been obliged 'to go drinking' following a funeral. A regular excuse is that 'I wasn't shown fair play.' This, however, can have wide-ranging implications that extend far beyond the two fighters and their clans. To accuse the fair-play men of not acting in the fighters' honest interest can in itself become the cause of a dispute which leads to yet another bare-knuckle fight.

The bout in Crossmaglen wasn't the only one that showed just how dangerous and chaotic bare-knuckle fights could be, especially ones that featured the great Dan Rooney. For another infamous fight, captured on video, Rooney travelled to London the same year to fight a member of the Cash clan. The night before he was to face Michael Cash he was at the centre of an adoring and boozy crowd who'd travelled from Ireland to watch the bout. The scene in the pub was akin to a crowd of sports fans heading for Twickenham or Wembley, getting tanked up on a weekend away from work and family. Rooney himself even looked a bit the worse for wear, not exactly the best preparation for an athlete the night before a tough contest. The original tape featured a number of well-known characters from South Armagh, both Travellers and 'country people' who had made the trip across the Irish Sea.

The fight was due to take place at a halting site in Hemel Hempstead, north of London. The camera caught Michael Cash in his tracksuit flanked by his close relatives as he strode to the rendezvous. Behind the fighter and his entourage there were hundreds more Travellers, mostly men in their Sunday best, and also a small number of women with children in tow. It was immediately apparent that a huge, expectant crowd was gathering – never a good prospect for two bare-knuckle boxers who want to scrap it out in a fair fight.

Early on tensions were high as Rooney again played the psychological trick of letting his opponent sweat it out, using up their energy with nervous adrenalin. There's never any guarantee that a bare-knuckle bout will happen until the fighters begin exchanging punches. The fact that a mouthy young fighter named Paddy Doherty and his cousin John Kiely were on hand that day didn't bode well for the chances of the fight going ahead without some incident. They were spitting the insults and the challenges. 'You know your hero, Dan Rooney? He's going to be history today. History off me or history off him,' said Doherty to the cameraman recording the event.

There was more posturing as Michael Cash was filmed on a phone giving the impression he was talking to Rooney. 'Get over here and fight, get it over with. Where do you want to fight? I'm only six miles from you. Talk sense with your big calf's head,' he said, hanging the phone up. Then he said to those nearby: 'He's coming.' Cash went into an empty halting bay and began swinging his arms ready for the fight. The roof of the bay's toilet block was covered with people, and even more were lined up on an embankment for a perfect view of the arena. When Rooney made an appearance he strode down the road with purpose, surrounded by a phalanx of his own close relatives and associates. A crowd of supporters followed behind, walking briskly. Immediately there was a flash of trouble when something was thrown and a young man jumped from a caravan roof. But Rooney got to the halting bay ready to fight as Cash reappeared and made his way towards the Traveller from Crossmaglen.

As Rooney stripped off his shirt for the contest there was a sudden surge from the crowd at the edge of the caravan bay. A vicious brawl broke out and one of Rooney's brothers became embroiled in a savage fight. It seemed that Doherty and Kiely, anxious to boost their reputations, had jumped the gun, wanting a chance to have a crack at the Rooneys before Michael Cash. The scene was one of complete chaos, with hundreds of men packed tightly together. At one point, Dan and one of his brothers had their backs to a truck as Kiely threw a series of punches at one of the men. He was seen then being shouldered by members of the mob as he lifted his arms in victory.

A bare-chested Paddy Doherty got into Dan Rooney's face, demanding that he fight. He was animated and aggressive, but Rooney played it cool, refusing the younger man's excited challenge. Doherty interpreted this as conceding victory and turned away, punching the air before he too was lifted up by the crowd. Doherty and Kiely, perched on the shoulders of their supporters, were almost brandished at the Rooneys as provocative totems. Rooney eventually extricated himself from the melee and walked away. The crowd trotted after him and he had to endure a gauntlet of puerile insults such as: 'You're a fucking queer,' as he made his way back to his car. His brother's face was cut and bleeding and his right eye was already swollen and shut. Even as Rooney sat in a car which slowly began to drive away, Cash taunted him with insults. As he left, Cash shouted: 'You big calf's head.' A woman then told the camera that the Dohertys and Kielys were 'the best people'.

The message was repeated later on camera by Paddy Doherty, who had changed into a bomber jacket, left open to reveal his chest and the religious scapular hanging from his neck. A scapular is worn by some Catholics as a sign of devotion to a particular saint. Normally it comes with a set of promises to which the wearer must adhere in order to receive benefits from the saint.

Elaborate and overt shows of Roman Catholic devotion are part and parcel of Traveller custom, although actual adherence to the Church's teachings attracts less enthusiasm. The irony of a devout Catholic violently hijacking a bare-knuckle bout and making threats against another man would, at the time, have been lost on Paddy Doherty.

More and more Travellers, however, have taken the route of genuine religious devotion, but have not gone down that path with the established Catholic Church. Where state institutions and mainstream churches have failed, charismatic and born-again Christians are succeeding like no one else in bringing Travellers into the fold. The Traveller evangelists exist side by side with those who remain faithful to traditional Catholicism. It is a fast-growing movement within the Traveller community which has already produced a number of pastors ready to deliver high-octane sermons. It's a route that Dan Rooney has chosen to take in his later years. He began to avoid the chaos that came with bare-knuckle fights and went to live in Coventry in the UK. Now he appears regularly at prayer meetings all over Ireland and the UK. He is becoming a leading preacher among Travellers and Gypsies, making the journey from street fighter to Christian soldier, a trend emerging among his people. As a pastor and preacher Rooney now fires off Bible quotes with all the strength he once mustered during brutal bare-knuckle clashes.

In August 2012 he appeared at a huge gathering of Christian Travellers in Selby, Yorkshire, where thousands of families from across the UK and Ireland had assembled. At a youth meeting hymns were sung and people took the microphone to give their testimony of how they had become devoted to God. Held in a huge marquee, rows of chairs faced a stage dominated by a large wooden crucifix. The youngsters seated in the audience included many dressed in typical Traveller fashion: girls wearing what people in the wider community would regard as revealing outfits. They clapped and joined in the singing, some standing holding the palms of their hands forward and their eyes shut with the intensity of the experience.

When it came to Dan Rooney's turn he strode purposefully on to the stage. The contrast with the video taken twenty-two years previously in Crossmaglen couldn't have been greater. While all eyes were on him, the crowd of young Travellers were calm and relaxed. The chaos and undercurrent of menace that had run through the crowd when Rooney had stripped off to fight McGinley was entirely absent. Most of those present were hardly old enough to have been born when the infamous fight took place in 1990, and more than likely had never heard of him except as Pastor Dan Rooney.

The steadfast gaze that he had once fixed on to McGinley was still there. But as he told the room: 'Tonight, it's all about Jesus.' Reading from the Bible, he warned the young congregation about the dangers they faced from evil and asked them to help others to pray. 'The devil is so wise and so clever. The greatest tool Satan has, [is] giving people plenty of time,' he said. In typical evangelist style he told the teenagers that: 'Jesus wants to set you free tonight.' Throughout the fifteen-minute sermon he maintained his forceful delivery. At one point when he paused to take a swig from a bottle there was a light-hearted moment when, to laughter, he said: 'Let me get a drop of water, I'm dying of thirst.' But otherwise it was fire and brimstone and a clear divide between God and Satan, safety and danger. As it was for the bare-knuckle boxer of old, it still came down to a simple choice between winning and losing.

These days Rooney has no interest in talking about his infamous bare-knuckle bouts, preferring to refer to the Bible, which he carries everywhere he goes. At a prayer meeting in the working-class Dublin suburb of Ballyfermot, Rooney was the guest of honour in a congregation who had gathered to listen to another Traveller preacher, Kevin Purcell from Newry. An inquisitive journalist who tried to broach the topic of Rooney's bare-knuckle boxing days became the next potential convert. Asked about the days when his fists did the talking, Rooney paused, unswerving in his duty to God, before replying: 'Are you saved? Is Jesus in your heart?' When asked about the story of Big Joe Joyce, who broke his leg during a bout and insisted on being tied to a truck to allow him to fight on, Rooney would only say that his former opponent 'is a good man'. While happy to evangelize about the need to turn away from sin, he didn't want to talk about the fights that made his formidable reputation.

Rooney's preaching has also meant action. He has contributed to various charity efforts aimed at helping homeless people deal with drug addiction, particularly among the Traveller community. When on the road in the UK or Ireland he calls into halting sites to speak with Travellers in a bid to convert them to his brand of Christianity. Some of the people he meets are involved in serious crime and have their own reputations among Travellers, but it doesn't bother Rooney, who has seen it all before. He may no longer be the bare-knuckle fighter of old, but to watch him deliver a sermon it would appear that Dan Rooney is still in show business.

8

It's Showtime

Irish Traveller bare-knuckle boxers instinctively know how to put on a show. They also know how to size up situations quickly and how to press the right buttons to provoke a reaction. It was inevitable that celebrity and Paddy Doherty would find each other. The hard man was already well known among Irish Travellers before he stole the show in an episode of *Big Fat Gypsy Weddings*. The reality TV series was a massive ratings winner for Channel 4, and for Doherty it was a springboard for a lucrative media career. His tight, black hair and clean-shaven square jaw marked him out as a real-life version of the only other Irish Traveller character to have made it to the screen in the UK. That character was Mickey, played by Brad Pitt in the hit gangster movie *Snatch*. Hollywood's ultimate alpha male stepped into the role of a hard-drinking, blindly loyal Traveller patriarch, who is unafraid to wear his deepest emotions on his non-existent sleeve. Above all he is a teak-tough, unbeatable bare-knuckle fighter, who is too wily even for the most sinister villains from the outside world. Mickey was admired by Gypsies, Travellers and menfolk across the board. Paddy Doherty then appeared as a real-life version of Mickey, showing that the movies, for once, hadn't gone overboard in dramatizing a menacing and volatile member of the underworld. Paddy even has the tattoos and the singlet vest.

In his book, *Hard Knocks and Soft Spots*, Paddy describes how he felt like a traditional Traveller from an early age. He fondly remembers his life on the road in the Midlands, near Birmingham, with Mummy and Daddy Ward. They had moved from Ireland to England, where Paddy was born in 1959. They eked out a living by collecting scrap metal or doing tarmac work. Even as a five- or six-year-old Paddy played his part, pushing leaflets through letter boxes and knocking on doors. Life was tough, but he loved being a nomad and never knowing what the next day would bring.

He recalls how he despaired when he was sent to live the life of 'country people' with an older sister in Manchester. He didn't want to be in a flat, where everything seemed so solid. Being stuck in school meant there was no way to escape the hostility of the wider community, who appeared to hold an abiding hatred for Travellers. It was only when he began training with a local boxing club that he started to feel confident and sure about himself. As a teenager he discovered that his true father was Patrick Doherty, a Traveller with a reputation as a fighting man. The woman he had known all his life as his big sister was really his mother.

As he explains in his book, this discovery of his true origins hardened the sense of displacement Paddy had felt while growing up. His aggression, which arose from years of being bullied and the apparent rejection by his biological mother and father, had been channelled by the rigid training schedule of the boxing club. Now that he knew his real identity he was only too happy to step outside the ring to prove his courage and to claim his place among Travellers. As the years progressed Paddy had to deal with the joys of marriage, becoming a father, and the sadness of grief when his eldest son Patrick died tragically in a car crash. Three other children died shortly after birth as a result of Fraser syndrome, a rare congenital genetic disorder.

In between the emotional highs and lows he cemented a reputation for reckless bravery and thuggery. He has been shot, almost died, and had his face smashed and rebuilt more than once. As he grew older he was called on by other Travellers to mediate in disputes as well as to referee bare-knuckle 'fair fights'. No doubt aware that the wrong comment could cause trouble, Paddy doesn't go into too much detail or mention specifics about the fights in which he officiated. Although based in the UK, he has played a role in facilitating bouts between the Quinn-McDonaghs and the Joyces as they went through a series of fights from the mid-1990s. One infamous fight between members of the Quinn-McDonaghs and the Nevins took place in Paddy's yard. He also featured on a videotaped message sent to members of the Oxford Joyces, in which the Quinn-McDonaghs accused the Joyces of cowardice for failing to turn up for a fight in the UK. They launched a foul-mouthed rant at the camera and sent the video to a relative living in County Meath at the time.

Just before he made it big on British TV he was on hand in the summer of 2008 for one of the most-hyped bare-knuckle fights between two Irish Travellers. He was there doing fair play for Paddy 'Jaws' Ward, who had challenged Barney 'The Gorilla' McGinley, who in turn had Big Joe Joyce watching his corner. This was the big time in terms of Irish Traveller bare-knuckle fighting. It was a clash between two fighters known among Travellers as real fighting men. On the day of the much-anticipated fight Paddy was right in the middle, but he wasn't the centre of attention.

His job as a fair-play man was to make sure the rules of bare-knuckle fighting were observed. The fighter selects his own fair-play man, usually from a neutral clan, to accompany him to the fight. The fair-play men are also there to keep spectators away from the fighters and to ensure the result is beyond question. They can also call on the fighters to shake hands and call it a draw. It's both an honour and a poisoned chalice to be called in to act as fair-play man. If things get out of control or if a fair-play man is accused of not doing the job without favour, it can lead to trouble. A fight without a fair-play man to supervise is known as 'a dirty fight' and Paddy has admitted that he has been successful at those as well.

Paddy Doherty's colourful character ensured that his reputation spread beyond the confines of the Traveller community. The people in TV-land finally came looking for him as he turned fifty. His first start on reality TV began with Danny Dyer's *UK's Deadliest Men* series, which aired in 2008. The actor interviewed Paddy at his yard in Salford, where 'PD' was painted in giant letters on the road at the entrance to the halting site. Doherty brought Dyer to the Appleby Horse Fair, where it was clear that the garrulous Traveller hard man had a spark of something special. The bi-annual fair is a huge gathering of Gypsies and Travellers from all over Britain and Ireland. Horses are bought and sold there. It's a place to meet other Travelling people, to show off and have a few beers, and sometimes it is a place where old scores are settled, too. Youngsters and older men alike clamoured to shake Doherty's hand.

Dyer hinted at an undercurrent of menace, but as Doherty encountered friends and acquaintances it was nothing but good-natured hand-shaking and back-slapping. There was nothing to indicate the dark part of Paddy's character, although he had earlier told Dyer that he'd have no problem biting a man's ear off in a fight and swallowing it so that it couldn't be surgically reattached. Later Doherty would complain that the show had been edited in such a way as to make him look as if he was talking about how he would fight in the present when in fact, he claimed, he had been talking about his youth.

Eighteen years earlier Paddy Doherty had made a cameo appearance on the video recording taken at a halting site in Hemel Hempstead, where Dan Rooney had been due to square off in his bare-knuckle fight with Michael Cash in front of at least a thousand Travellers. It was a scene of heaving chaos as a young and lean Paddy told the camera: 'I rate myself as the best man in the country, apart from my own people.' When asked how the fight will go, he answers with unbridled aggression: 'I'll tell you how the fight will go. I'll fuck Dan Rooney, I'll fuck any fucking man. If any man wants to jump in and take his place, do it now.'

When the TV cameras came back after Danny Dyer it was for *Big Fat Gypsy Weddings*. The show had begun as a mini-documentary on the Channel 4 *Cutting Edge* series in which a short documentary snippet is aired. In 2010 a clip of *Gypsy Wedding* proved to be an incredible hit in the ratings. It was enough for Channel 4 to commission a five-part series from Firecracker Films. The producers had tapped into the intense curiosity on the part of the wider community about Gypsies and Travellers and their lifestyles. It was the first time any significant TV airtime was given to Travellers. It was young Travellers and Gypsies celebrating their life and embracing their own way of doing things. The outrageous dresses of some brides provided more than a few water-cooler moments for the viewing public. The competitive nature of Traveller families was shown driving the need for even bigger and more lavish wedding celebrations. Tiny teenage girls were literally outweighed by the ornate gowns they demanded from their indulgent parents.

Amid the seemingly ludicrous and never-ending desire for glass carriages, bejewelled tiaras and eye-catching outfits, Paddy Doherty emerged as a counterbalance. Usually, the men from the Irish Traveller clans stayed in the background or didn't even appear in the show. The father of the bride, brothers and male cousins stayed out of shot or had their faces pixellated in the finished cut that was broadcast. They were obviously keen to protect their identities and certainly weren't forthcoming as to the source of the cash used to pay for the lavish celebrations. The dresses alone could cost in excess of €50,000, not to mention the outfits for the bridesmaids. Then there were the cakes, limos, fireworks, liveried horses or whatever else the young bride asked from her father.

Paddy, on the other hand, revelled in his moments in the limelight. His obvious charm made him an immediate hit. Despite his hard-man image he wore his heart on his sleeve. He let his affection for his wife, whom he referred to as 'the woman', shine through even as he played the part of the tough Traveller patriarch, protecting his family and holding his own with good cheer in a hostile world. In one episode, Doherty couldn't hold back the tears as he drank at his son Patrick's graveside to mark the anniversary of his death. His visceral grief quickly surfaced when he talked about his son. The youngster had taken off with his friends in a car after saying goodbye to his father in July 1996. Within minutes news had filtered back that there had been an accident. Paddy had rushed to the hospital but it was too late. Years later on Irish TV, at the height of his celebrity, he described how he had touched his son's bleeding body in the hospital and put his fingers into his own mouth so that he would have part of his beloved son inside his own body.

After *Big Fat Gypsy Weddings* delivered Paddy Doherty to a wider audience it was obvious they wanted more. In the summer of 2011 he was invited to take part in *Celebrity Big Brother*. In the house Paddy Doherty emerged as a rock of common sense and the steadiest personality. He kept his head down and was friendly with everyone, but it was former Atomic Kitten Kerry Katona who quickly recognized in him what the rest of the viewers would soon see. Consciously or otherwise, she attached herself to the Traveller hard man, who found himself cast as a roguish fatherly figure.

The final vote came down to Kerry or Paddy. He won. He roared his delight, and so did many other Travellers in both the UK and Ireland. It was seen as the moment when Travellers were finally recognized as being as much a part of society as everyone else. From his humble origins in Birmingham, as the son of an unmarried Traveller woman, Doherty had found his way to the top of Britain's celebrity culture. He came, he talked, and by 2012 he had conquered. The next TV project saw him team up with fellow *Big Brother* contestant Sally Bercow, the wife of the Speaker of the House of Commons, John Bercow.

But even as Paddy tasted the success of his media career, the shadows of his violent past never seemed far behind. The year before *Big Brother* he had been drinking with a young member of the Oxford Joyces, John Joyce, along with other Travellers. The much younger man had previously been involved in a fight with Paddy's son-in-law. Later, back at Paddy's caravan, Joyce launched an attack after words were exchanged. Caught off guard, Doherty was badly beaten and suffered shocking facial injuries. The case went to court, where the interviews he gave to Danny Dyer were brought up to show the jury his violent nature. Doherty blamed the producers, claiming they had told him what to say and to play up the hard-man image. He said in court:

> All that's for the cameras, all that crap, it was just having a laugh. It's all nonsense, it's just for a joke. The crew sort

of tells you what to say and you play along. Danny Dyer made me out to be a very different person than I was. It was just for the cameras, it's not true.

Joyce was found not guilty.

Then in June 2011 Doherty and Joyce clashed again. This time Doherty had been out jogging when Joyce and his brother Dougie demanded he fight them there and then in the road. Paddy ended up in hospital again with a cut ear and eye and all three were charged with affray. The fracas was captured on camera and posted on the internet. At court hearings, members of the families clashed with each other, and there was a heavy police presence whenever the case came up. The final sentencing date didn't happen until after *Big Brother*, when Paddy, who pleaded guilty to affray rather than put his family through the ordeal of a trial, got a suspended sentence. John Joyce was jailed for fifteen months, while his brother got a hundred and fifty hours of community service.

Determined to give up any connection to bare-knuckle boxing, Paddy stopped acting as a fair-play man and moved to a new halting site in north Wales in 2012. He continued doing TV with the well-received *When Paddy Met Sally*. But again fate intervened and Paddy almost lost another son, David, in another fatal car crash in March 2012. The youngster slammed the Mitsubishi Shogun he was driving into a parked van on a lay-by. Young Doherty's best friend, James Loveridge, who was in the passenger seat, was killed instantly. Three other pals in the back of the SUV were also seriously injured, as was the driver of the van who had pulled in to get forty winks. At the time David had been serving a driving ban for driving without insurance. To make things worse, he fled the crash scene and then stole a Land Rover to get home. In June that year David was sentenced to three years and ten months for causing death by careless driving and other offences, including leaving the scene of an accident and driving without insurance.

In his typical forthright style Paddy later spoke of the devastation the accident had caused. He told *Wales on Sunday* how he had spent the week after the accident with the Loveridge family. After the grief of Patrick's death in a car crash in 1996, Paddy took comfort in the fact that while David was injured and jailed, he hadn't lost another adult son in such tragic circumstances:

> I'm lucky I don't have to visit him in a graveyard. I know he got prison, but he's going to come home to me. I've got a son eighteen years of age, Patrick, who is dead and buried and what would I give for him to be in jail so I could go and see him.

Paddy Doherty's life story is an exceptional one. He makes for good TV and his book is a good read. The pub fights, the incredible emotional highs and lows, the family tragedies are stories that many other Traveller families can understand. But his story is an atypical one. It's as if Paddy Doherty lived the extreme version of the modern urban Irish Traveller's life. When he is on TV Paddy represents Travellers well, showing his fierce commitment to family and his outspoken honesty. They are qualities admired by all Travellers and people from the wider community.

His story goes some way to providing an insight into the Traveller life, but as in all communities, there's no single individual that can be said to be the archetype. Even among the fighting men, who are no strangers to casual violence and to suffering as well as inflicting serious injuries, Doherty's life has been more colourful than most. There are many blood-curdling anecdotes about the well-known fighting men, but none seem to have engrossed themselves so deeply in keeping up a reputation as a hard-man boxer as Doherty did. From his run-in with the Rooneys in 1990 up until his recent media success, Doherty kept himself at the heart of Irish Traveller bare-knuckle boxing through his connections with the likes of Ainey McGinley, Big Joe Joyce and James Quinn-McDonagh. While Doherty became the best known bare-knuckle fighter in the wider community thanks to his TV appearances, among the Travellers that dubious honour belonged to others.

9

The Bare-knuckle Dynasties

One man keen to enjoy the adulation afforded Dan Rooney was Big Joe Joyce. He was known as a tough bare-knuckle boxer and had already consolidated a reputation from his teenage years, when he had first thrown his fists in anger. The contrast between Big Joe and Dan couldn't be greater, even today, with both men in their sixties. There is no way Big Joe would let his fists do all the talking. He has never been short of a few words when it comes to letting people know what he thinks of former rivals and the fighters who now take on his sons. While Rooney is a man of few words, Big Joe strives for colour and can be almost poetic in his description of fights and former opponents. He might enjoy a comparison with Muhammad Ali because when it comes to talking, Big Joe is international class.

As his nickname suggests he is a big man. His grey gaucho-style moustache and mop of hair make him easy to pick out in videos of bare-knuckle fights, where he still turns up as a spectator and occasionally as a fair-play man. When he appears on camera, delivering challenges or talking up a fighter, he doesn't hold back. Joyce gets animated and pulls every possible insult out of the bag. It's designed to infuriate and provoke opponents, and it works. Big Joe has his detractors, as do all the fighting men, but only a fool would underestimate him in any regard. He has experienced all the violent chaos a bare-knuckle fighter can expect in a lifetime. He's done time in jail, while his face and body bear the scars of conflict. His house outside Moate has been smashed up and petrol-bombed. The family's old home in the town was also the scene of various assaults, including one shotgun attack.

Joyce was certainly well able to do more than just talk. He learned the basics of boxing at St Aloysius Boxing Club in the 1960s in Manchester before returning to Ireland aged sixteen. He fought and beat a member of the Maughan family in a clash in Longford in 1968 that would put him on the road and make him one of Ireland's best-known Traveller fighting men. His chance to test his mettle with Dan Rooney came in 1981 in Epsom, a full nine years before Paddy Doherty would try to skip the queue at Hemel Hempstead. Although Rooney was younger than Big Joe Joyce he was already more widely known. Before they fought they had a couple of pints together and the man called on to show fair play was Famous Paddy Cash. Despite being on Rooney territory, with just a brother-in-law for company, Big Joe was allowed to get the fight on unmolested. They went at it for fifteen minutes, swapping punches toe to toe. Then Rooney delivered a punch to Big Joe's left-hand side and he went over on his leg, shattering the bone. Big Joe demanded that he be propped up and tied to a truck to finish off the fight, but the fair-play man intervened and gave victory to Dan Rooney.

Big Joe's fight in Longford in 1968, a bout against Nicky Kiely in Manchester in 1977 and the subsequent fight with Rooney make it clear that fighting Traveller men will travel anywhere to take up a challenge. No one cares about the 'King of the Travellers' title. It doesn't really exist, except in the minds of some 'country people'. It's about one fighter winning bragging rights over the other and proving that they are the best man. There's no rematch unless an argument is made and accepted that somehow fair play wasn't shown. Even accidentally breaking a leg in a fight is no excuse for losing. Neither is it about money. While large sums of cash can be staked on a fighter, there's no question of a fighter winning a purse. Big Joe was told that one gambler lost £70,000 backing him to beat Dan Rooney.

In the years that followed, the two fighters' paths through life considerably diverged. While Dan Rooney found religion and eschewed the violence of bare-knuckle fights, Big Joe has supported his sons, who have followed in his footsteps. He himself even continued fighting right up until 2010, at an age when most athletes would consider themselves well past their prime. Living in a country cottage on the edge of the town of Moate in the Irish midlands, he enjoys the Traveller lifestyle even if he is one of those who stay put in the same house.

Big Joe Joyce has sired a bare-knuckle boxing dynasty like no other. His youngest son, also Joe Joyce, is a fearsome fighter who is now regarded as among the best, every bit as good as his older brother David. As a teenager David won a reputation in the licensed ring as a juvenile boxer, representing Ireland well over a dozen times. But it is Big Joe's grandson, Joe Ward, who has carried the torch farther than any other member of the Joyce clan as far as the wider community is concerned. In his first senior fight in February 2011 he beat another County Westmeath Traveller, David Joe Joyce, at the National Championships in Dublin to win a place in the final.

For his second senior fight, six days later, he was up against Kenny Egan, an Olympic silver medallist, the title holder for ten years in a row and a household name in Ireland. Young and fearless, Joe Ward brushed the old champion aside. He was so far ahead on points by the third round he visibly relaxed and he still had too much power for Egan. Anyone watching who hadn't already heard of Ward was witnessing a boxing prodigy at work. This stunning performance came when he was just seventeen years old and still eligible to fight in the youth ranks. At his tenth senior fight in March 2012 Ward beat Russian Egor Mekhontsev 20–14, becoming European light heavyweight champion.

It was an astounding and meteoric rise to the very top echelon of international amateur boxing. From being a Junior European Champion in 2009, by 2011 Ward was a hot Olympic-medal prospect and his name began appearing in the newspapers. But he still had to fight in a qualifying tournament in Turkey ahead of the Olympics. He duly got to the final, which he needed to win to book his place on the Irish team. However, Ireland's high hopes of Ward making the London Olympics unfortunately came to a bitter end when he was controversially eliminated by Turkish light heavyweight Bahram Muzaffer. The Turk, who was beaten by Egan at the 2008 Olympic Games, was handed a shock 18–15 decision. The result was upheld after an appeal from the Irish team, and so the teenage sensation missed out on the chance to compete at the highest level. The Russian, Mekhontsev, who lost in the European final to Ward, went on to take gold at the London Olympics. It was a real sporting 'What if?'

Claims of fixing, unfairness and cheating abound in the boxing game, whether of the bare-knuckle variety or the official gloved kind. In 1989 Big Joe and another serious fighting man, Anthony O'Donnell, came to blows in Dublin. The story goes that it was a spur-of-the-moment encounter that happened outside a pub. The result of that fight was never agreed, although the O'Donnells claimed that Anthony emerged the winner. A rematch was organized later in the year. It went ahead in Clondalkin, amid a big crowd that attracted the attention of the Gardaí. The youngsters kept the Gardaí at bay by throwing stones, amid claims that big money had been staked by gamblers on the outcome of this heavyweight clash. This time it was O'Donnell who fell, breaking a leg, according to their side of the story. The other version, as told by Big Joe, was that O'Donnell was forced to give up after being cut by a crushing blow to the nose. Joyce claimed victory and, still covered in blood from the bout, posed for a *Sunday World* picture that was used with the headline 'Fists of Fury'. It was a headline that would have ramifications more than twenty years later.

For sixteen years after that, Big Joe Joyce stayed out of bare-knuckle fights. His last match had been in 1990 and since then the only scraps he had got involved with were so-called 'dirty fights', usually when young Travellers full of booze fancied their chances of making a reputation. Then in 2006, out of the blue, Big Joe was called on to go out and take on an old contemporary of his, Ainey McGinley, the man who had fought and claimed victory over Dan Rooney in his Crossmaglen stronghold. The two old heavyweights were set to square up to each other again. Within two months, a series of fights between the Joyces and the McGinleys were lined up to take place in December that year. Top of the bill were the heads of the respective families, who should have been thinking about retirement.

Although both men were now in their late fifties, Ainey McGinley and Big Joe Joyce wanted to get it on. Despite the fact that they had sons who were already formidable bare-knuckle boxers, the old-timers insisted they wanted to go head-to-head. There was no way it was ever going to be a trip down memory lane or a nostalgic veterans' match. This was all-out war. The same rules would apply to them as they would to the men less than half their ages who would be fighting on the same day. Even though they were at this stage grandfathers, being the best still mattered to them both.

Big Joe voiced his opinion about Ainey, who had gone to a newspaper to issue a challenge. Ainey had complained that Big Joe had laid claim to the title of 'King of the Travellers' in a book by this author, *The Outsiders*. Even though no such claim was made, once the challenge was out it was impossible to put it back in the bag. The squabble gathered its own momentum and was generously helped along by Big Joe, who found his own media outlet in which to respond. He summoned a reporter and photographer to his house and the story ended up in the pages of the *Sunday World*. In his customary style he said:

I'm back in training, Ainey, and I will put you in hospital when I fight you on 1 March in Dublin. You were a bully all your life, only beating opponents who were nine- or ten-stone weight or men who were drunk. I will show you who's King once and for all. You're not in my league. The only man alive who can give me a fight is Mike Tyson. I hear you have gone to England already – I hope it's to do some training because I'm coming to get you. I will take your money too in a bet. Sure, a woman could beat you in a fight.

Ainey says he beat Dan Rooney. I have the video of Ainey and Dan fighting in Crossmaglen in 1990 and it shows Ainey running away. Dan beat him like a rag doll. Ainey was never a good fighter and I will prove it in March. I'm back running four miles on the road every morning. I am swinging at the bags here at the back of my house. [He was referring to the punching bags that hang in a shed at the back of his house in Moate.]

The fight was organized to take place in Edenderry, County Offaly, in December 2006. It attracted a large and excited crowd keen to watch the spectacle of two old men ready to hammer the hell out of one another. Johnny Nevin acted as fair-play man for the Joyces, while another well-known bare-knuckle boxer, James Quinn-McDonagh, was there on behalf of Ainey and his sons. As expected, Big Joe was all business. He took off his leather jacket and, with his fists already bandaged, he was ready to fight in his white vest. The fair-play men had their hands full keeping Big Joe quiet. He was already stirring things up, shouting: 'I'll bate you, boy.' McGinley was getting his hands wrapped with red bandages while Joe kept up the verbal pressure. He was told, 'Whisht, now,' in a vain attempt to keep him quiet. One of the fair-play men told the crowd to move back and added: 'No cheering on, on both sides.'

McGinley in his T-shirt was ready to go as Vaseline was applied to his face. Big Joe immediately launched himself at Ainey with a deliberate onslaught of heavy jabs. The crowd couldn't contain itself, breaking out with roared exclamations. He had done all the talking, and for the first while it was Joyce who did most of the punching. But McGinley stood firm, and countered with his own punches whenever he could. When he slid out of the way of one of Joyce's onslaughts, Big Joe stumbled over and hit the ground. The spectators, cameraman and fair-play men all crowded in on the fighters, which gave them time to snatch their breath. Joyce landed some more heavy digs on McGinley, who managed another counter-attack. Then, just three minutes after the chaotic fight started, the fair-play men dived in to separate the clinched fighters and the shout was heard: 'He's biting!' A full-scale brawl threatened to break out amid a heaving mass of bodies. Ainey's son, Barney, who was standing behind his father, raised his arms in victory.

But the fight got going again, and again Big Joe landed a clean punch. He didn't, however, have enough in the tank to follow up immediately, and Ainey caught a vital breather. Joyce launched another flurry of energy-sapping punches as McGinley managed to fire one off before closing in and getting hold of Joyce. After just four minutes of fighting, the accusation came that Big Joe had bitten his opponent again. Ainey backed away, clearly bleeding from his left ear, the blood dripping down on to his chest. 'You fucking won it!' roared a supporter at McGinley. This time the fight didn't restart.

Later Ainey, his supporters and his fair-play man, James Quinn-McDonagh, gathered in a large industrial unit nearby. A bloodied but happy Ainey was videoed as he spoke down the phone to someone, telling them how the fight had gone. He said delightedly:

> I had a better fight with Joe than I did with Dan Rooney.
> It was all heavy clouts. I'd say I need about three stitches
> in the lip. He bit the top of my ear off twice. He got away
> with it the first time, then we got him on the second one.

The old-timers weren't the only men fighting that day. Occasionally when boxers from opposing clans want to set up a 'fair fight' other members of the family get caught up in the excitement and look for matches against their opposite number. For practical reasons, such as the likely arrival of the Gardaí and the dangers of having too many keyed-up fighting men hanging around for too long, the number of bouts is normally kept down to just a handful. As well as Big Joe and Ainey lining out for the pride of their family, there were also two each of their offspring. John Joyce was lined up to take on Barney 'The Gorilla' McGinley, and their younger brothers David Joyce and Trevor McGinley were also on the card. All four sons had kept close to their fathers during the punishing opening four minutes of fighting.

Big Joe was still standing bare-chested when the call was made for 'the young lads' to fight. After the high-octane grudge match between the grizzled warriors, the fighting space was full of men milling about. It took a few minutes of shouting from the fair-play men to clear a ring of spectators for the next bout. There was still confusion among those watching as to who had been declared the winner of the clash between Big Joe and Ainey. The next fight was to be John and Barney, two big men with the training and experience of the official boxing ring. His face in a grimace of concentration, Barney kicked away a few rocks from the fighting area as the fair-play men went about their work. When finally the two boxers were ready to square up Barney held his hands high and commanded: 'Can you hold that position, lads, and less of the women roaring, now that's it, shit talking. Let two men box.'

Like his father, John Joyce took the fight to his opponent, seeking the early hammer blow that would give him a winning edge. But McGinley cannily backed away, waiting for his chance to land counterpunches. For the most part those watching managed to stay quiet, and the only sound was the constant chirrup of mobile phones going off every few seconds in the spectators' pockets. The first two minutes was almost like a ring boxing match with plenty of combinations being thrown. Joyce was doing most of the work and landed some hard body blows. Barney managed to protect his head and weave away from a couple of savage jabs. He still had enough spare energy at one point to remind the men watching to 'stay quiet, give us respect' as partisan shouting began to creep back up.

Four minutes into the bout Barney started firing off more punches as John Joyce seemed to tire following his high work rate in the early stages. By now Joyce was on the back foot and ended up going through the line of spectators. The fight had slowed down to a pace that better suited McGinley. He tried to finish off the contest with an onslaught of blows that Joyce did well to avoid; Joyce even managed to land a counterpunch. By now the roars from the crowd were full-blooded and the fair-play men, spectators and cameraman got mixed together in a smaller and smaller circle as Joyce tried to hang on. For thirty seconds solid the pair, literally head-to-head, swapped a series of heavy punches. It had been Joyce's last-ditch effort to snatch a win, and when it failed to deliver a knockout blow, he had nothing left to give. He had no choice except to 'give best' and concede the fight. Barney was hoisted upon shoulders amid roars of delight. Then, as he slid back to the ground, Ainey locked his arm around his neck and told him: 'Fair play, son.' It was high praise for any Traveller son to hear from his father. By any standards it was a good fight, and those who had been watching muttered in approval.

Yet straight away there appeared to be some tension. The McGinleys had got back into a car and were ready to leave, but Big Joe was at the window. There was a discussion. There was argument over the result of the fight between David Joyce and Trevor McGinley and who had won. 'It's a drawn fight,' shouted one of the men. The McGinleys got out of the car and the two older men expected their sons, as they had done, would shake hands. But David was fired up. The champion licensed boxer had claimed victory because he said Trevor had held him illegally.

When that fight had taken place, the order had gone out for video cameras to be turned off. This was to protect David Joyce's official boxing career. Taking part in a bare-knuckle fight is a criminal offence and for licensed boxers committing any form of violence outside the ring could lead to suspension from the sport. At that time he was still a promising amateur boxer who had successfully fought his way through the junior ranks and represented Ireland. Since the age of eleven he had taken part in eighty fights, and had been the Irish Amateur Boxing Association Boxer of the Year. His fight against Trevor McGinley, who was four years older than him, was his first bare-knuckle one. It was his first attempt to follow in the footsteps of his father. Some of the fight was caught on camera and appeared to show young David getting well on top of his opponent. Like his father's bout, it ended in chaos, and with the result in dispute among the crowd. The fair-play men had called it a draw. Later, a copy of a DVD which showed David fighting was forwarded to the boxing authorities and his licence was suspended for six months as a result.

As the arguments continued, Barney 'The Gorilla' McGinley strode up amid the milling crowd. His face was marked from his tough win over John Joyce. David wanted to talk to him and get up close to Barney, who also was expecting a handshake or some of the fair praise that traditionally cools down tempers. Instead, Barney was taken by surprise when David told him: 'You done a good bit of training, obviously in another four or five years you'll be ready for me.' Cooler heads understood the insulting jibe before Barney realized what had been said, and moved in between the pair.

An infuriated Barney immediately demanded that nineteen-year-old David fight him there and then. 'I boxed "Jaws" Paddy when I was eighteen. I'll fight you if you want it now. I won't jab around, I'll knock you out, you shit.' More jibes were aimed at McGinley. All the time the distance between the two grew wider. Yet McGinley became even more enraged as he was chaperoned away by his own people. They stood in a protective semicircle and watched him scream, his voice cracking with emotion and fury. 'They're going too far now,' he roared at the top of his lungs. 'Where's the knife? I'll drive it into his forehead.' His threat succeeded in finally keeping the crowd quiet, most of whom couldn't leave until other cars and vans had been moved out of the way first. There was a sudden chill that lasted for a few seconds until enough people realized that the chances of a crazed knife attack being allowed to happen were slim. Still, it was time to leave.

10

The Mighty Quinn

Over the last twenty years the bare-knuckle boxing scene among Irish Travellers has been dominated by a handful of families and individuals. One of those key figures has been James Quinn-McDonagh, who acted as fair-play man in the rematch between Big Joe Joyce and Ainey McGinley. A friend of Paddy Doherty's, he too has courted publicity while being centrally involved in many of the most talked-about fights. He has the relaxed physical presence that many extra-large-sized athletes share. He moves with casual assurance, yet with a deft touch which hints at faster gears for use as and when they are needed. He may not be aware of it but James has the habit of watching the doors and windows, his eyes darting back and forth, although there is nothing in his calm, well-spoken tones to suggest that he is troubled or stressed. By normal standards, however, his life has had some colourful interludes. They range from being shot in the leg in a punishment-style shooting, to having his home razed to the ground by a criminal gang, to being the star of a documentary that impressed audiences at Utah's Sundance Film Festival. He's no ordinary man and he's no ordinary Traveller.

Like Paddy Doherty, James Quinn-McDonagh enjoys the limelight, albeit in a much more understated way, although these days he is taking steps to remedy that situation. In his fighting prime, when he appeared on camera before and after fights, his language was considerably more toned down compared to that of Big Joe Joyce. Any chance he'd get, James would say: 'This is it, I'm not fighting any more.' James gave the impression that he was a reluctant fighter, forced to answer the insults levelled at his family name. He was the first of the Irish Traveller bare-knuckle fighters whose name became more widely known outside their own community.

Fights had been videoed in the past, and the likes of Ainey McGinley, Dan Rooney and Big Joe Joyce had all appeared on tapes and in newspapers. But James brought a little bit of showbiz sparkle to the mix as he squared up to an opponent on damp country back roads. The tattoos on his chest and arms added another outlaw edge that registered with people from the wider community. But what really got people sitting up and taking notice was when, at the end of a fight with Lurcher Joyce, he was handed a paper bag stuffed with cash. The fight featured on VHS tapes – and later DVDs – sold through casual Sunday-morning markets all over Ireland. Whatever James made from bets staked on his fights, cash was also earned from the copies hawked from stalls along with the latest pirated releases from Hollywood. The effect was to bring James Quinn-McDonagh to a wider audience.

For James, as for many Irish Travellers, the early years were tough. He is from the last generation to experience life on the road in the traditional barrel-roof caravans, living off the land and depending on casual work and kindness from farmers to make a living. Life was made even harder when his father was jailed in England. He explains in his autobiography, *Knuckle*, how, as one of the kids, he would sleep in shelters made from birch poles with straw added for warmth. Food came from vegetables given by farmers or sometimes taken from the field for that night's dinner pot by a youngster already clued into living by his wits. Rabbits, caught by snares or dogs, were added when they were available, but otherwise it was a precarious lifestyle punctuated by regular moves to new campsites.

School for James, like most Travellers of his generation, was almost non-existent, with the state unable and unwilling to make allowances for the Traveller lifestyle. Religious orders notorious for their violence towards schoolchildren showed an even sterner side to Travellers. Work came from picking vegetables and potatoes during the harvest season for the market-garden farmers in north County Dublin and north Leinster. For a while he showed promise as a young boxer at a club in Dundalk before the family moved on again. Later James, like his father, would find work with a building firm in London in the 1980s and then go on to make a living driving, doing haulage and running a scrap business with his father. He lived with his wife Theresa and together they had two boys. He took up boxing at that time, training with a local club in east London.

James attributes his decision to become a bare-knuckle fighter in part to family pressure but also to having been inspired by watching the videos of Dan Rooney and Ainey in action in Crossmaglen in 1990. But the real reason came one night in 1992 when a pub booze-up in London ended in tragedy. James explains in his autobiography that he wasn't even there when it happened, having opted to stay at home with his wife and their newborn child. As his brother Curly Paddy was being dropped back to his halting site in Peckham by one of the 'Bronx' Joyces, a short but violent row broke out in the back of the van. Brian Joyce suffered a fatal stab wound and was declared dead on his arrival in hospital. Curly Paddy was among those arrested, and he admitted the 'accident'. It meant the end of James's time in London, and the next day, fearful of revenge attacks by the Joyce clan, he fled the city with other members of his family. It was the start of a bitter enmity that has lasted over three decades and launched James Quinn-McDonagh's career as a bare-knuckle fighter. Curly Paddy served his time for manslaughter and later returned to Ireland.

It wasn't long before a challenge came for James Quinn-McDonagh to fight. The first was from a gnarly old adversary from the Nevin clan, Christy 'Ditsy' Nevin, who also lived cheek by jowl with other members of the Quinn-McDonagh family in his native Mullingar in County Westmeath. Back then Ditsy had a reputation as a fighting man, and even in his late middle age still actively defended it. As it turned out the fight, at a wedding in 1993, lasted just a few minutes. James Quinn-McDonagh was too young and too fit for the older man, who couldn't even land a punch on his adversary. As is usual after most fights, the stories came thick and fast about how the loser hadn't been ready or was sick or some other excuse. With Ditsy it was the fact that he had fought with broken ribs. It left the door open for more fights for James Quinn-McDonagh, whose reputation as a fighter had suddenly grown throughout the Traveller community.

The next challenge came a few months later from a cousin of Ditsy's, Patrick 'Chaps' Nevin. The fight took place on the picturesque shores of Lough Ennell, where James faced a far tougher and younger opponent than on the last outing. He had to work hard to keep out of range of Chaps's punches, and for thirty minutes or so looked to be in trouble. Eventually, James took his chances as the other fighter began to tire, and towards the end knocked Chaps down four or five times before he was forced to concede. Although the two men shook hands and didn't appear to hold any animosity towards each other after the fair fight, things gradually grew worse for both families thanks to the festering feud between various members.

During a Travellers' football tournament in Dublin's Phoenix Park a disagreement blew up between James's uncle and cousin and another Traveller over some heavy tackles being made on the pitch. One of the Joyces, amid claims that he had pulled a knife, was hit with a pair of crutches. In the middle of the melee was James, and so another challenge to fight came from Jody's Joe Joyce, a second cousin of Big Joe. This time James was up against an aggressive fighter who already had a couple of bare-knuckle bouts under his belt. James, however, was much bigger and able to fend off most of his attacker's punches, although he did have to take more than a few solid shots to his head. He managed to cut Jody's Joe badly above both eyes and after nine minutes the vicious but fair fight was over, with James Quinn-McDonagh victorious again. His win was celebrated by the wider clan while on the other side the sense of grievance and offence among the Joyce and Nevin clans increased.

The fights were coming thick and fast for James. In 1996 he got another challenge from the Joyce clan, this time from Big Joe's brother, Lurcher Joyce. He was another fighter who came with an impressive reputation but in the end seemed to have little to offer in terms of a contest. On the video of the fight Lurcher appears out of condition compared to James Quinn-McDonagh, who knocks him down four times in as many minutes. At that point the fair-play men stand in to stop the fight and a paper bag of cash staked on the outcome is handed to Quinn-McDonagh. It contained IR£19,000, a substantial sum which made more than a few people sit up when later watching the video.

He wasn't in a hurry to fight again, but later Paddy Doherty was on hand to organize his next fight. This time it was to be in Manchester, with reports that various Travellers had staked £60,000 on the outcome.

Fate, however, intervened before the contest could take place. At the Spinning Wheel pub in Dundalk in 1996, James Quinn-McDonagh found himself looking down the barrel of a gun. A five-man armed gang had come to the pub looking for the boxer. In the ensuing struggle James was shot in the leg, but a second shot missed as the masked gang fled the scene. The reasons for the attack have never been made clear, but luckily enough James didn't suffer any lasting damage from his injury. It meant, however, another move for his family, and they settled into Dunsink Lane in Finglas, west Dublin, where a large number of other Traveller families had also set up home.

James, however, couldn't resist making comments on camera after every fight. Although the remarks sounded conciliatory to outsiders, they had the effect of winding up the Joyce and Nevin clans to even greater levels of emotion. What was being said on the videos was leading to more challenges. Despite his insistence that he no longer wanted to fight, James Quinn-McDonagh's comments and the subsequent stories in the newspapers were interpreted as unnecessary gloating over clans whose pride had been deeply wounded.

Constant challenges were being sent to James, but he chose his battles carefully. He was well aware, as Ditsy found out to his cost, that fighters get older and slower and young men want their chance to beat the man with a big reputation. His final fight, in 2000, was to be against Ditsy's son David, a young man determined to avenge his father's defeat years before. It took place in a farmyard in Edenderry, County Offaly, watched by a small crowd of neutrals. Patient, and aware that he had to use his energy carefully, James Quinn-McDonagh settled into a long-drawn-out and boring fight in which the younger man circled looking for an opening that rarely came. Eventually, as the referees and spectators were losing their patience, David Nevin began to run out of steam. James Quinn-McDonagh took his chance and launched a flurry of punches. The fight continued for another few minutes, but the younger man was finished and stuck out his hand to shake.

Always in James's shadow was his younger brother Mikey Quinn-McDonagh, who was determined to carve out a name for himself. As a teenager he suffered a defeat by Paul Joyce and it was something that he could never forget. Joyce was a big man and Mikey, although brave, couldn't find a way through to land punches on Joyce. At one point Joyce was able to literally throw him aside as Mikey tried to get inside the bigger man's guard. With the fight going downhill rapidly he couldn't help himself, and while caught in a clinch he bit Joyce. When he was pulled off, Joyce raised his arms in victory. The fair-play men, however, let the fight restart, but when Mikey sank his teeth in a second time, it was all over.

In the subsequent years he morphed from a skinny teenager into a tough fighter ready to punch his way through walls to get to his opponents. In another encounter he fought David, the son of Brian Joyce, who had died from a knife wound inflicted by Mikey's brother Curly Paddy in 1992. A clip of the fight shows Mikey eager to win, as if it is him who is out to avenge his father's death, not his opponent.

One of his last fights saw him pit his strengths and boxing skills in a rematch against Paul Joyce at a halting site in Luton, London. Fought under a blistering sun and the watchful gaze of a police helicopter, he went toe to toe against the much bigger man. There was a huge crowd watching, but it was well managed, with fighters, referees and cameramen in an area enclosed by construction fencing. Mikey looked the part of the bare-knuckle fighter, his face a determined mask of concentration, his muscles taut and covered with tattoos. He sprang into action against Joyce, who was both taller and far heavier. Joyce looked hopelessly out of shape compared to Mikey's chiselled physique, but he was an experienced and clever fighter. Joyce was also well able to take a punch as well as deflect some of Mikey's powerful jabs. Despite his speed, Mikey couldn't get through Joyce's defence often enough. After forty minutes, with both men bloodied and bruised, it was declared a draw. The fight finished with both men's pride and honour intact. It also meant the £120,000 staked on the fight would go back to the relieved clan members who had put up the cash.

Mikey's fighting days were brought to end when he was charged with the murder of his wife Jacqueline, who died in August 2012 at their Dundalk home. During 2013 he was on remand in prison awaiting trial.

Throughout his fighting career James Quinn-McDonagh, one way or another, ensured that news of his victories ended up in the newspapers in Ireland. Possibly with an eye on how history would view his exploits, he ensured film director Ian Palmer was a regular at his fights. Over a decade Palmer filmed the key moments in James's boxing career: from his fight with Lurcher Joyce until he boxed David Nevin in 2000. The footage, which included Mikey's fights as well, when put together as the film *Knuckle* created a powerful visual story of the Traveller brothers' fighting history. It proved a hit with the wider community on the art-house cinema circuit, winning plaudits when it was premiered at the Sundance Film Festival in Utah. Nothing like it had been seen before. Finally, James Quinn-McDonagh was on track to get the audience he deserved.

The release of *Knuckle* coincided with James leaving

Ireland again to move back to London, where he had been happy in the 1980s and early 1990s. The move had nothing to do with any fallout from the documentary. Any fears that old wounds could have been reopened were unfounded. If anything, his comments at the end of the documentary, suggesting that he was going to a wedding, were taken as meaning that he wanted to put the feud between the McDonaghs and the Nevins to bed.

But trouble never seems far behind James Quinn-McDonagh, and he and his family had got into an entirely new scrape with a criminal gang running an illegal waste-disposal business. The area where James's family lived in Coolock, a northern suburb of Dublin city, was becoming surrounded by the collected waste. His brother Curly Paddy took exception to the growing piles of debris and the acrid black smoke as items were burned to retrieve copper wiring and scrap metal. Relying on his formidable reputation, Curly Paddy intervened and complained about the behaviour that was affecting not just his family, but several others living in Traveller accommodation in the area at Coolock.

The thugs' response was extremely violent. Curly Paddy was shot in the leg, one of his sons was beaten up and petrol was poured over a female relative. James Quinn-McDonagh's house nearby was already surrounded by mounds of rubble which had been deposited there and com-pacted with machinery. Now it was firebombed and left badly damaged. When James didn't return after a few weeks, the gang literally took apart the small dwelling, which was owned by Dublin Corporation. The garden walls were left standing, but the house was completely demolished and the rubble trucked away, presumably dumped with the rest of the rubble piling up around Northern Close. Even a statue of the Virgin Mary which had been concreted to a pillar was broken off. Later, ramshackle stables for trotting ponies were built where James had lived with his wife Theresa.

Aerial photographs later showed the extent of the criminal gang's illegal waste-disposal business. Skips of rubbish were simply dumped on parkland and compacted down in a professional manner using earth-moving machinery. One Traveller housing development, which had been built at considerable expense to the taxpayer, was completely destroyed in the process. It had been constructed especially for Travellers, with small chalets and concrete hardstands that had room for caravans and houses. Now it was empty, with rubble piled up in banks as high as the roof apexes. Families had suffered violence and been the subject of threats. They upped and left the council accommodation which they had probably waited for years to get.

The response by the local authorities was less than overwhelming, and there were admissions that officials had also been subjected to threats, including at home. As a result Dublin Corporation had been unable to access the site and monitor the situation. The scene at Coolock was a testament both to official Ireland's ongoing failure to find ways to accommodate Travellers and to the capacity of a domineering criminal element in Traveller society to screw things up for its own people.

During 2012 and 2013, following exposure by the *Sunday World*, efforts were made to stop the illegal dumping. There were a number of investigations carried out in multi-agency operations, backed up by armed Gardaí, which effectively shut down the operation.

Spurred on by their unexpected success in seeing off the Quinn-McDonaghs, the hybrid mix of Travellers and criminals with links to former republican paramilitaries embarked on an extortion racket in which wealthy members of the Traveller community in the Dublin region were targeted. It was a sudden and unusual shift of power that had several Traveller dodgy dealers and rogue traders running for cover. In some cases Traveller traders were ordered to cough up as much as €50,000 or face potentially lethal attacks. They were left in no doubt that cash was going to the Real IRA and that not paying would have had terrible consequences.

A move to London was the only sensible decision for James Quinn-McDonagh, who wanted to keep his family out of any more trouble. It has meant an end to his direct involvement with the Irish Traveller bare-knuckle fighters. The quest for glory in that arena has been taken over by other contenders such as the sons of Ainey McGinley and Big Joe Joyce. Now in his late forties, James has tried to re-launch himself as a fight promoter from his London base, first attempting to get a bare-knuckle reality TV show off the ground and then making a bid to start a legal version of bare-knuckle fighting. Embracing social media, James Quinn-McDonagh has yet again shown his skill at public relations, building up a core of loyal fans from the platform afforded to him by the film *Knuckle*. He has also tried his hand at TV presenting, interviewing the son of another famous bare-knuckle fighter for an online TV channel. Intelligent and media savvy, James Quinn-McDonagh is the thinking man's version of the bare-knuckle boxer.

11

Unfinished Business

Fighting men don't enjoy a quiet life. The violence that defines them in the bare-knuckle bouts tends to follow them into their everyday circumstances. Paddy Doherty has lost count of how many times he has been hospitalized, and he has had more than one close brush with death. James Quinn-McDonagh has been effectively exiled to London. Big Joe Joyce has been shot at and had clumps of flesh ripped from his arm and face.

In that regard Paddy 'Jaws' Ward is fully qualified as a Traveller fighting man. Jaws inherited his nickname from his father, who was given it after he lost his teeth at the age of thirty-six. Jaws and his father were once the targets of an assassination attempt at the funeral of Patrick 'Skillet' Ward in Sligo in 1999. The Wards claimed that they had tried to approach members of a rival UK clan – the closely related Bumbee McDonaghs – at the funeral, when they were ambushed and gunmen opened fire. One man, Patrick 'Deuce' Ward, was shot in the back and died.

Four men were charged with the murder but acquitted after a series of trials. An independent eyewitness claimed Jaws had been armed with a slash hook, which the defence barrister said he had 'wielded like Harry Potter's wand'. When the McDonaghs were acquitted, Jaws senior was heard to shout: 'The state done us down. An eye for eye, lads.'

Around the end of 2006, when Big Joe Joyce and Ainey McGinley were finishing off old business, Jaws Ward was serving time in Castlerea Prison in Roscommon. He had been jailed for threatening to shoot his cousin John 'Jokes' Ward in Ballybane, County Galway, in March 2006. He had been spotted by officers dumping a shotgun and a machete after a shot had been fired at John 'Jokes' Ward. At his trial he admitted possessing the weapons, but denied threatening to kill his cousin. Ironically, the violence had erupted after Jaws's brother Laurence was shot at a bare-knuckle fight in Manchester in 2005. Following that there were a number of incidents and skirmishes between the two factions which led to guns being used both in Ireland and the UK. There was tight security at Jaws's trial in Galway, with thirty uniformed and armed Gardaí on duty at the courthouse. Everyone going into the court building was searched, including lawyers and journalists. Jaws got a three-year sentence.

Meanwhile, as Barney 'The Gorilla' McGinley was strutting his stuff after his victory over John Joyce, Jaws was getting restless in jail. During his tantrum after being taunted by David Joyce, Barney had mentioned that he had fought Jaws when they were eighteen. The implication that he was a better fighter than Jaws was something that Jaws couldn't let go. Jaws took advantage of the prison gym to get into serious training, reportedly working out twice a day. From behind the prison walls in the west of Ireland his challenge went out in April 2008. Once he had been released he would take on Barney. Immediately, the followers of Traveller fighting men knew this was going to be a big fight. In his youth Jaws had been a handy amateur boxer and had represented Great Britain at U21 level. The hype began to build.

A date for the clash was finally settled, and it took place on a bog lane in County Westmeath. It hadn't been the first-choice venue as decided by the fair-play men. The Gardaí, concerned at the potential for disorder, had mounted a series of checkpoints in a bid to stop crowds gathering and to force the fighters to call off the event. It went ahead with a small knot of spectators in attendance, including reporters from the two Irish TV stations and a press photographer. Paddy Doherty, yet to become a celebrity outside of the Travelling community at this stage, was acting as the fair-play man for Barney 'The Gorilla' McGinley. Big Joe Joyce was the fair-play man for Paddy 'Jaws' Ward, which made the gathering a veritable who's who of the Irish bare-knuckle world. The two showmen, Big Joe and Paddy, were delighted to be at the centre of things. Doherty gave the fighters a quick rundown of the rules: 'The first one that puts in dirt, you're beat. May the best man win and shake hands.'

Jaws and The Gorilla touched their fists off one another's in the style of licensed ring boxers. It was a mark of the respect from the two men towards each other. Then they got down to business. It was immediately apparent that Paddy 'Jaws' Ward had a significant height and reach advantage. He was able to land jabs without Barney 'The Gorilla' McGinley getting anywhere near him. For the first three minutes McGinley was on the back foot, but he went in low on the counter-attack and did his best to avoid Jaws's straight-armed jabs. 'Good fight, boys. Good fucking fight,' shouted one of the spectators. After six minutes the two fighters were still going at a fast and reasonable pace. The fair-play men, Doherty and Joyce, were wound up and anxious to be seen giving the men equal treatment. They moved the boxers away from a pile of stones and kept telling those watching to stay back and 'show respect'. It was a big fight and a lot of reputations were at risk.

Ten minutes into the fight both men were breathing hard but still trading blows. At this stage Ward looked fitter, benefiting from the training regime and clean-living lifestyle behind bars. As the fight wore on Barney was caught by a combination of punches and he took one hard jab square in the head. It knocked him off his feet and he hit the gravel hard. He got up quick with his back to Jaws as one of the fair-play men roared: 'Get it on, boys, no time.' There's never a break in bare-knuckle, no standing count to give a downed fighter a chance to recover his senses.

Jaws went in for the kill, but he too was feeling the pace, and a couple of wild haymakers went well wide of the mark. Yet still, Barney was connecting with punches and far from being beaten. But then Jaws found the target again and McGinley stumbled. He stayed on his feet and tried to stay close to Jaws to get under his guard and negate his opponent's reach advantage. A minute later McGinley was down again when Jaws connected with a solid right hook to the side of his head. Even then McGinley got back up as Jaws threw his last reserves of energy into finishing the fight. McGinley had absolutely nothing left and was in danger of being knocked unconscious. He 'gave best', conceding the fight. Then he turned his back, the defeat a bitter blow. Big Joe was in quick to shake his hand, but McGinley's eyes were down. Jaws was congratulated by the fair-play men, and even got a hug from Doherty. The two fighters shook hands, but there was a sense that already there was unfinished business. It was a cursory shake and Jaws was turning his back even before releasing his grip.

Back in the square at Moate, Jaws was given a hero's welcome by his supporters, who had travelled to share in the victory. The towering fighter maintained a quiet grin and even appeared embarrassed by the adulation. 'You knocked him out two times, you destroyed him,' said one man to him for the benefit of the crowd. Big Joe was invited to talk on camera. 'Barney McGinley was claiming he was best in the world. Paddy was too strong for him. He broke up Barney McGinley,' he said, to rowdy cheers. As Big Joe was being encouraged to add more, Jaws stepped in between Big Joe and the camera. 'There's nothing else to say. There's no point kicking a man . . .' he said, leaving the sentence unfinished.

That sense of unfinished business was soon to become apparent for Big Joe Joyce and his fighting sons. Nothing much had ever been said about the Anthony O'Donnell versus Big Joe Joyce fights in 1989. For years any issue about the clashes had stayed dormant, but in October 2011 things changed thanks to the advent of YouTube as a method for sending public messages between the bare-knuckle fighters. Once the goading messages would be circulated by word of mouth, and then it was via VHS tapes, and later DVDs, copied and passed around.

This time it was Anthony O'Donnell who appeared to be the first to start goading Big Joe into a rematch, decades after their original fights. An angry phone conversation was recorded and posted on the popular website. Among other insults O'Donnell told Joyce: 'You dirty shite, I'm the boss.' Furious at what he saw as the rewriting of bare-knuckle history, he accused Big Joe of lying about their fights in 1989:

> You said you gave me such a bad beating and the blood you had on you was off me. Didn't I beat you until you cried in my face and said you couldn't fight any more? Six months you were in Ballinasloe Hospital. You cried into my face, you dirty tramp, and said you would never fight again.

The puerile insults didn't stop there. The online exchanges sparked a series of YouTube messages which have notched up several hundred thousand views. Obviously more than just members of the Travelling community had decided to follow the build-up to another clash between the Joyces and O'Donnells.

David Joyce's uploaded reply to the initial message from the O'Donnells was memorable for all the wrong reasons. He spat out angry insults as he demanded the O'Donnells fight sooner rather than later. Even though it had been just a couple of weeks since David and Anthony O'Donnell's nephew Simon had acted as fair-play men together for a clash between members of the Stokes clan, they were now in a war of words. David's choice of 'shite in bucket' as a sobriquet for O'Donnell became an internet hit. Another reply from Anthony O'Donnell and his sons Anthony and Martin poured more venom into the mix. Between them they had also ticked all the boxes when it came to using politically incorrect language, dragging in references to people with disabilities and 'black fellas'.

The publicly traded insults and challenges had the desired effect. Twenty-two years after Anthony O'Donnell and Big Joe Joyce clashed outside a pub in Dublin their sons decided they wanted to settle the matter of who had been the better fighter. It was a question of pride. One of the posted videos had even been entitled *Fists of Fury 2*. Although the two older men, Big Joe and Anthony, thought better of togging out for another round of bare-knuckle fighting, two brothers from both families took up the challenge. It was organized for a Sunday in February 2012.

The O'Donnells travelled from their London home to take up the challenge against David and Joe Joyce junior. A convoy of cars left the Joyce family home just after 11 a.m. It was a cold, grey morning. The initial venue for the fight was at the end of a bog track just outside Kells in County Meath. It was a bleak spot, the ground a dark peaty brown surrounded by scrub and twisted trees. Bits of junk poked from the vegetation. About fifty Travellers kicked about, waiting for the O'Donnells to arrive. While other people saddle up their horses for a Sunday morning hunt, or make their way to a Gaelic football match, these guys were looking forward to a bloody bare-knuckle fight between two pairs of hulking boxers. The Joyces were in situ and ready to rock. The dozen or so cars that had been parked close to the venue, however, were visible from the main road.

Before the O'Donnells could arrive a Garda sergeant turned up with another officer and told everyone to move on. 'It's only a fair fight, we'll be gone in an hour,' said one of the men.

'There'll be no fight here today,' said the sergeant, unfazed. There was no sign of movement from the crowd until he added: 'If you want I can stand at the end of the lane and take everyone's name as you leave.' Included in the crowd were a few people who still had live suspended sentences for taking part in feud violence in the midlands. There were others who had been recently cautioned over public-order offences in Longford. And then there were some who no doubt would prefer that the official boxing authorities didn't know what they got up to in their spare time. Among those who would rather avoid an official sanction were members of the Nevin clan from Longford, who had been prosecuted under the Public Order Act for making threats to a rival family via YouTube clips. Intended to provoke a bare-knuckle contest, the comments had gone overboard, with a suggestion that an individual would be kidnapped and murdered. The charges, against sixteen men, were dropped after they agreed in court to stay out of trouble and avoid bare-knuckle fights. It had been the first such prosecution in Ireland.

After the arrival of the Gardaí, the fair-play men had to find a new venue for bare-knuckle fights between the Joyce and O'Donnell brothers. A madcap convoy of a dozen cars followed, driving the twisting roads of Westmeath and Louth to a newly appointed location near Drogheda. It was a grim concrete yard with an industrial shed. There was junk scattered around, a rusting shipping container in one corner, and a pile of rubble that afforded a better view for at least one spectator. Under dark rain clouds the fighters got ready to do battle with a minimum of fuss. This time the O'Donnells were ready to go, and the sons of Big Joe Joyce and Anthony O'Donnell squared off to settle the row over who won the bragging rights after the 1989 bouts. A crowd of up to two hundred spectators was there to witness the fights.

First up was Joe Joyce junior against Martin O'Donnell, both stripping off to fight bare-chested. Even though they are young men, they are big. O'Donnell had the longer reach, but Joe junior was able to stay out of range and produce his own counter-attacks. Both men landed heavy punches into each other's faces as the fair-play men shouted for the spectators to keep back. Near the end, as the combatants tired, there were muttered accusations of breaking unfairly when the two clinched. Even though the fighters kept going forward looking for the knockout blow, neither could find a way to end the fight. They were bloodied and weary, yet were still finding the strength to land blows with sickening thuds. There was a collective sigh of relief when, after more than thirty minutes of non-stop fighting, a fair-play man grabbed their wrists and had them shake hands. He declared it a drawn contest. The crowd, appreciative of the hard-fought bout, broke into polite applause.

Next up was the older of the two sets of brothers, David Joyce and Anthony David O'Donnell, who faced up to each other straightaway. Early on, both fighters circled cautiously but didn't hold back once hostilities began for real, with six-foot, four-inch O'Donnell fighting southpaw. Although they kept their distance from each other, when the combatants closed in the combination punches landed with serious intent. Both well-trained and experienced ring fighters, they tried to play the tactical game, waiting for the other to tire and make a mistake. At times the fair-play men, not seeing any punches being thrown, told the boxers to shake hands and call it a day. The crowd managed to keep their emotions in check and there was little egging on of the fighters or partisan roaring of encouragement. Compared to the contests the Joyces had had with the McGinleys, and considering the level of animosity in the YouTube messages, the bouts were well-managed sporting affairs. The fair-play men prevailed after half an hour, persuading the two bloodied boxers to shake hands. It appeared to be a genuine hand-shake.

None of the old-school men like Big Joe or Paddy Doherty were there to see the fight. Although one or two grizzled veterans were among the crowd, it represented a changing of the guard. It was also two young men, contemporaries of the combatants, who acted as the fair-play men. As David Joyce and Anthony O'Donnell shook hands at the end of the fight Joyce declared: 'We're different men to our fathers.'

Two of the McGinley clan from Longford, Ainey and Patrick, who had been at the original Fists of Fury fight in Clondalkin twenty-two years previously, were also there. Asked by David Joyce who had won the original fight, the unequivocal answer was that Big Joe had been the winner. It had taken nearly an hour of tough bare-knuckle fighting to end the latest flare-up in the simmering tensions between two fighters that had fought decades before. The fighting DNA had well and truly been passed on to the next generation, and YouTube had found a new meme.

Years after a bare-knuckle fight, questions over who actually won can remain a source of friction between rival fighters. As the Joyce and O'Donnell sons found out, it can also be the reason for another generation to start off a rivalry anew. It's no wonder that it became popular to video the fights so that the result could be seen by everyone, whether impartial or otherwise. On the flipside of the argument, the videos also mean there is a permanent record of a defeat that can't easily be erased. The only way to restore honour is to seek and win a rematch. Another downside to the videos is the commentary that often comes in the aftermath. David Joyce's taunts at Barney 'The Gorilla' McGinley will ensure a lasting enmity between the two that at some point may well result in a bare-knuckle fight.

As far as Barney 'The Gorilla' McGinley was concerned, he too still had unfinished business with Paddy 'Jaws' Ward after their fight in August 2008. Despite being knocked down twice and forced to 'give best', it wasn't long before Barney was back looking for a rematch. Jaws hadn't been sitting on his behind. Fresh out of jail and with a family of six, he took the opportunity to start a professional boxing career. He had shown himself to be in good physical condition in his fight with Barney. He had also shown he was well able to take a punch as well as deliver one. Jaws had been hitting the gym hard, and for a heavyweight boxer being in your early or mid-thirties is no reason not to consider a pro-career. With the experience of his amateur days, he was signed up to make his debut in December 2010 on a boxing card at the National Basketball Arena in Tallaght, County Dublin.

Considering his colourful background, there was

naturally a respectable amount of interest in Jaws. Asked at a press conference about details of his bare-knuckle record Jaws jokingly suggested contacting the hospital accident and emergency departments around Ireland, who might have them. His opponent, Pavels Dolgovs, was a 31-year-old Latvian journeyman who had won just one of his previous six fights. Jaws also had some height and weight advantage over the Latvian, but in the end, despite the fighting talk, it wasn't such a good start to a career. Over four rounds the smaller man was quicker and more accurate than Jaws, and he took the judges' decision on points. Yet still Jaws persisted and lived up to his contract for a second fight, this time on a card at City West in Dublin where it was his turn to win on points over a Lithuanian fighter, Igor Borucha. Since then Jaws hasn't made a return to the professional ring.

Barney had been training hard, too, putting in the hours at a gym in Bradford, Lancashire, where he was living. He made a long DVD which showed him boxing with sparring partners, and it finished off with him running the roads Rocky-style, in a sweatsuit, through the streets of Bradford. In his efforts to goad Jaws into action he said: 'I am the greatest man among Travelling men. I am still the King and always will be, Paddy.' The DVD was sent to Jaws's home in Galway. It continued:

I'm here in Bradford at this present moment. I made a challenge last year for to box you. I rung you up on the phone and I sent a challenge to you and you wouldn't accept my challenge. You carried on on the phone, you acted like a little baby with name-calling. I sent my challenge twice to you, this is my third challenge to you. I made this TV, Paddy, especially for you to look at it. Are you going to box me? Are you afraid to box me? Are you able to bate me? I don't think you'll be able to bate me.

Barney claimed that because he had given Paddy 'Jaws' Ward a chance to fight in 2008, he was owed the opportunity of a rematch. He says in the video clip:

> Fair enough, we did box when we were eighteen years of age for thirty-seven minutes. The two of us drew. Twelve years later you sent a challenge to box me again. I gave you a shot at the title. Fair enough, you got the title on the day. The world knows that. When I boxed you I wasn't the man I am now. So all I'm saying is if you are game enough as I thought you were game, oul fella, if you want to box get the fight on.

He also claimed he should get a rematch because the fair-play men didn't do their job properly. To turn on the fair-play men in that way is to open up the possibility of a whole new enmity with another Traveller clan. In full bridge-burning mode, Barney attacked Big Joe and Paddy Doherty, whose TV star had just begun to rise at the time. 'Back in '08 when I boxed you, Joe Joyce and his sons did not show me proper fair play. That little man from Manchester, Paddy, I got no fair play from him either,' he said, reserving his contempt for Doherty. McGinley said that this time he would opt for another burgeoning star of the screen to act as a fair-play man, James Quinn-McDonagh. 'This time I'm getting James Quinn to show me fair play, he'll show me the world of respect and fair play,' he said, implying that the others hadn't done so. But then he warned that he would find a way to force the fight if Paddy 'Jaws' Ward didn't accept the challenge. 'If you don't, I promise you I am landing back to Galway where you live, and I'm going to bring you out by the back of the neck. I'm going to make you fight me, it's as simple as that,' he warned.

The rising tension prompted extra security measures for

Jaws's fight against Borucha at City West Hotel in March 2011, when another Traveller fighter, Willie 'Big Bang' Casey, was going for a world bantamweight title. Still, Jaws was in no mood to give McGinley a chance to regain the honour he felt he had lost. With his fledging professional career underway the Galway man had no intention of jeopardizing his prospects through injury or a possible suspension of his licence by the boxing authorities. Jaws remained resolute, but McGinley was equally persistent in demanding a fight. For his next round of challenges he opted to go for the increasingly popular YouTube so the entire world could watch. By now, after a half-dozen messages, McGinley claimed that Jaws was a coward for not fighting. 'Make no excuse, you can run, Paddy, but you cannot hide. I'm the King and you know it. Get your ass to Appleby. I'm not the man you fought four years ago, I'm prepared for you now.' He also told the author at that time: 'I was definitely not fit then. I had been sick.' Surprisingly, he said a challenge had also been issued by Ainey McGinley to fight Paddy Doherty. 'Celebrity Paddy never fought in his life. He's done a lot of talking but he's never fought anyone,' said Barney.

In June 2012, Jaws broke his silence with a terse video message which was also posted on YouTube. He stood alone in a gym, in the middle of the boxing ring. It was empty, there was no else throwing in their tuppence worth or standing in support, grim-faced and arms folded, as they do in many such videos.

> You're going around England telling people I'm going to Appleby to fight you. I never spoke to you about Appleby. I never spoke to you since I beat you, as a matter of fact. I've no problem fighting. I'll give you a date in twelve weeks' time if there's not a fighting man in England or Ireland who'll fight.

The short message was clear. It meant that McGinley, by claiming to be the best in the world, had to take on any other challenger before he could fight Jaws.

But that wasn't enough for Barney 'The Gorilla' McGinley. He lived up to his promise and within a week arrived uninvited at the halting site in Galway where Paddy 'Jaws' Ward was living. Although Barney arrived with a small entourage of just a handful of relatives, including a brother, the prospect of the two men fighting a rematch immediately drew a crowd to the Circular Road area of Galway. The two finally squared off at Carrowbrowne halting site on the edge of the city, watched by a group of interested spectators and a couple of Garda officers who arrived on the scene just after the sparring began.

Kitted out in dark shorts and T-shirt, with his fists bandaged, McGinley looked sharp. In his running shoes, jeans and dark vest Jaws looked as if the fight had been suddenly sprung on him. Traveller honour meant that he couldn't back down. Obviously, the training for the professional fights had worked well, and if anything both fighters looked fitter and sharper than when they had last met in 2008. Jaws maintained his style, relentlessly moving forward; McGinley kept moving back, waiting for his opportunity to counterpunch. There were no fair-play men and the small group of spectators steadily grew as the fight continued. Nearly four minutes in, when a bruising body shot from Jaws hit the target with a thud, raucous cheering broke out. Jaws was fighting in front of home supporters, and McGinley, struggling, was in the middle of hostile territory. Immediately Jaws closed in with a flurry of punches to the head, but McGinley stayed on his feet.

The lack of an obvious fair-play man became glaringly apparent when both fighters delivered punches while holding each other. They broke off, each literally pointing the finger at the other. McGinley survived but Jaws delivered a number of left jabs without reply, all the time edging after his opponent. 'Come on, Paddy, he's tired,' shouted one spectator. Then, as McGinley got in to throw a combination, Jaws caught him with a left hook as he went to dance away. The crowd roared as McGinley hit the ground. Jaws didn't wait and followed up with a right-hander while McGinley was still on his knees trying to get up. It was a straightforward foul when it comes to bare-knuckle boxing, and meant that McGinley, by default, had won the bout. With his blood boiling at the effrontery of McGinley turning up in his home town, Jaws hadn't been able to resist going for the *coup de grâce* when the other man was on his knees.

Immediately a crowd of men flooded on to the tarmac playground where the two fighters were battling. Amid the screaming and roaring the two men battled on, but chaos broke out around them. A number of other fights began, and eventually they stopped as one group began cheering loudly. In the melee that followed a number of people were injured, some suffering slash wounds from knives. Both fighters were arrested shortly afterwards and charged with affray. In March 2013 Jaws, who pleaded guilty to affray, was told to prove his fighting days were over when the judge adjourned his case for a year. Barney, in the mean-time, had left the country after being initially charged along with his opponent.

That wasn't the only trouble to follow Barney in 2012. His self-declarations of greatness and his claim to the nebulous 'King of the Gypsies' title attracted other Traveller fighting men to issue challenges, just as Paddy 'Jaws' Ward had expected. Among the first on to YouTube was Northampton-based Hughie Doherty. One of the 'Punk' Dohertys, he is a first cousin of Celebrity Paddy. Like his famous cousin, Hughie had also had his fifteen minutes of fame when he featured in the stylish documentary *Gypsy Blood*. The film, shot by Leo Maguire, followed the exploits of Irish Traveller Hughie as well as English Romany Traveller Fred Butcher. It focused on the relationship both men had with their young sons, against the backdrop of violent and sometimes bloody clashes.

There was some controversy when it aired on Channel 4 in 2012. In one part Hughie's seven-year-old son is asked what would happen if he were to lose a fight. The kid replied: 'He'll drown me if I lose.' Hughie laughed off the comment as a joke, but then he emphasized that to be a Doherty was a heavy burden because it came with a reputation that had to be defended at all costs. *Gypsy Blood* also showed Hughie Doherty fighting a much bigger non-Traveller man, who, after taking a few shots from Hughie, puts his hands up to 'give best'. The clip showed Hughie to be a useful fighter, but in reality fights against 'country people' carry no value among Travellers. As far as the Travellers are concerned they are a breed apart.

The question of just how far apart was raised in the documentary's final scene, where Hughie lets his son spar for well over forty minutes against an older, bigger cousin. Even when the youngster falls and smacks his head off the concrete, Hughie intervenes to stop his wife from ending the fight. The scene provoked a couple of hundred viewers into complaining to Britain's broadcasting regulator Ofcom. It is a disturbing insight into the unrelenting need to prove the family's honour that hangs like a dark shadow over Traveller fighting men. There is little doubt that the importance of demonstrating prowess with their fists, and so maintaining their reputation, is a central tenet in their lives.

The videos uploaded to YouTube don't have the same production values as Maguire's top-class work, but Hughie Doherty's all-consuming desire to forge a reputation as a fighting man shines through just the same. His challenge to Barney 'The Gorilla' McGinley came with a nice line in provocative Traveller humour: 'You say you're the King, you're nothing but a burger king.' The videos accuse McGinley of having backed out of a challenge previously laid down in the UK:

> You were arguing on the internet about another Doherty
> man in Birmingham. You said you'd do to them what you
> done to the Punk sons. You did fuck all. You wouldn't
> fight us. If you are man enough to fight me I'm putting
> it straight to you now. You hid from my brother for five
> year, the whole world knows that, and you are going
> around the place telling everyone you are the king. I beat
> scobies like you seven days a week. You're nothing but a
> sausage. You know for a fact that you wouldn't last five
> minutes. If you want to fight, ring me and get it on. I
> don't need any dates and times, I'm ready to get it on now.
> I'm giving you seven days to ring me or I'm coming to
> find you, sausage boy.

His taunts brought a predictable response from McGinley. At this stage McGinley and his family were in Belgium. From there, they posted a riposte on YouTube. Barney's father was first up, giving a history lesson and casting doubt on the Doherty clan's pedigree. 'The London Dohertys and the Northampton Dohertys didn't come from a fighting breed of people,' he said.

His son Barney was equally dismissive of the challenge and claimed there were no DVDs of Hughie Doherty's fights, no proof of any fighting record to boast of. 'I have every proof in the world. I'm the greatest, I'm not a sick man now. I had to go to Galway after four year and get my title back,' he said. Describing Hughie and his family as 'leprechaun people', he addressed Hughie's father: 'Punk, do me a favour. Before I give them brain damage, just drown them. End of story. We are number one.'

Claims by the Dohertys that Ainey McGinley suffered a broken jaw and lost teeth in the fracas in Galway were disproved by Ainey, who gritted his teeth for the benefit of the camera and then proceeded to punch himself in the jaw to demonstrate the absence of any injury. One of Ainey's sons wearing boxing gloves then pounded his father's midriff as he shouted encouragement: 'Come on, drive them into me!' Midway through the clip the McGinleys' focus switched to Big Joe Joyce and his son David, and Ainey issued another challenge for a rematch. The clip finished with a younger brother hammering punches first into Barney's torso and then Simon McGinley's, to show off their toughness and preparedness to fight.

As if to prove the old saying, 'Be careful what you wish for', Hughie Doherty eventually got his fight with one of the McGinleys. In March 2013 he faced Barney's brother, Trevor, under a motorway bridge in England in a brutal slugging match that went on for thirty minutes. He gave as good as he got, but Hughie didn't have the power to damage the bigger McGinley man. In the end, bloodied and battered, and after taking a series of heavy jabs to the face, he lashed out with a kick at Trevor McGinley. Doherty hadn't been knocked down, but his kick meant he had lost the fight.

Since 1990 the individuals at the centre of the bare-knuckle boxing scene have changed. Dan Rooney and Paddy Doherty have new careers, while James Quinn-McDonagh has looked for ways to bring what he learned from bare-knuckle boxing into the mainstream world. There has also been a changing of the guard as the Joyce sons have taken up where their father left off, just like the McGinleys and O'Donnells. It's no longer primarily a way of solving rows: it has become an underground sport among an exclusive club of Traveller families. They fight for pride. It's not about money, although big sums of cash might be gambled on either side. For the fighting men and their families, there is an ever-present risk of violence. Disputes over results can lead to feuds, and then there is the chance that fighters could end up behind bars for their efforts. Yet, despite such drawbacks, those clans who embrace bare-knuckle fighting look as if they will preserve the practice for at least another generation. There's still unfinished business to sort out.

12

The Road to Glory

Ever since rich and powerful men paid to watch others fight, the prizefighter has existed. The gladiators of ancient Rome, if they were good and survived long enough, could become wealthy in their own right and enjoy the fruits of fame. Lauded by the mob and rewarded by their patrons, the professional combatants who reached the top were the superstars of their time. They came from among slaves, captured soldiers or from the ranks of disgraced military who sought an alternative to death as the path to redemption. Few ever found it, but the dream fuelled the desire to escape the drudgery of slavery or the penury of dishonour. Their honed bodies and their skill in the lethal arts made the gladiators desirable to both men and women, who sought to bask in the reflected glory of their martial prowess.

Today's professional combatants don't have the short sword, the trident or lance; instead they use their fists. Although there are risks, professional boxers can reasonably expect that they won't be given a fatal *coup de grâce* if they perform badly or lose a limb in the course of a bout. They do, however, share the sense of being outsiders who have chosen one of the few routes to success that remain open to them. Many professional fighters, certainly those in Western Europe and the United States, come from tough neighbourhoods, from the ghettos and from communities that live on the margins.

An Irish Traveller halting site on the edge of town slots into anyone's definition of a life on the margin of wider society. For many, the male role model is the tough guy who can rise above the domestic din, to impose their will or to inspire others to follow. The hard men among the bare-knuckle fighters provide a template for young boys to emulate and to which they can aspire. The story of the young street tough who overcomes all challenges to become a champion in the ring is romantic. It's a narrative beloved of Hollywood and maudlin sportswriters peering through the cigarette smoke and soft focus of whiskey vision. From *The Cinderella Man* to *Rocky*, it has always been a box-office hit.

The story of Francis Barrett, a Traveller from a halting site at Hillside, on the eastern edge of Galway city, reads as if it was written by a scriptwriter keen to cash in on the formula that works so well. At the age of eleven a young Francis was asked by barber Michael Gillen if he wanted to join his Olympic Boxing Club. The popular barber, known as 'Chick', was a corner man straight from central casting. Training in a metal shipping container that had been transformed into a lock-up gym without electricity or running water, young Barrett would go on to have an amateur boxing career that encompassed 250 fights. Among those he would beat in the three-round amateur bouts was future UK boxing superstar Ricky Hatton.

When Francis Barrett qualified to represent Ireland in boxing at the Atlanta Olympics in 1996 there was genuine delight across all walks of life for the young Irish Traveller's success. He was the first among the community to make such a breakthrough, a Traveller who was featured on prime-time television for his guts and achievement. Regardless of the fact that the bookies had him at 100–1 to win the gold medal, the entire country rallied behind the flag he carried at the head of the Irish team during the opening ceremony. As the youngest member of the contingent, nineteen-year-old Barrett was the plucky kid who had fought his way to share a piece of the big time. He totally outclassed his Brazilian opponent, Zely Fereria Dos Santos, winning 32–7. Hopes were high but in the next round he more than met his match in Tunisian fighter Fethi Missaoui, going down 18–6. He had the spirit and fitness, but the North African was a clever technical fighter who picked off points for a comfortable win. During the fights TV cameras caught the live reaction of his family from their halting site in Galway where family members were interviewed about the doughty young Olympian. Everyone was happy to welcome this Irish Traveller into their home, albeit through their TV.

In Francis Barrett's story there are all the elements of the complex and sometimes contradictory nature of the relationship between Travellers and the wider community. Just months after his return from Atlanta, he married Kathleen McDonagh at a church in Wembley. It was a triple ceremony and there were thirty-six bridesmaids in pink taffeta, ribbons and lace, along with four hundred guests. In the days before *Big Fat Gypsy Weddings* it was an eye-catching event. But the press photographers who turned up to record it were regarded as an intrusive annoyance by some of the wedding guests. Although Francis was lionized by the Irish media thanks to his heroics in the ring, not all the Traveller guests welcomed the presence of photographers at the church. The outsiders were threatened, and one young man tried to slash a camera bag with a knife. A protective group of young Travellers stayed outside the church, even after the police had arrived to help calm the situation. The spectacular ceremony went off without any further hitches.

Francis's popularity, however, survived the altercation and was to be enhanced by the release in 1999 of *Southpaw: The Francis Barrett Story*, a documentary which charted his rise from the ranks of amateur boxing to carrying the flag for Ireland. It was a rare insight into the Travellers' world and the tough conditions Barrett had had to endure just to get as far as the boxing ring and compete at an equal level. In the ring Francis Barrett continued to work hard, but he didn't qualify for the Olympics in 2000, prompting his decision to go professional. At light welterweight he had the potential to do well.

The same year there was a well-publicized incident in which Francis was slashed with a knife during an altercation with members of the 'Smurf' McDonagh clan in Galway. There had been a long history of animosity between members of the two families, and with Francis's reputation as a boxer there was no shortage of eager volunteers who wanted a chance to establish their own reputation by taking on the nearest thing Irish Travellers ever had to a mainstream superstar.

As a professional he fought twenty times, suffering three defeats near the end of his career which eventually led him to call it quits. It's a tough life as a lowly ranked professional, even if he did notch up some minor titles. While training he made ends meet by laying cables for water companies and telecoms around London, hoping that a shot at a serious title would come his way. Francis also tried his hand at fight promotion and staged a well-attended card in Galway in 2009. That same year, however, he spoke of how, despite all he had achieved, he was still turned away from a city hotel when in the company of an English businessman and boxing promoter. Travellers are still not wanted.

Yet Barrett is proud of his Traveller roots and took part in another award-winning documentary in 2011, *Blood of the Travellers*. For years Irish Travellers have demanded recognition from the Irish government as a separate ethnicity, which would give them equal standing when dealing with the wider community as well as a greater sense of self-esteem. *Blood of the Travellers* saw Francis travelling through the Traveller community, collecting DNA samples which were then tested by a panel of eminent scientists. The programme sought to make the argument that Irish Travellers are literally a breed apart, and have a separate ethnic identity from the wider Irish community.

Francis Barrett's influence as a role model for other young Travellers cannot be underestimated. Although he never got his shot at the big time, Francis created a boxing legacy that has and will have an impact for years to come. He blazed the trail that others are now following all the way to the Olympics and the medal rostrum. He has inspired a generation of young Travellers who flocked to boxing clubs all over Ireland and the UK in the years after 1996, and who have in turn encouraged others to work hard at becoming elite athletes.

One of those is his first cousin, Coleman Barrett, who showed early promise to win a bronze medal in the World Junior Championships in 2000. The London-based fighter went professional in 2003, notching up six wins without defeat in two years. He took four years off fighting before re-emerging as a force to be reckoned with, and getting two more victories under his belt. Barrett was invited to take part in a Sky Sports Prizefighter tournament in November 2009, and turned out to be the dark horse of the tournament, reaching the final and having a crack at Olympic gold medallist Audley Harrison. The Galway native was the 25–1 outsider but started well enough to have the bookies worried until Harrison found the punches to beat Barrett on points.

Coleman Barrett came back again the following February at a fight in the National Stadium in Dublin to claim the Irish heavyweight title by beating Colin Kenna. Since then Barrett has been quiet, his last outing being a win in October 2010. There had been high hopes that a mouth-watering clash against another Irish Traveller, Tyson Fury, would go ahead. Instead Coleman Barrett had to vacate his Irish title without staging a defence. In 2013, at the age of thirty-three, it is possible that he might yet make another comeback.

Tyson Fury, in turn, had to fight more than one battle eventually to claim the Irish title. The massive Manchester-born fighter first had to convince the Boxing Union of Ireland that he had enough Irish roots to qualify him to fight for the title under an Irish licence. It took an affidavit from his uncle, the father of another top professional fighter from Limerick, Andy Lee, to convince the authorities that his grandmother hailed from Galway. Fury, who stands six foot nine inches tall, is an impressive pugilist. He is currently, without doubt, the leading contender among Irish Travellers to have a chance at claiming a world title in boxing. Neither is Tyson Fury reticent about expressing his own confidence in his ability to snare a title. He's not shy, and likes to get involved in a bit of verbal combat well before a fight even takes place.

Tyson Fury didn't lick his fighting prowess off the stones. He is the son of Gypsy John Fury, who was also a professional fighter. He decided to name his son after 'Iron' Mike Tyson, the infamous US boxer and world champion. Gypsy John was born in Tuam, County Galway, and moved at an early age with his family to Lancashire where he lived the Traveller life. His professional boxing record is more modest than his son's, having been stopped twice and knocked out twice in a pro-career that spanned all of eight bouts. Gypsy John's last fight also made headlines, but for all the wrong reasons.

It started in a car park at an auction house when he bumped into an old adversary, Oathie Sykes, in July 2010. According to Sykes's version of events Fury attacked him in a brutal onslaught that culminated in his eye being gouged out. On his side, Fury claims to have been bitten, and says the shocking injury happened as he tried to prise himself loose. He was tried, convicted by a jury and handed down an eleven-year sentence, which was later cut to nine after an appeal. Tyson was in the public gallery throughout the trial to support his father who, until then, had been his coach and trainer. For those regarded as 'fighting men' among Travellers such violent street fights are a frequent hazard in a lifestyle that can suddenly and spectacularly spin out of control.

Drama seems to follow Tyson around. Boxing pundits are divided about his talents. One commentator, before his fight with Martin Rogan for the Irish heavyweight title, described Tyson as 'an accident waiting to happen'. In that sense, he's a true representative of the Travelling man's fighting spirit. Tyson's early training, however, had obviously been effective: he won his first professional bout at the age of nineteen, after six rounds in December 2008. Within a year he won the English heavyweight title from John McDermott in controversial circumstances. Complaints about how the referee scored the fight, after the judges were deadlocked, saw a rematch in June 2010 which Tyson also won.

A victory over Steve Cunningham in New York in April 2013 pushed Tyson Fury further up the world rankings and closer to a title shot.

★

If Tyson's life story so far is dotted with episodes of violence or chaos that afflict many Traveller families, it has been a fairy tale compared to that of fellow Irish Traveller and Mancunian Michael Armstrong. The story goes that Armstrong was born in Longford, Ireland, as his partially sighted father crashed the car while his mother gave birth. After moving to Manchester, the family broke up when Armstrong senior's illness got worse, and Michael ended up in various care homes and became involved in petty crime. He turned to professional boxing at the age of eighteen, adopting the name 'Michael Gomez' because a fighter called Michael Armstrong was already registered in his weight category. He called himself after Puerto Rican boxer Wilfredo Gomez. On the night he went out to celebrate his eighteenth birthday, and the birth of his first child, Gomez and his friends got involved in a fight with another group outside a nightclub. Gomez punched a man who fell, hit his head and later died. He was tried but acquitted of manslaughter after it was accepted he had acted in self-defence.

In 1999 he won the British featherweight title, but his career suffered amid stories of a wild, boozy lifestyle. In 2001 he was stabbed in the arm while out with a fellow boxer. On the operating table he almost died after having an allergic reaction to the drugs administered to him. His apparent lack of professionalism meant that in 2003 he went into a fight as the rank outsider against a title contender, Alex Arthur. He was also fighting the Scot on home territory in what was seen as a stepping stone for Arthur towards better fighters than Gomez. Erratic and brilliant as ever, Gomez produced an explosive and aggressive display, tearing apart Arthur's defence and stopping him in the fifth round after knocking him down three times.

After that victory Gomez appeared to knuckle down and work hard in the gym, winning an impressive string of fights. He won the World Boxing Union super featherweight title and defended it three times until he lost it to Javier Osvaldo Alvarez in 2005. His next fight, however, provoked more controversy. Fighting in Dublin for the Irish title against Peter McDonagh, Gomez was knocked down in the sixth. He got up but turned his back on his opponent and returned to his corner, effectively giving up in the ring. He said afterwards that he had decided there and then to retire from boxing. There were immediate claims that there had been unusual betting patterns, and the prize money due to both fighters was initially withheld until an investigation found neither man had any questions to answer.

Even then Gomez's reputation was solid enough that in 2008 he was given a second chance of a title fight with Amir Khan, an Olympic silver medallist who had turned professional to great fanfare. Gomez had won three fights in a row and was matched against Khan for the Commonwealth title. In an interview with the *Manchester Evening News* before the fight with Khan, he spoke about the apparent turnaround he had made in life.

> My brother is in jail doing a long term, and so are my cousins. It's where I should be, and I have done a few stupid things. But these days I am more proud of the fact that I have provided a better life for my kids than I am of winning British titles or WBU titles. It doesn't even come close. When my little girl looks me in the eye and tells me she loves me, it means more than any Lonsdale Belt. It might be because she wants an ice cream, but it still melts me. But it hasn't changed me as a fighter. I still wear my heart on my sleeve, but these days it is not to show everyone how tough and macho I am, but that heart is on my sleeve for my kids.

The boxing showman in him wasn't far behind, however, and in one TV interview Gomez reminded viewers how he had almost died after being stabbed: 'If death doesn't scare me what chance does Amir Khan have?'

Gomez fought bravely, and for a while exposed Khan's defensive frailties. The undefeated young champion was expected to sail past the 'has-been' Gomez, and knocked him down in the first round. Not long into the second round, however, Gomez connected with a hard left hook which had the young fighter on the canvas. In the third round Gomez was getting punished but was successful in keeping much of the fighting at close quarters. In the fourth Gomez delivered a body shot that again shook the young fighter, with the ITV commentator remarking: 'This is almost like a *Rocky* film.' The crowd roared and maintained the high-octane atmosphere, knowing that they were witnessing a truly exciting professional bout. In the fifth round Khan's accuracy was devastating, even as Gomez continued to look for the knockout blow, managing to land a couple of hard punches. But as Gomez tired, Khan threw out more well-placed and powerful combinations, with Gomez's head snapping back from the force of the blows as he teetered into the ropes. Khan was on top of him, ready to kill off the contest, when the referee got between them and called an end to the fight. It wasn't Gomez's turn to be *The Cinderella Man*.

Gomez continued to fight, and won another Commonwealth title shot in 2009, which he lost to Ricky Burns. There was a plan for Gomez's life to be the subject of a movie, with his character being played by *Shameless* star Jody Latham. An impressive trailer was made, which is still on YouTube, although the full movie has yet to surface. It does, however, finish with the line from Gomez: 'Don't tell me I'm finished. I haven't even started yet.'

★

There is no shortage of film-script material when it comes to the professional boxers among the Travelling community. They come from tough backgrounds and have had to overcome serious disadvantage and deal with difficult issues. When Willie 'Big Bang' Casey takes to the ring his family's hard history is literally inked on his chest. It's impossible to miss the tattoo that runs from his collarbone down the left side of his chest over his heart. The portrait is of his older brother, Paddy, one of twins, who died after an unsuccessful struggle with drugs. Willie and his brother are just two of twenty-three siblings who grew up in Clonlong on the edge of Southill in Limerick city. In the past decade the estate has become synonymous with gang violence and drug-dealing, giving rise to Limerick's reputation as a city pocked with enclaves of dangerous criminality. The fact that Willie became the first member of his family to leave school with his Junior Certificate qualifications gives a hint of the man's mindset as he went from a rookie professional to a world-title contender in just ten fights as a super bantamweight. As an amateur he fought well but he was never going to reach the heights of an Olympic squad. When he was on the cusp of hanging up his gloves for good, promoter Phil Sutcliff persuaded him to go professional.

In October 2008 'Big Bang' made his pro debut in Killarney, County Kerry, at the age of twenty-six when he stopped Brazilian fighter Carlos de Jesus. Just four fights later, in Toronto, he beat the Canadian champ, Tyson Cave, and earned himself a ticket on to the high-profile Sky Sports Prizefighter circuit. His all-action, hard-punching style made for good television. By May 2010 he reached the final of the competition when he beat Scottish boxer Paul McElhinney. There was more to come when in November he fought fellow Irishman Paul Hyland for the EBU (European) super bantamweight title and lifted the belt.

Suddenly Willie 'Big Bang' Casey had become an 'overnight' success. He was the man who could overturn the Irish sporting public's great disappointment when Bernard Dunne lost his world title to Kiko Martinez. (Dunne, an eloquent and popular sportsman, was a favourite son of the Irish sporting public and media. In 2007 he had fought Martinez in Dublin, but lost.) Casey himself had watched the fight on TV at home before he had even thought about turning professional. Now it was his turn to step into the big time. His success had been years in the making despite his apparent meteoric rise through the ranks of the professional fighters. 'The boxing comes from my father's side of the family. All my older brothers started out in the Southill boxing club, but the worst thing was they all gave it up too soon. I gave it up myself as well,' he said in an interview with the *Sunday World*. He had married in his late teens and had four children with his wife Mary. To provide for his family he had worked as a welder, and it wasn't until his mid-twenties that he had returned to the boxing ring, winning an All-Ireland intermediate title. 'I hadn't even thought about going pro at that stage, never mind getting up to the level he's at,' he said, referring to Dunne.

In the end Martinez was unable to defend his champion's belt, citing a rib injury. Instead Casey fought Guillermo Rigondeaux for the vacated title. Like the Dunne versus Martinez fight, there was a lot of hype and expectations were high. The tough, wiry fighter, however, had met his match in the Cuban, who opened with a flurry of body punches that left Casey wincing in pain. Then as the shots came down on his head the referee stepped in and stopped the fight twenty seconds before the end of round one. Casey, undefeated in eleven previous fights, was simply outclassed, and any hopes that he could have taken over the reins as boxing's golden boy faded away.

The tough Traveller from Limerick has been back in the ring since, winning his first two comeback fights, then losing one and winning again in 2012 for a still-impressive 14–2 record. In his fight against Jason Booth in July 2012, he claimed the WBO Inter-continental super bantamweight title. He may not be a world champion contender but Willie 'Big Bang' Casey is every bit the type of positive role model that so many young Travellers need to look up to.

The Irish international amateur boxing squad has seen the fruits of Francis Barrett's inspirational performance to reach the Olympics in 1996. There are scores of young Travellers training every day now in boxing clubs across Ireland and the UK. It took eight years before an Irish Traveller took up where Francis Barrett had left off in Atlanta in 1996. That honour fell to Andy Lee, a cousin of Tyson Fury, who was the only boxer on the Irish team in Athens in 2004. Born in London, Lee moved back to Limerick with his family at an early age. Fighting as a middleweight, he got through to the second round only to be beaten after a controversial countback decision went against him. He was still welcomed home as a hero, and soon after began his professional career. After a decade in the professional ring, Lee has notched up thirty wins and just two defeats as a middleweight.

One of those defeats was against Julio Cesar Chavez in a WBC middleweight title fight which pitted him against a fighter who had won forty-five of his previous forty-six fights at the time. He started well, but the fight came to an end in the seventh round after Lee was caught with a powerful uppercut and the referee intervened.

Based in the United States, Lee has carved out an impressive reputation for himself. Since the Chavez defeat in June 2012, Lee has bounced back with two victories in early 2013.

*

In 2008 two young Travellers burst on to the international scene in the shape of John Joe Nevin and John Joe Joyce, both from Mullingar. They each boxed in separate clubs outside their home town and both qualified for the 2008 Olympics in Beijing. It was a strong boxing team, with Kenny Egan winning a silver medal while Darren Sutherland and Paddy Barnes finished with bronze. Joyce and Nevin, who finished in the last sixteen, were the only ones not to win a place on the medal rostrum. In both cases, however, they lost to the eventual gold medallists in their categories.

Four years later in 2012, still aged only twenty-three, Nevin put things right when he went all the way to the final, to finish with a silver and become the first Traveller to win an Olympic medal. Ironically, even as fans crammed pubs to watch the fight, Nevin would complain that members of his own family were being refused entry into the same bars and clubs in his home town of Mullingar.

Nevin's ability to dodge his opponent's punches lends itself well to amateur boxing, which is all about scoring points rather than the capacity to soak up punishment and deliver a knock-out blow that's needed in the professional game. A member of the Irish elite boxing squad and signed up to the British Lionhearts team in the World Series of Boxing, Nevin has become a household name in Ireland.

Another young light heavyweight, Joe Ward, the grandson of Big Joe Joyce, has also put down a marker as a future prospect. As described in Chapter 9, he beat the long-term Irish champion and silver medallist Kenny Egan in convincing style, but then failed to qualify for the London Olympics, where he would have been a medal prospect. Under the Olympic rules he didn't qualify, even though he was the senior European Champion and ranked as one of the world's top ten boxers.

★

Top-level boxing, whether professional or amateur, is a tough business. But it's one that many Traveller fighters are well prepared for, driven and supported by family pride to win the plaudits of both their own people and wider society. Current evidence suggests that Irish Travellers are entering a golden age of professional boxing, and it is a matter of time before an undisputed world champion emerges from within an Irish Traveller clan. It is one area where Travellers are entirely integrated with the wider community. They train and work closely with people who aren't Travellers. The elite boxers all maintain their Traveller roots and are proud of their heritage. The support the boxers get from sports fans shows that people are more than capable of seeing past the casual prejudice usually applied to Travellers. Even the bare-knuckle fights between Travellers attract a wide audience on YouTube. When it comes to building bridges, the boxing ring is as good as any place to start.

THE TRAVELLER
TRADERS

13

Home Sweet Home

The frightening stories of feud violence, and of the hardened fighters who dominate the bare-knuckle boxing clique, could be seen as symptoms of a community with deeply ingrained social problems. The failure of the education system to attract Travellers plays no small part in that. The dreadful infighting is ultimately self-destructive and holds back the community from making progress in the eyes of wider society. But the horror stories and lack of formal education don't reflect the deep intelligence which many Traveller traders demonstrate. Among the Traveller traders there are those who are proficient in several languages and who have made millions of euros, but there are also those who have shown an aptitude for a style of organized crime that defies official categorization.

There are Travellers who are teachers, writers, soldiers, Garda officers, lawyers, labourers and every other kind of profession, but they are in the minority. Most Travellers, one way or another, are self-employed. In the past, Traveller breadwinners would have worked as tinsmiths or done casual labour on farms, while the business elite dealt in horses. Today, many combine a nomadic lifestyle with work such as driveway paving, home repairs, landscaping and gutter cleaning, dealing directly with householders.

Others deal in vehicles including cars, vans and caravans. Carpet and furniture sales are other areas where legitimate business people from the Traveller community have done well for themselves. Members of the community also make a living as market-stall traders, turning a profit on whatever can be bought and sold. There are antique dealers whose level of expertise is every bit as good as that of the top professionals working for well-known auction houses.

There is a sophistication and a capability to the Irish Traveller traders that belies the oft-mooted image of lumpen, poverty-stricken families stuck in a cycle of deprivation and condemned to worsening living conditions. Travellers, and others advocating the need for greater opportunity, equality or access to social services, have quite rightly championed those who are dispossessed. But the idea of wealthy and successful businessmen doesn't fit the poverty narrative, which delivers only part of the real picture. While the world of Irish Travellers is indeed a troubled one, there exist in it the same extremes of poverty and wealth, criminality and altruism found everywhere else.

Irish Traveller traders embrace the nomadic lifestyle and combine it with a fierce entrepreneurial spirit that has carried them all over the world. Yet many of them also operate in the black economy, usually combining it with legitimate trading. One popular income stream comes from cigarette-smuggling into both Ireland and the UK, importing products from Europe and the Far East. Another is to scam householders who agree to some kind of work on their property. This section of *Gypsy Empire* deals with those Traveller traders who cut corners, pull strokes or commit crimes in their relentless pursuit of profit.

The Traveller clans considered as being among the elite of the traders are those who regard the town of Rathkeale, County Limerick, as their spiritual home. They have developed into a unique group, willing to do business on any continent, moving quickly from one deal to the next, following the trail of euros, dollars or pounds sterling. Goods are shipped from anywhere in the world, the traders' nomadic lifestyle no handicap to sourcing shipping agents to send maritime containers from one side of the world to the other.

The activities of the Rathkeale Travellers, sometimes known as the Rathkeale Rovers, were virtually unheard of outside Ireland until 2011, when a row over an illegal halting site in the UK put them under the spotlight. A decade-long planning wrangle at Dale Farm, Basildon, Essex, provoked a lot of curiosity. This stemmed from reports that some of the homeless Irish Gypsies involved were in fact wealthy traders, who owned extensive properties in Rathkeale.

Reporters from abroad suddenly wanted to find out for themselves about the Travellers who had created such a stir. They found in Rathkeale a town faced with much the same issues as the authorities in Essex. Wealthy traders had built compounds and houses without planning permission and bought sites that had been left neglected. Other houses had been subjected to lavish attention, with expensive ornate stonework, wrought-iron railings and French-style windows, while yards had been carefully paved with stylish cobble-locking. Residents from the wider community were concerned that the Travellers in many cases hadn't been subjected to the full force of planning regulations. It wasn't just 'country people' who felt aggrieved by the behaviour of the traders, because those Travellers who had made Rathkeale their permanent home felt they had been left to bear the brunt of the fallout.

Years ago Rathkeale was a thriving market town, where farmers brought their livestock to sell in a cattle mart which has since closed down. Now parts of the town, such as Fairhill and Roches Road, are comprised of properties almost exclusively owned by Traveller families. Houses in the town are aggressively sought after by Traveller traders, and stories abound of owners being repeatedly offered large amounts of cash to sell. Many of the Traveller-owned buildings remain locked up for most of the year, secured by padlocked gates and steel window shutters until the owner returns. It doesn't make for a pleasant atmosphere. In 2012, Limerick County Council were pursuing dozens of active cases against property owners from the Traveller community over breaches of planning regulations.

There is no reason why Rathkeale has produced so many prolific Traveller traders. Rathkeale just happened to be the place where some Traveller traders put down roots less than thirty years ago. They could easily have settled in any other nearby town if property had been available. Many have done well through various means, but the most lucrative business has been the antiques trade. Several individuals from the Rathkeale Traveller community have become true experts when it comes to dealing antiques. Chief among them is Simon Quilligan, also known as Sammy Buckshot. He runs a shop in the tourist village of Adare, a few miles from Rathkeale, but his reputation as a canny operator has spread right across the UK and Europe. The likes of Michael 'Levan' Slattery have followed in Buckshot's footsteps, looking for niches to exploit in the antiques market. Richard 'Kerry' O'Brien is another member of the business elite whose imposing mansion is at Fairhill. Like many others among the traders, he is multilingual and prepared to travel far and wide in search of business opportunities.

At Christmas the town is packed with trailers and vehicles bearing licence plates from all over Europe. Families who have been on the road for ten or eleven months will return for the festive season. Parking space in the town is at a premium during December, when the streets are crammed with high-end vehicles. It is not unusual to see Mercedes-AMGs worth in excess of €200,000 in the town. Range Rover Sports are virtually ten a penny, and one year a rare Porsche Panamera, complete with a personalized plate, was parked in Rathkeale. Those who are less successful have to settle for BMW X5s and various models from the Audi marque.

On holiday and with nothing to do all day, the youngsters spend their time cruising about in the cars. They think nothing of stopping to chat with pals in oncoming vehicles, oblivious to the fact that they are blocking Rathkeale's narrow streets. At times it can be an anarchic place as the town's population is doubled by the sudden influx of Travellers from around the world. During Christmas 2012 the Garda Traffic Corps were on hand to curb the worst excesses of the young drivers. Two young men, however, couldn't resist trying out what their high-powered cars had to offer, and held a drag race on a public road on Christmas Day. The pair were caught by Gardaí as they arrived back in the town. They were brought before the District Court, where they were jailed for two months and banned from driving for five years, although both were released soon after successfully seeking bail to launch an appeal.

The holiday atmosphere and the boozing that goes along with it can lead to other problems. During the year most of the younger members of the trader families are scattered across Europe or the US. Nothing much can be done about disputes over cash until they see each other. When that happens in the heightened atmosphere of the festive period in Rathkeale, it can lead to trouble. On New Year's Day in 2013 there was what appeared to be a sudden attack by a large group of people on a house at Fairhill, the home of Brigid Ryan, who lives there all year round. She had previously been involved in a row over debts owed between Rathkeale families, and at one point she was charged by the Gardaí with extortion, although the case was later dropped.

The attack on her home was caught on security cameras that showed a group of men, some armed with bars and slash hooks, smashing windows. Two were clearly visible brandishing knives. During the hour-long assault others threw rocks at the property and even continued the attack after Gardaí had arrived at the scene. Both the front and back doors of the house were pounded with weapons. A car parked in the driveway was also badly damaged. One man, who just days earlier had been given bail after being convicted of the high-speed road race on Christmas Day, was caught on camera as a ringleader in the attacks. It was a matter of good fortune that no one suffered a serious injury.

It may be just as well, then, that many of the Travellers who are regarded as Rathkealers only spend a few weeks every second year in the small County Limerick town. However, the manner in which funerals are staged clearly demonstrates how the Travellers see the place as their spiritual home and, if possible, their final resting place. The cemetery contains several rows of twelve-foot-high granite memorials constructed from imported materials, with some costing well in excess of €100,000. While some Traveller clans like to indulge their daughters' penchant for fairy-tale-style weddings, the Rathkealers like to leave their mark after death. Their expensive gravestones aren't just about showing respect for the dead, they are also a statement of a family's wealth and standing in the highly competitive world of the Traveller trader. No expense is spared, with life-size statues of the Virgin Mary and St Christopher, the patron saint of Travellers. In some instances, huge rosaries with beads bigger than tennis balls are draped over stone representations of the pearly gates, while book- and heart-shaped slabs are engraved with messages from loved ones.

It is an ostentatious show that Travellers make no apology for, like their unconcealed love for the Virgin Mary. In that regard the Rathkealers share the open devotion to their Catholic faith that many Irish Travellers display. First Holy Communion ceremonies, weddings and funerals are celebrated as important milestones and social occasions. In the summer of 2009 that devotion could not have become more apparent. Trees were being chopped down in the grounds of Rathkeale's small church where the weddings and funerals of the Travellers are held. On the stump of a felled tree an image of the Virgin Mary became visible to many people. Immediately vigils were held, with candles lit and decades of the rosary recited while hands clasped prayer beads. Thousands of people, not just Travellers, turned up to pray at the tree stump in St Mary's Church. If ever Rathkeale Travellers needed proof of their special status anointed by God, then this was it.

While the Traveller traders' adopted town may have given rise to the occasionally used moniker 'Rathkeale Rovers', their real reputation was forged well beyond the town boundaries. The story of Michael 'Levan' Slattery illustrates just how far they rove, and their ability to operate anywhere in the world. His limp, a reminder of childhood polio, makes it easy to recognize Levan. A rotund redhead with typically fair Celtic skin, he has the air of a crumpled small-time businessman or a pub owner from the remote end of the Irish countryside. His manner is gruff and changes quickly to downright rude when he isn't getting his way. His foul-mouthed manner sometimes gets him into trouble. But behind the unappealing exterior is a sharp mind, one that is quick to recognize an opportunity and capable of setting up international transactions.

During 2004, Levan was scouring antique shops and dealerships in the eastern United States. In May, when he ran into Elmer Mack, a tough-talking American of Polish extraction, Levan wanted to do a deal. At E. A. Mack Antiques on North Howard Street, which is effectively Baltimore's 'Antique Row', Levan tried his usual mixture of cajolery and brash persuasion to get what he wanted. The object of his desire was an eighteenth-century card-table worth $29,000, according to Mack, who had no interest in Levan's initial derisory offer. The lacquered Georgian table represented a professional coup for Mack, who had spotted it at an estate sale in 2001. It had once belonged to a member of a Baltimore blue-blood family, which had made its fortune as Alexander & Alexander Insurance. Mack had snapped it up for $6,700. It was his prize catch, the type of find every antique dealer dreams of making. The dark wooden table is a distinctive piece, painted with playing cards and flowers. The King-George-II-era lattice work and King-George-III-era ball and claw feet make it an unusual item and the type of object wealthy collectors love to acquire. Levan's expert eye was drawn to the fine piece of antique furniture in Mack's premises and the possibilities for profit which it represented. The Traveller wheeler-dealer wanted to pay $10,000 in cash and swap two antique turf buckets in return for the period piece. It only took a glance from Mack to determine that the buckets had no value and that Levan was out to pull off a swindle.

Two years later, in 2006, on a return trip to the store in Baltimore, Levan arrived with some associates in a renewed effort to clinch the deal, in spite of Mack's obvious reluctance to agree to the transaction. This time peat buckets and reproduction Georgian wine coolers were put up in a part-swap deal before Levan offered to pay $28,000 for the table. In the meantime William and Kathleen Holden, two of Levan's associates, kept firing questions at Mack while others hid the table under moving-mats and loaded it on to a truck. As far as Mack was concerned it was a classic distraction theft, while Levan and the Holdens would later claim that a verbal contract had been agreed. Mack was able to get $10,000 from the Holdens in September 2006 after putting pressure on them through his lawyer.

Levan may not have reckoned on Mack's tenacity in trying to recover his losses. A former US Marine, the antique dealer also had long experience in the risky trade of dealing with luxury goods seized by the US authorities from drug-dealers. In other words, Mack was no shrinking violet and certainly wasn't going to let Levan get away scot-free with the antique table. But Mack was to discover that the Irish Travellers he had encountered were no ordinary grifters, pulling off scams for quick profits. Levan was an accomplished international trader, while the Holdens were closely linked to the elite Rathkeale Traveller traders. Born an O'Brien, Kathleen Holden's brother, Richard 'Kerry' O'Brien, is one of Rathkeale's most successful Traveller traders. The family has close connections to the United States. Another of Kathleen's brothers served out a career in the New York Police Department before retiring to Ireland.

Elmer Mack filed criminal charges against the couple and Michael 'Levan' Slattery in a bid to get the rest of his cash back. For their part, the Irish Travellers denied any wrongdoing, claiming that Mack had agreed to the swap-deal. They countersued Mack on the grounds that the antique dealer had used criminal charges to enforce a civil contract. They also claimed that Mack had sold the wine coolers for $22,500 and had made a profit on the deal. After a week-long hearing in 2008, a Baltimore City Circuit Court jury didn't buy their story and found in Mack's favour, awarding him $58,000 in damages.

As far as Mack was concerned, the fight had only just

begun. He went on to win further damages for the malicious lawsuit by the Holdens against him. No doubt Levan was somewhat surprised at Mack's tenacity when a private detective turned up at his Ballywilliam house in Rathkeale one Christmas to serve him legal papers. It wasn't the first time Levan's past had been waiting to catch up with him on a trip home to Rathkeale. The Revenue Commissioners once took the opportunity to seize a camper van and four-wheel-drive vehicle on which the requisite import duty had not been paid. The American antique dealer had also set about trying to identify Levan's assets in order to recover the cash spent on the legal battle. Unfortunately for Mack, the walnut card-table has yet to resurface. In 2012 the legal case Mack had against Levan and the Holdens was still alive and kicking.

What Mack had discovered, to his cost, was a community of well-connected and well-resourced international traders, prepared to trample over anyone on their way to a quick profit. They consistently show an ingenuity and resourcefulness that belies the lack of formal education among the community. Their nomadic lifestyle stymies the efforts of law enforcement to catch up with individuals who routinely do business across international borders without any problems. There are several among that specific community who have shown a talent for sharp business practice like no other. They include cigarette smugglers, dodgy antique dealers, sellers of counterfeit electrical goods and those who run tarmac-paving schemes that deliberately rip off customers. The Rathkeale Traveller traders operate regardless of any language or cultural barriers, whether it's in Hebei Province, China, the outskirts of Helsinki or the foothills of the Italian Alps. In business-speak their business model is culture-blind.

14

The Wizards of Oz

In the summer of 2009, it was business as usual for the Rathkeale wheelers and dealers on the road in the UK, continental Europe and beyond. God's chosen ones, as usual, were busy dealing antiques, laying tarmac, selling electrical goods and furniture and smuggling tobacco. One group of salesmen, however, went a bit further than would normally be expected. They booked tickets for themselves, without their wives and children, to Australia.

A consignment of diesel-powered electrical generators had been sourced in China and was due to be shipped to Europe. Instead, the cargo was redirected to Australia. The generators were shoddy and substandard, but coming straight out of the box they looked shiny and new. The average punter, thinking he had got a bargain, wouldn't be able to tell the difference. By the time anything had gone wrong, the gifted salesmen from Rathkeale would be long gone. The dodgy generators were even branded with a name that sounded suspiciously similar to another well-known established manufacturer. The salesmen also had a supply of power tools for sale, which like the generators were cheap copies and possibly even counterfeit versions of well-known brands.

The traders' modus operandi was very simple. The

consignment was cached in a small number of lock-up storage spaces in different places. Each trader would load up his rental car or van with a supply and hit the road. They set up in car parks near shopping centres, or simply knocked on doors looking for customers. Having learned their trade from an early age at their daddy's elbow, the Rathkeale salesmen are skilful and pushy. They are brilliant entrepreneurs, and never shy about closing a deal once they have a customer on the hook. There was no shortage of punters willing to hand over their dollars in Australia. It wasn't all work and no play and, by one account, the trip was the Rathkeale-Traveller-trader equivalent of a rock-band road tour, complete with boozing sessions and trashed hotels.

The first group of Rathkealers arrived in June, during the Australian winter. Like most immigrant Paddies just off the plane, they stood out with their shorts and pasty white legs. Starting in Sydney, several traders made their way north and set up another 'base camp' near Brisbane. They rented space from a Storage King outlet in the town of Durack for their supplies. From there they hit the unsuspecting residents of the Gold Coast with their charming, pushy sales spiel. When one group rolled up in Darwin, Australia's most northern city had just been hit by a series of rolling blackouts. In the tropical zone, electricity keeps the air-conditioning on and beers cool so the prospect of a bargain generator was irresistible. As one buyer found out to his cost after buying ten of the machines, the deal was indeed too good to be true.

As the consumer complaints began to stack up, an Australian government Fair Trading official issued a public warning to the media, pointing out that the products had been bought for $129 and were being sold off for between $400 and $1,500 each. The low-quality units also posed a serious safety issue, while it was pointed out in polite official language that the people selling them were quite likely lying about how good they were. The statement read:

> Tests conducted on the generators have revealed they are not capable of performing in accordance with the representations made at the time of sale and in the signage on the packaging. These are not made by reputable companies. Consumers should not buy these generators, but if they have purchased one, they should have it tested by a qualified electrician. There is no warranty offered and there is no chance of obtaining a refund on any items purchased because these people quickly leave an area after they achieve any sales.

The Aussies, famous in this part of the world for their laid-back cynicism, had never seen anything like it. Even Australians, it appeared, were not immune to the Traveller traders' sales spiel on full power.

After a couple of weeks, police had also taken notice as a number of reports began to filter through of the Irishmen going door to door selling electrical goods. Fair Trading investigators traced the centre of operations back to the storage facility in Durack. Throughout the month of August they kept close watch to see who was visiting. By 1 September 2008 the authorities had enough information to act. They moved in and arrested more than two dozen Travellers. Those taken into custody held a mix of Irish and British passports, some with addresses in Rathkeale, as well as Dale Farm and Smithy Fen, another site used by the Rathkeale Travellers in Cambridgeshire in the UK. Luckily for the Traveller traders, the Australian government had recently changed the rules, which meant that anyone caught working illegally was no longer automatically held in custody. Having escaped ending up in jail, the entire group left the country before they could be officially and unceremoniously kicked out.

However, another gang was still operating successfully, prompting mutterings back in Rathkeale that they might have even sabotaged their rivals by tipping off the authorities. As it turned out, that group had their own troubles, as officers from Fair Trading were also keeping a close watch on them. Surveillance pictures showed a number of men, including Danny 'Bishop' O'Brien, beside a rental car. The car's hatchback was open and visible inside were boxes of the generators being sold across New South Wales. At this stage the Aussie authorities figured the Rathkealers had sold at least €300,000 worth of merchandise without any licence, and without the goods being approved. A Federal warning was issued in October, again advising consumers not to buy anything off the Irish Travellers.

Fair Trading investigator Michael Cooper said it was one of the best-organized scams they had seen hit Australia for years. 'People believe they are getting a bargain, when really it's just rubbish from China or Taiwan. Their whole modus operandi is to fly under the radar. They deal only in cash, and if the authorities question them they move very quickly,' he said. Cooper dealt first-hand with one gang when he approached them at their lock-up facility in Sydney, accompanied by a TV camera crew. The Traveller traders didn't hang around as soon as they realized that Cooper wasn't a policeman, speeding away without locking up, leaving their stash of generators behind. In their haste to get away, they even drove off with the door of the rental van wide open.

Within days, Danny 'Bishop' O'Brien and others had left the country and were back home in Rathkeale for the Annual Blessing of the Graves ceremony in November. The Aussie authorities followed up the case, managing to identify most of the group through their passports. Some were then phoned and written to, being told that they were no longer welcome in the country and would be deported at the airport if they tried to return.

A small band had also ventured as far as New Zealand during their stint of southern-hemisphere trading. Four young Rathkealers travelled to the North Island selling power washers. Their excursion came to an abrupt end at Dargaville when they were held up at gunpoint and robbed of their merchandise, cash and their rented vehicle. They left for home after the robbery, after more than meeting their match.

One member of the group who had been to Australia had a lot more in store for him when he reached Britain. While he had been away, results from the UK's national DNA database had linked him to the unsolved attack and rape of a disabled woman in May 1991. A man who had called to her house in Deepcar, Sheffield, selling furniture, had asked to use her toilet. The woman, then in her forties, suffered from cerebral palsy and had to use a wheelchair. After gaining entry, the man locked her dog in a room and launched a sexual assault on the woman. She was so badly injured that she required emergency surgery and endured a long period of recovery. It took her a year before she could pluck up the courage to return to her own home. Police had taken DNA samples at the time, but they were unable to track down her attacker. What they didn't know then was that the rapist was eighteen-year-old Jeremiah Sheridan.

In the meantime, Sheridan had got married at the age of twenty and had had three children with his wife. Then in 2005, Sheridan allowed a sample of his DNA to be taken when he was arrested over a public-order offence in Cambridge. No one had foreseen that in 2008 a review of the 1991 sex attack would match the two DNA samples. While he was in Australia the police made an appeal for information about Sheridan's whereabouts on *Crimewatch*. One of the investigating officers stressed the importance of keeping such cases open:

> The whole point of reviews is not only to protect the public and bring people to justice, but to help victims get some closure if the person responsible is caught. People affected by offences like this never get over them or forget them, and they can affect the rest of their lives, but if they can see the person responsible sentenced it can bring an immense amount of relief knowing they are off the streets.

By the time Sheridan left Australia in September 2008 he must have realized he was facing serious criminal charges when he landed back in the UK. Arrested at Heathrow, he appeared in court in Sheffield in July 2009. The then 37-year-old changed his plea shortly before his trial was due to begin and admitted raping the woman. Sentencing him to sixteen and a half years at Sheffield Crown Court in September, Judge Graham Robinson said:

> As an act of kindness she allowed you into her home. Her physical and communication difficulties must have been obvious to you. The victim said she was shouting but nobody could hear her. She said you hurt her and blood was spurting everywhere. This was a grave crime of sexual violence. The victim was a vulnerable woman attacked in her own home. She was subjected to life-threatening violence and you abandoned your victim, leaving her with serious injuries.

Half the sentence would be served under licence. However, Sheridan successfully appealed the length of his sentence, and in 2010 the Court of Appeal reduced it to nine years.

In Australia, the process of wrapping up the Rathkealers' excursion also continued. New South Wales Fair Trading Commission destroyed a consignment of the seized generators in July 2009, on the grounds that they were not safe enough to be auctioned off to members of the public. Using a huge bulldozer, the generators were lined up for the photographers and publicly crushed flat to put them well and truly beyond use. The Fair Trading Minister at the time, Virginia Judge, again warned householders to be on their guard, but also warned the con artists they'd be jailed if they ever set foot in Australia again.

These scammers are very cunning, operating across Australia, generally targeting rural areas in NSW in a 'hit-and-run' style. Fair Trading investigators conducted a highly successful covert surveillance operation on these rogues last year and confronted members of the group at a storage facility in Sydney. The Travellers subsequently abandoned their rented accommodation, motor vehicles and remaining goods and fled the country. Officers contacted gang members overseas and warned them they could be prosecuted under the Crimes Act, for obtaining money by deception, if they come back to NSW. If proven guilty, the offenders could be sentenced to five years in prison. So far the warning has made its mark. We believe they will not be coming back to Australia, which is a great outcome for consumers.

Although the Rathkealers didn't return to Australia, others did, travelling from the UK to do house-repair work. Irish Travellers based in the UK have been turning up on the radar of Fair Trading officials since 2010. In response, a national travelling conmen taskforce was set up specifically to target the traders who arrive in Australia. Two Irish Travellers were caught red-handed in Sydney when they tried to charge the equivalent of €1,400 for painting the eaves of an 89-year-old woman's home. The elderly woman's son alerted officials as the pair were due to call back for their money. The encounter was caught on video. One of the men asked: 'Am I going to get my money after working my rocks off?' He was told that as an unlicensed trader he was not entitled to get paid. Asked about where he was living he was elusive and claimed to be 'staying in different hotels here and there'. When asked which one he was currently booked into he replied: 'I'm staying in the car at the moment.' His explanation for the other men who had turned up while the painting job was being carried out was equally implausible: 'I had a few friends here, they were just standing around doing nothing, visiting. They were on holidays, you know what I mean? Just watching me work, basically.'

In 2012, more Irish Travellers were flagged by Fair Trading officials as they entered Australia. One man, Felix Moorehouse, who had already been convicted in Ireland of attempting to extract €6,000 from a farmer in Cork, was stopped at Melbourne and served with a number of court summonses. Moorehouse had previously been caught and fined over dodgy building work in Australia in September 2011, shortly after which he had left the country. When he turned up at Melbourne Airport on 17 January 2013 he was served with court summonses to answer outstanding charges in relation to rogue building work in a Sydney suburb. On the same day a 26-year-old Irish Traveller, Jerry Connors, was stopped at Perth Airport, where he too was served with a number of court summonses. Unlike Moorehouse, he was refused entry. He had previously come to the attention of Fair Trading officials in 2011 and as a result his name was flagged when he tried to enter Australia.

In an official statement Fair Trading Commissioner Rod

Stowe said both men were involved with a gang of Irish Travellers who had been on the radar of the national travelling conmen taskforce for some years: 'In 2011, NSW Fair Trading Minister Anthony Roberts established this taskforce and has led a relentless national strategy against travelling conmen, and we are determined to continue to track these gangs and hold them accountable for their crimes against vulnerable Australians.'

Tight immigration and working-visa rules have meant that the rogue traders among the Irish Travelling community haven't gained a permanent foothold in Australia. Those Traveller traders who insist on bending and breaking the rules have been well and truly marked out by the Australian authorities. The swift response in setting up a specific taskforce is in marked contrast to many European countries, where authorities usually leave such matters to the police or the civil courts. Continuous publicity campaigns when known scam artists enter Australia give Fair Trading officials a great chance to track them down. Their use of the media and videotaping of their encounters also means the scam artists are subjected to the kind of publicity that makes it harder for them to do business and to exploit vulnerable homeowners.

To outsiders, it may seem like a hard way to earn a living, but some rogue traders can make thousands of euros or Australian dollars in a single day. The scams have been refined over and over to produce the best results, and despite the best efforts of the hard-working Australian Fair Trading officials, the traders don't usually get caught. In those countries where the authorities don't have the same capability to react, there is even more chance of rich pickings for the rogue Traveller traders.

15

Black Gold

It's not all glamour for the Traveller traders from Rathkeale. The basic earner for many of the traders is doing tarmacadam work all over continental Europe. Antique trading, cigarette smuggling and furniture sales can produce a big payday, but only a few traders have the skill and contacts to rely entirely on such high-risk transactions for their main income stream. All the Traveller traders are on a constant lookout for such a deal, which could provide the means to allow them to step up among their clan hierarchy. But when such a lucrative scam isn't on the cards, it's a matter of getting up in the morning and knocking on doors touting for business.

One of the favourite lines of work is to offer property owners a once-in-a-lifetime offer of some top-quality tarmacadam work at a knock-down price. The sales patter is always the same, no matter what language it is being delivered in. A potential customer is told that a work crew is in the area doing a large project on the nearby motorway. They have material left over and can pave a yard, car park or driveway just for the price of the labour. Surprisingly, plenty of people still fall for it.

In 2013 the Rathkeale trader regarded as being the best in the business when it came to drumming up customers for this scam was just a teenager. Able to make the deal in a variety of languages including Swedish, Polish and German, this youngster, along with his father and brothers, can generate in excess of €100,000 in a good week. It may sound like an astounding sum, but each householder they persuade will pay out around €6,000. Then there are commercial properties, whose bigger yards offer much greater prospects for profit. Once they figure a customer is good for the cash, the crew piles in, working furiously to get the job done as quickly as possible before anyone can change their minds. They lay a thin veneer of a tar-like substance over which gravel or chipping material is rolled. Invariably it's a botched job, but the Travellers are gone with the cash before the hapless victim realizes they have been duped.

Every so often they make the newspapers in a country where they are operating. Usually they manage to stay under the radar, but when the police take an interest in the tarmac crews, warnings go out to the general public. In Germany they are known as '*teerkolonne*', in France as '*les faux bitumeurs*', and '*asfaltari Irlandese*' in Italy. It may sound stressful, with angry customers and police breathing down your neck, but a single crew can generate millions. Considering that there are at least twenty-five such tarmac gangs from Rathkeale operating around the world, although mostly in Europe, they have cornered a significant business possibly worth close to a hundred million euros annually.

There could be as many as ten men in a single crew. Often two or three will be Rathkealers, possibly a father and two sons, or brothers working together. Also among the group will be one or two Irish labourers they may have picked up along the way, usually recruited back in Ireland through a classified ad. Sometimes men they meet in Irish bars are hired if they happen to be short-handed. The rest could be Polish workers recruited in Ireland in previous years, but now directly from Poland where these crews also operate.

A number of Irishmen have spoken about their experiences of working with the tarmac crews. One such is Liam, a tough-looking wiry labourer from the Irish midlands, in an interview with the author for the *Sunday World*. Like some of the other Irishmen who made up part of the Rathkeale crew, he had spent time in prison and found it difficult to get regular work. He spent the best part of six years travelling back and forth between Ireland and the Continent to labour and drive trucks for one of the Rathkeale crews.

> I was working for them in France doing chipping and tarring. It isn't tar at all, it's a scam. They don't put it on a proper surface. The tar isn't proper tar, it's called emulsion. This is like the stuff they use to water down tar. It's not the correct thing. They have their hawkers, the boys who go out and get the work. That's an illegal thing they're doing in France. They found a kind of loophole in French law with this thing called a bond of command which you sign. What they do is find people, usually someone who is a bit vulnerable. Here's one example, we did a job for nuns at a retreat near Toulouse. Basically they charged nine thousand nine hundred euros for this job, and it was worth three hundred. They are the most religious people in the world, and then they go and rip off nuns. The hawkers are the ones who go out and find these vulnerable people, some of them eighty or ninety years of age. They would think they are getting tarmac. I did one job where there was no tar at all, just chippings. We could go on a job and the people wouldn't be there and the job would be done. They are put into a position then that's intimidating. They wouldn't be going up to a strong-looking man and trying to scam him.

Liam worked long enough with one father-and-son team to get a good insight into how they did business and the level of money they were making.

We're talking about serious money. On a bad week they make fifty to sixty thousand euro. On a good week they'll make a hundred and fifty to a hundred and sixty thousand euro and that's between five or six of them. Then they take out the overheads paying for the chippings and the tar which isn't the real stuff at all. The jobs don't last. Our gang had two tarring lorries. They were built for them in England. They're not a proper tar and chip lorry, there's actually no such thing. One truck usually spreads tar and then the chippers come behind it. A proper tarring lorry will have sixty jets, our tar lorries have eight. Everything is fake. A lot of the motors they have with them are ringers, stolen from England. They have fake papers made up for them.

On average they charge ten euro per metre. If they were measuring up a job they'd be: 'Roll out the tape, roll out the tape.' By rolling out the tape five metres, that would be our wages for the day. They were charging cash, this was part of the scam. They said they would include the tax when looking for the job, then afterwards they would double the price of the job to include the tax. They were never paying the tax, of course. They are the best people I've ever seen to make money. It's all illegal. The most jobs we did in a day was seven. The cheapest one out of that was five grand and the next one was seven grand. We'd stay around for three weeks and then we'd be gone. I was arrested twice at hotels in France at six in the morning. Pulled out of the hotel, forty gendarmerie around, very rough. They're obviously pissed off with them.

One common tactic used by the Rathkealers is to use a builder's tape measure with a long section cut out of the middle and then stuck back together. The customer is shown the tape when the area to be covered in tarmac is measured, and a price is agreed based on the deliberately wrong, but longer, measurement. It's a simple but effective scam.

Anyone from the wider community working for the Rathkeale clan bosses is very much a second-class citizen as far as the Travellers are concerned. They are hired help, to be used or discarded as demanded. As Liam says:

When I first started my pay was a hundred euro a day cash. The deal was they would pay half the hotel, which they never did. These weren't nice hotels, fairly basic, fairly disgusting some of them. The abuse they give to people working for them is unbelievable. Like, they'd ring you up: 'Get up at five.' And you could be sitting there waiting for them for three or four hours while they're off having their breakfast, a fry-up or whatever. You'd be brought off to work, working up the mountains or somewhere, no food, no water. Now in France it can get fairly hot over the summertime. I worked in forty-degree heat. I got the job through a relative, I was desperate for work. I didn't really realize what I was getting myself into. There were always problems with wages, there were always arguments about money, they were supposed to pay for the hotels. If we didn't work we didn't get paid. We could go and do two or three jobs and if they didn't get paid, we wouldn't get paid. It's a win-win situation for themselves.

When crew members were arrested by the police, the Travellers usually got a head start to get away from the police. They would stay separately in campsites away from the labourers, keeping their families and their work life entirely distinct. As Liam explained:

> I'm not good enough for the Traveller people. Travellers distance themselves from the likes of us. They don't like their women being around us at all. I don't know why, they were rough-looking women. The lads come out in January and set things up, they stay in hotels. When the weather gets better, they come out with the trailers, the wives and all the family. They all stay in the same camp, but they won't work the same area. One crowd will go a hundred kilometres in one direction and the other will go the other way. When we got arrested one morning at six, they had their site and were gone before the police could catch up with them.

It's not all plain sailing, and some suppliers refuse to sell material to the rogue Irish operators. Liam described how:

> They had a lot of trouble buying stuff. There was one day I had to drive over a thousand kilometres just to get this stuff called 'taco', the supposed tarmac. One place we had to give the guy a five-hundred-euro backhander and he'd set up the tanks for us, he knew it wasn't good quality.

In the aftermath of falling victim to the rogue tarmackers people are furious. There is a sense of being duped and of feeling a bit stupid. At that point most victims are too embarrassed to tell anyone else, and simply decide to write it down to experience and never again fall for such a scam. Some, however, angry at the pushy and often aggressive demands for cash, will turn to the police or the media to warn others of how the tarmackers work.

Around the time Liam's crew were operating in France in 2009, one gang turned up at Château de Cayx near

Cahors, a picturesque castle and vineyard property owned by the Danish monarchy. They did a tarmac job, got paid and then disappeared. A few weeks later so too had most of the 'tarmac', which had dried out and turned back into mere dust and gravel. Residents in nearby Castlenaudary also had encounters with a Traveller tarmacking gang. A number of locals were caught by the fraudsters, but reported their concerns to the media and encouraged other victims of the scam to come forward. One woman explained that the salesman came across as 'very serious', which gave her confidence that she was dealing with a reputable operator instead of one of *les faux bitumeurs*. She paid out €3,500 to have a stretch of driveway tarmacked. Six months later the Irish had long gone and the grass was regrowing where the tarmac should have been.

In the summer of 2009 one crew got into trouble and made the local TV station news when they approached the Immaculate Missionary Sisters in Monza on the outskirts of Milan. Tarmac in Monza is usually associated with the Formula One Grand Prix, thanks to its famous motor-racing circuit. The canny nuns sensed something was up when pushy workers approached, offering to tarmac their driveway for free. The nuns suggested they tarmac an area in front of the convent gates, which was in fact owned by the local authorities and not part of their property. When the job was over the Rathkeale crew demanded €5,000 for the work they had originally said they would do for free. The sisters, however, put the Travellers off, saying they would have the money ready the next day, despite a number of increasingly intimidating visits from the work crew. The nuns contacted the local police, who decided to set a trap for the rogue operators. One officer dressed up as a priest while others took up position in the convent and waited for the Travellers to return. When two men arrived at the convent looking for their cash, the 'priest' made his move and, backed up by his colleagues, arrested the suspects. One of those was named only as 'John G' and described by police as an Irish nomad. They were given bail and subsequently disappeared.

Liam's story is typical of what happens to 'country people' who go to work for the Rathkealers. Some Travellers, however, are better than others when it comes to paying for accommodation and ensuring their workers get a sandwich and water. One of those is Johnny 'Bottles' Sheridan who, with his crew of Irish and Polish workers and his three sons, also worked around Milan and the surrounding area during the summer of 2009. Bottles got his nickname from collecting deposit bottles in his early days when he lived in his native town of Rathkeale. He now owns a property in the town's square which features some elaborate stonework paid for by his entrepreneurship across Europe. The family are well known in the County Limerick town, where his brother 'Ouzel' Sheridan bought the old Garda station on Roches Road.

Ouzel previously featured on national media in Ireland, when he put himself forward as a spokesperson for a group of Rathkealers responsible for a series of 'invasions' at sites around the country. With his back to the camera Ouzel moaned about how Travellers suffer prejudice, are homeless, and have no choice but to create illegal halting sites. There was no reference to how many of the same Travellers made their cash during the rest of the year, when they were on the road.

Luckily for his workers, Bottles is regarded as one of the better bosses among the Rathkeale crews, buying food for his employees and paying part of their nightly hotel bills. Those working for him have a better time of it than Liam did with the crew who hired him.

Yet even Liam's boss was far from the worst: others have a reputation for intimidation, physical violence and refusing to pay workers their wages. Although they might be working for a scam artist, non-Traveller labourers see little of the profits and put in long days without rest laying the 'tarmac', as well as enduring interminable road journeys.

Customers' cheques are almost always cashed by non-Traveller members of the crew, some of whom have also been ordered to open bank accounts. They get paid extra to take the risk. One of the workers is usually asked to pose as the boss of the operation and given a flash car to drive. If, as they often do, the local police come calling, the non-Traveller who was paid an extra €50 a day and who got to drive the boss's car is the scapegoat who ends up in jail while the police do their best to track down the phantom traders. In these ways, non-Travellers in the crews work hard for their money, even if it is ultimately obtained by deception.

On the other hand, some of the Traveller traders make little secret of how much cash they are making. As if to underline their authority they'll flash large wads of €100 and €200 notes, which they'll pull out of their pockets to pay for the day-to-day expenses and wages. When they were in France the rogue traders used company bank accounts to transfer money back to Ireland, but usually they prefer to deal in cash. Their women are regularly sent home to Ireland from whatever part of Europe they are in with cash packed into their hand luggage to be safely deposited.

Stories of the road crews' exploits are swapped when the millionaire Traveller traders gathered in the Limerick town of Rathkeale over Christmas. The frontman of Johnny 'Bottles' Sheridan's operation is his son Patrick, known as Paper Face, who is a skilful hawker, adept at getting customers to agree to having their driveways tarmacked. Two other sons of Bottles are also part of the crew, and between them they were operating three tarmac trucks and transporting their workers in the back of a Ford Transit. Working in the forty degrees centigrade heat of the Italian summer, Bottles's crew were praised for their speed by one customer, who paid in cash and even gave the labourers gifts of beer and whiskey. Little did he know at the time why the crews worked fast.

In one week alone in June 2009, Johnny 'Bottles' Sheridan's crew made a staggering €190,000 in cash, according to sources in Rathkeale. But a job at a convent close to Milan nearly went wrong. The Carabinieri were called in when the €75,000 bill presented by the Travellers was questioned by the Italian customer. However, as far as the police were concerned the job looked perfect, and they told the hapless victim he had to pay up. Within days the thin layer of tarmac had come apart, but Bottles had fled the area by then, along with his crew. In a series of midnight phone calls the workers were roused from their sleep and told to get on the road to Genoa two hundred kilometres to the south. Down there things didn't go smoothly either. The entire crew and their fleet of vehicles were escorted to the police station in one town south of Rome. It took several hours, but Johnny 'Bottles' Sheridan eventually persuaded the Italian cops he was a lowly illiterate labourer and was sent on his way along with his workers.

Earlier in the year, the crew had worked their way through Europe, with jobs going well in Poland until two workers were arrested and a Traveller had a gun put to his head by an irate property owner. Then there were jobs in Germany, Holland and Austria. Wary of the French police thanks to stories of heavy-handed tactics from other Rathkealers, Bottles steered clear of France.

After the usual Christmas break in Rathkeale, he and his sons returned to the road in January 2010 and began operating in the historic town of Bergamo. Nestled in the foothills of the Italian Alps, it is a wealthy town and an upmarket tourist destination, just under an hour's drive from Milan. In February that year it was cold, and temperatures were dropping below freezing at night, but it was dry and bright. Paper Face went door to door seeking out business for the tarmac crew run by his father, using his basic Italian to sell the prospect of a cheap but professional job. The picturesque town of Bergamo features many stunning hillside properties with long unpaved driveways, making perfect pickings for the unscrupulous traders. Any language or cultural barriers posed no problem to Paper Face.

One of the doors he knocked on was that belonging to local fireman Claudio Bianchi. His impressive home was part of a large building that had been divided in two and shared with a neighbour. It was reached by a long, narrow driveway up a steep slope. Claudio's neighbour also agreed to pitch in for the tarmac after hearing how the crew could do a quick, efficient job at a cheap price. Speaking through an interpreter just a day after Johnny 'Bottles' Sheridan and his crew had been on site, Claudio explained how, despite some worries, he felt they had done a good job. 'At first they seemed pretty good but then things started to go a bit wrong. I began to think it was strange to do this kind of work in winter,' he said. The unfortunate householder said that because they were Irish he had felt the work crew could be trusted. He explained how the job was carried out non-stop with one half resting while the others continued laying and rolling the tarmac. He said the work seemed to be of a good standard, and he paid up on the day, although he admitted that he felt he was overcharged after initially agreeing a price of €20 per metre. 'When they finished they wanted cash. They were very insistent they wanted cash but in the end they accepted two cheques,' he said. Both cheques were drawn down by the Travellers by the following day at a nearby bank. Claudio said the crew had no mobile phone number or any kind of business card. He recognized the Rathkealer Johnny 'Bottles' Sheridan, from photographs shown to him, as being among the group of thirteen workers who had laboured on the driveway he shared with his neighbour.

Although Claudio said he was happy with the job, it was obvious just the day after that it had not been sealed properly. In their haste to get everything done quickly, the crew had left uneven sections and partially covered drain covers. Cement dust was even spread over some bits in a bid to disguise gaps and shoddy work. Together with his neighbour, Claudio ended up paying €7,000 for the work, which was done in four hours. It was, as it happened, one of four jobs carried out by Bottles's crew that day, for which they charged between €4,000 and €7,500. It wasn't all profit. Bottles did have some overheads, as investigations later found his crew had bought tarmac material from quarries all over Italy, with up to €20,000 being spent in cash in a single day. A twenty-tonne load in Italy usually cost Bottles's drivers €2,000, always paid in cash.

Of course, as we have seen, the Traveller tarmackers don't always make a clean getaway, despite their precautions. A worker employed by Travellers told how on one occasion his boss abandoned an expensive Mercedes when police approached as they laboured on a property in the French Alps: 'He just got out the door and ran down the mountain. He left the car behind for the police.' A crew arrested near Lyon in early 2010 had been in twenty of France's ninety-six departments and, according to French media reports, appeared to have made €97,000 the previous October.

French cops also identified eleven victims in Craponne, Francheville, La Tour-de-Salvagny, Sainte Consorce and Bessenay, targeted in just six days from 19 February 2010 by the same gang. On another occasion an arrested Irish Traveller was found in possession of €180,000 in cash. Then, in 2011, John Kealy, then aged forty-three, and his son Michael Kealy were convicted of ripping off householders who had hired them to carry out driveway work. They were given suspended sentences of six and eight months at St Malo and ordered to pay back €13,800. In 2011 six Irishmen were also arrested in France close to the Swiss border, and the authorities seized two cars and machinery worth €200,000.

A year later, Irish Travellers doing the same scams in Norway were classed as that country's most active criminal organization. They were found to have operated in twenty of the country's twenty-seven police districts.

16

Rhino Hunting

The tarmac business brings the Traveller traders on to every highway and byway as they seek out customers and discrete campsites. It provides plenty of opportunities for those with the knowledge to hunt for antiques at bargain prices. The antiques trade is littered with both possibilities and pitfalls. Sought-after collectibles can be in high demand one year, then fall out of fashion or become unprofitable when a collection is dumped on the market. Classic items will always sell and hold most of their value, but for the small-time trader it pays well to get into the market ahead of the latest fad. Big-game hunting trophies, where the heads of exotic animals are stuffed and mounted, became trendy for a while, with interior decorators seeking interesting curios. Demand for rhino horns, in particular, went through the roof during 2009 and 2010. But it wasn't the decorators who were chasing the rhinos, it was the Rathkealers. What legitimate antique dealers and taxidermists didn't realize was that the Travellers were keen to supply an avaricious Chinese market for the ingredients needed for traditional medicinal concoctions.

In 2000 there were seven rhinos butchered in the wild, killed by poachers on the hunt for their horns in South Africa. The level of poaching remained a constant until a sudden surge in 2009 brought the total to 122, according to statistics from South Africa's Department of Environmental Affairs. Another huge increase in 2010 saw 333 animals die in South Africa to feed the Chinese market. That soaring upward trend was evident in 2011 with 448 rhinos butchered and then 668 in 2012. It prompted the South African government to start using an army unit in the Kruger National Park in a bid to slow down the rate of poaching, with lethal consequences for some of the illegal hunters. For conservationists it is a disaster and a crisis, fuelled by the bulging bank accounts of the increasingly wealthy Chinese, who want to buy medicinal products that contain rhino horn, even though there is no evidence of any medical benefit arising. Rhino horns are effectively the same material as hair or fingernails.

Some Rathkealers saw an opportunity in the crisis. For years animal head mounts had gathered dust in private collections in ageing houses and hotels. Their value was limited and buyers were thin on the ground. They might sell as curiosities, but as an in-demand 'medicinal' ingredient their value grew out of all proportion. Antique rhino horns also came without the risk of being shot at by the South African army.

Like all international traders, the Rathkeale Travellers seek to buy at a low price and sell high to make a profit. Ideally, things that are light and easily transported offer the best returns. While antique furniture can offer great rewards, tables and chairs can't be placed in hand luggage and easily brought across the Atlantic. The horns of a rhinoceros, however, fit the bill perfectly. Dealers in Chinese traditional medicine are reported to pay anything up to 00 per kilo, although in reality the price is usually o €20,000. Years of colonial big-game hunters the African savannah means that stuffed rhino heads can turn up in the unlikeliest of places, tucked away in the homes of old aristocrats. They are also a favourite exhibit in natural history museums all over Europe.

A number of the Rathkeale Traveller traders were quick to spot this niche market and began bidding for rhino horns at auctions all over the world, sometimes against one another. Like twenty-first-century Indiana Joneses, they also used their antique-tracking skills to seek out potential sellers. The only drawback to this lucrative new income stream was the fact that trade in the body parts of endangered species is illegal. Under the Convention of International Trade in Endangered Species (CITES) the import and export of items such as rhino horns is against the law in most countries. Similarly, the elephant population has been imperilled by hunters' greed and the international market demand for ivory. A shoot-to-kill policy operated by security forces detailed to protect endangered animals ensures that the price for such illegal objects remains high.

It was in this shady market that members of the Rathkeale Traveller traders began to do well. Using a Chinese and an English dealer based in the UK, they were richly rewarded for supplying the eager buyers. In January 2010 the involvement of Rathkealers in the illicit global trade became public knowledge when customs made a series of arrests. Three men, all Irish Travellers from Rathkeale, were caught as an attempt was made to move eight rhino horns through Shannon Airport. The previous month, two rhino horns had also been intercepted at Shannon. The consignment is estimated to have been worth up to €500,000 on the black market and remains one of the biggest such seizures by authorities anywhere in the world.

Among those targeted by the traders in a hurry to get their hands on rhino horns were taxidermists. In fact, so many emails and requests went in their direction that in July 2010 the European Taxidermy Federation (ETF) issued a warning to its members about the illegal trade. It was a warning they had to repeat. The problem wasn't confined to just Europe. Members of a US-based online taxidermy public forum revealed that several members had been contacted by people seeking items for hotels or museums. The posts from members also included an email from a 'John Sullivan' seeking a rhino-head mount for the opening of a hotel. Rough around the edges, with basic spelling mistakes, it gives a hint of a cajoling, yet resourceful way of approaching business:

> Hi, this is John Sullivan here from Ireland, I'm having a grand theme opening of an African seen here in my hotel in Kerry, Ireland. The thing is I'm having grate trouble in locating a real rhino head or horn in Ireland and a local taxidermy told me to email u on the off chance that u might be able to locate this item for me or refer some person or company or even auction that might have one for sale, it has to be the real item and not a fiberglass reproduction. It would be very much appreciated if u could get back to me with good news within a week or 2 as the grand opening will be on 4/sep/2010 and we really need this item.

During 2010, a man based in Commerce City, Colorado, received such an email from John Sullivan in Ireland. Ignoring the warnings from the taxidermy world, he made contact with the Irish buyers who were keen to get a deal done. The man, however, was an informant for the United States Fish and Wildlife Service, which then took over communications to lure the buyers into a sting operation. Special Agent Curtis Graves emailed 'John Sullivan' that he could do even better and could secure four rhino horns.

Sullivan was clearly aware it was illegal to trade in the objects, but he was confident in his emails that there would be no problem smuggling them out of the US. 'We never loses a horn to Customs, we have so many contacts and people payed off, we can bring nearly anything we want out of any country into Europe,' he boasted.

On 13 November, Richard 'Kerry' O'Brien junior and his brother-in-law, Michael Hegarty, turned up in Commerce City to complete the deal and hand over the cash. O'Brien told Special Agent Graves, now acting in undercover mode, that he was a cousin of the 'John Sullivan' who had sent the emails seeking to buy the rhino horns. He told Graves that they would be able to hide the items in a consignment of furniture being shipped to the UK. 'Listen, we got furniture going back to England every couple of weeks, we can put it between the chest of drawers or something like that,' he told the agent. He and Hegarty handed over €12,850 and went back to their rental car, no doubt delighted at the prospect of making a massive return on their money.

Their joy quickly turned sour as the federal agents sprang their trap, arresting both men and taking back the four black rhinoceros horns. A search of the pair's rental car turned up passports, luggage, a chest of drawers, four large packing boxes and shrink wrap that agents believed was going to be used to pack the horns. Held in custody, O'Brien and Hegarty were indicted by a grand jury in Colorado on 29 November and brought to Denver District Federal Court for pre-trial hearings. They, along with the mysterious 'John Sullivan', were all indicted for smuggling. 'John Sullivan' either doesn't exist or is a pseudonym used by a colleague of the Rathkeale pair. Released on bail, the duo were electronically tagged and had to stay at an address supplied to the court.

It was a tough time, especially for Hegarty, who had

to stay in the US throughout Christmas at a time when his family was being targeted by extortionists back in Rathkeale. A pipe bomb had been used in an attack on his mother's home in Ballywilliam. It had been one of a series of attacks against different Rathkeale families who had returned to Ireland for the festive season. Hegarty sought to use these as a reason why his bail restrictions should be relaxed to allow him to return home, but there was no budging the court.

In April 2011, lawyers for the Irish Travellers tried to have the case dismissed on technical grounds, claiming that the entire prosecution was based on an accusation of smuggling which hadn't actually occurred. 'The platform on which this prosecution is built is a platform that shouldn't exist,' said Defence Attorney Virginia Grady. Prosecutors argued that O'Brien and Hegarty had talked about their plans to smuggle the rhino horns back to Ireland. 'It was clear that their intent was to purchase rhinoceros horns and smuggle them out of the United States illegally,' said Assistant US Attorney Linda McMahan. The defence argument was ruled against by Judge Wiley Daniel, and in May the pair decided to face the music and pleaded guilty to the charges in the hope that they would escape with a fine. Richard 'Kerry' O'Brien senior flew over to the States with high hopes that he would be able to use whatever influence he had to help his son and son-in-law escape any more jail time.

There was an additional anxiety on behalf of Hegarty, whose younger brother Patrick had died tragically just a few days earlier during a large Easter gathering in Cologne, Germany. *Bild* reported how groups of Irish Travellers had run riot through the city's party area, leaving drink bills unpaid, being unruly and fighting with each other and locals. It culminated in a stand-off between dozens of German cops in riot gear and the Travellers, who had camped under a flyover close to the city centre. Tragedy then struck when Patrick Hegarty collapsed and died from a heart attack, despite being quickly rushed to hospital. Police had to intervene again when it was claimed that some of the Rathkealers wanted to drive back to Ireland immediately with his body for burial. His family intervened and handed over the job to professional undertakers, who shipped his remains back to Cross's Funeral Home in Limerick. There was a delay in burying Patrick Hegarty while the family waited, hoping to hear that Michael had been freed and would be home in time for the ceremony.

However, there was no good news to come from Denver, where Judge Daniel wanted to make a point to any others who might be contemplating getting involved in the ever more lucrative trade in rhino horns. He ordered the cash, worth $17,000, to be forfeited, and sentenced both men to six months in jail. Their release was to be supervised for three years on completion of their jail time. The two men and the handful of supporters who had made the trek to Colorado were shocked by the jail sentence. It was also greeted with dismay back in Rathkeale where, with no reason to delay any longer, Patrick's funeral went ahead the next day. Several hundred mourners followed the ornate casket being carried in a horse-drawn hearse with glass sides. There were flowers and wreaths and, flanking the coffin on either side, were two large bottles of Jameson whiskey. Patrick was laid to rest in the cemetery just outside the town, among the outsized marble memorials preferred by the Irish Travellers from Rathkeale.

The agents who had made the case were delighted with the result of their hard work. In a statement, Steve Oberholtzer, Special Agent in Charge for the US Fish and Wildlife Service, said:

The illegal trafficking in rhinoceros horns fuels the dangerous poaching situations we see in Africa, and that poaching has contributed to most species of rhino being listed as endangered. We will continue to pursue investigations into the unlawful trafficking in imperilled wildlife, and we're pleased that these men were held accountable for their crimes. We hope these sentences serve as a deterrent to others involved in this unlawful trade.

*

It could be said that Richard 'Kerry' O'Brien junior has a habit of being in the wrong place at the wrong time. His arrest and conviction happened just as the international clamour about the need to clamp down on the rhino-horn trade got underway. The case against him and Hegarty was prosecuted under a new law from the Patriot Act which the prosecutors for the Fish and Wildlife Service were determined to enforce.

Six years earlier, when he was just nineteen, young Kerry had also suffered from a backlash – this time against tobacco smugglers hassling truckers in Belgium as they stopped off near ferry ports that would bring them to Britain, an episode recounted in *The Outsiders*. A restaurant owner, fed up with his customers at Jabbeke being put off by the harassment, complained to the police, who launched an operation to catch the tobacco bandits in action. 'Kerry' junior was one of four arrested and later convicted of being part of an organized crime gang and sentenced to two years in jail.

There is a parallel to be drawn between the arrests in Commerce City and those at the Jabbeke services stop in 2004 which offers an insight into the typical Rathkealers' cultural approach to life and death. One of the tobacco bandits convicted along with Kerry junior was Daniel 'Turkey' O'Brien. Although sentenced to two years, the two O'Briens spent just nine months inside, because in Belgium time spent in custody on remand is treated as double. Daniel 'Turkey' O'Brien's father died when he still had two months left to serve in jail. He made the decision to keep his father's embalmed body at Cross's Funeral Home in Limerick until such time as he was back in Ireland and the funeral could go ahead. On his release Turkey travelled back to Ireland to see his father's remains finally interred in Rathkeale Cemetery. Funerals and wedding are important celebrations which, if possible, will be delayed until the important principals can attend.

While O'Brien and Hegarty were kicking their electronically tagged heels in Denver, there were others doing their best to break into the new and lucrative business of rhino-horn smuggling. All through 2010 the number of reported thefts and burglaries targeting antique rhino horns slowly began to increase. The *Sunday World* published a story highlighting the arrests and convictions in the US and the fact that rogue traders were actively targeting the horns. Many of the antique horns on the market had already been snapped up, and legitimate traders were becoming wary of being targeted by criminals.

By early 2011, it had become an epidemic, and in response, the UK banned the sale of antique rhino heads. Just days after the ban was announced, in February 2011, Sworders Fine Art Auctioneers in Essex suffered a break-in. Although their rhino artefacts were kept under lock and key and security guards were due to come on duty, burglars broke into the premises in a well-planned raid. The break-in came after the firm posted details of a mounted rhino head on the internet. The thieves forced open doors, grabbed the trophy which had been bolted to a wall, and made their escape across a field. The black rhino's head was valued at £50,000 as an antique, but was worth as much as £200,000 to the illicit Chinese medicine market.

Following the arrests of O'Brien and Hegarty in Colorado as well as the seizures at Shannon Airport, the chief suspects behind the sudden spike in rhino-related burglaries were members of the Rathkeale Traveller-trader community. By this stage the canny operators had already sewn up the black market, buying rhino trophies before anyone else had realized their value. It was not just rhino heads that were the focus of the Rathkealers' attention. Antique ornamental dagger handles and wine goblets had often also been fashioned from rhino horns, and were therefore just as valuable.

The break-ins could happen anywhere in Europe. In March 2011, the Muséum d'Histoire Naturelle de Rouen in France was targeted. Then two eighteenth-century horns were stolen from the Museu da Ciência da Universidade de Coimbra in Portugal. By now museum curators were aware that an Irish gang were the main suspects behind what, on the face of it, appeared to be a series of bizarre thefts. As O'Brien and Hegarty were jailed in May 2011, the burglaries continued throughout Europe. Early one morning that month, burglars broke into the Haslemere Educational Museum in Surrey, England, and stole a mounted rhino head. It was the only artefact targeted by the thieves, most likely acting on the orders of a senior Traveller trader.

The next month, there were a series of thefts in Germany. First, six rhino horns were stolen from Zoologisches Museum Hamburg. In the wake of that theft, staff at Naturkinde-Museum, Bamberg in Germany, discovered that a rhino exhibit had gone missing. Visitors are allowed to walk around Naturkinde-Museum unsupervised. It was found that a glass case had been broken and the rhino horn removed. In the next incident, two men bought tickets and walked into a museum in Gifhorn, where they broke two horns off rhino-head trophies and ran away. It was a crude but effective plundering of German museums that could have generated as much as €2 million.

Another three specimens were taken from La Specola Museum at the University of Florence. It is thought that the thieves hid in a courtyard near the museum and then after closing time forced the front door, making their escape out the back. In Liege, Belgium, two would-be thieves subdued security guards with tear gas. One of the robbers managed to tear a horn off a trophy head but police were able to respond quickly and the two men were arrested at a roadblock. They claimed that they had been promised €3,000 for the theft and were to leave the horn at a prearranged dead-drop in Holland.

At this stage the Natural History Museum in Ireland still had rhino exhibits on display. As it is located next to the Oireachtas, the Irish parliament building, the presence of police and army security personnel probably put off any potential thieves. A notice from Europol had been sent out to police forces around Europe, warning about the gang's operation, and a local crime prevention officer had called to the museum. The Keeper at the museum, Nigel Monaghan, said at the time that they were aware of the spate of thefts at museums in Europe. 'All museums are aware rhino horn has increased in value. But it only has a high value in the Far East,' he said, warning that it would have been standard practice to preserve rhino horns using a variety of chemicals, including arsenic. 'It has been proven that they are of absolutely no medical value whatsoever,' he added. Not long afterwards, the museum took the rhino exhibits off public display amid fears that copycat criminals or even armed raiders could endanger the safety of visitors.

In July 2011 the rhino gang struck again in Belgium. This time the thieves were successful, snatching a stuffed head from a museum in Brussels, and reaching their getaway car as security guards chased them on foot. On 7 July Europol issued a public statement in which some members of the Rathkeale Traveller traders were designated an 'organized crime group'. The international media took an interest in the Europol statement, which described the gang as being active across Europe, South America, Australia, China and the United States. According to Europol, members of the same gang were also involved in drug-trafficking, the sale of counterfeit products and money laundering. Europol's spokesman, Søren Pedersen, admitted that other criminal groups might be involved:

> We can't say that every rhino-horn theft from now on or earlier can be linked to these people. I think others have also realized how valuable these horns are. But it seems that this Irish gang has been very good at identifying rhino horns all over Europe. So far, these cases have mainly occurred in central and northern Europe.

The Rathkealers had gone from being able to operate quietly under the radar to being listed as one of Europe's organized crime gangs. The senior Traveller traders who had orchestrated the scam, however, had already cashed in. Sources suggest that a small number of individuals had made 'millions' selling rhino horns via middlemen. Those late into the game had to resort to smash and grabs, with all their associated extra risks and unwanted publicity. Yet still, the thefts continued.

A rhino head was taken from a natural history museum in Blois, dragged along the floor and loaded into a vehicle. The theft, in July 2011, was discovered when staff arrived the following morning. Three more were stolen from a Czech castle during a nightly tour, prompting publicity in a country where it is thought hundreds of such trophies exist thanks to the nineteenth-century Czech aristocracy's enthusiasm for big-game hunting. Another raid in the Czech Republic, however, only netted a replica horn, which were increasingly being used by museum staff to replace genuine exhibits taken off display as a security precaution.

In just six months there had been more than thirty burglaries and robberies targeting rhino horns around Europe. Despite the publicity and the extra security precautions, there was no let-up in the demand for rhino horns; people were still willing to steal them. At Ipswich Museum a popular stuffed rhino known locally as 'Rosie' was next to fall victim. The thieves ripped the horn off and also took another rhino-head exhibit stored on a shelf.

The thefts and burglaries continued throughout 2012, although in some cases not everyone made a clean getaway. Michael Kealy, then aged thirty-six, was the subject of extradition proceedings in the Irish High Court during 2012. Detective Sergeant James Kirwan told the court he had arrested Kealy in a car park in County Kilkenny. The officer said he told Kealy he had a warrant from the UK which alleged he had been involved in the robbery of a rhino horn from an antique dealer at Newark, a market town in Nottinghamshire. On his arrest Kealy had told the Garda: 'I know what it's about, I just witnessed the crime.'

Details from the warrant were heard in court, in which it was alleged that the antique dealer had driven with the rhino horn to a meeting with a number of men at a McDonald's restaurant. The horn had been grabbed from him and the group had attempted to drive off in their car. The dealer had wrestled with them through the car window, but had been beaten up and knocked unconscious. Kealy, who denied his involvement in the snatch theft from the dealer, was initially released on €15,000 cash bail to await trial on a European Arrest Warrant. In March 2013, Kealy consented to his extradition, but his request for bail was denied by the court. It was said that he had lied about an upcoming medical appointment, and he was remanded into prison until he surrendered to the UK authorities.

In January 2013 another Traveller from Rathkeale was also arrested on foot of a European Arrest Warrant. This time John Quilligan, aged thirty-one, was wanted by authorities in Austria investigating the theft of rhino horns in Vienna estimated to be worth €300,000 on the black market. The Austrian authorities had requested Garda assistance in tracking Quilligan, after a number of arrests following the theft of the rhino horns from a museum and an antique dealer. He was arrested at a Garda checkpoint in north County Dublin and then brought before the High Court where he was released on bail on condition he hand over his passport.

Early in 2013, two of the traders arrested while trying to smuggle rhino horns through Shannon Airport back in 2010 appeared in court in Ennis, County Clare. Brothers Michael and Jeremiah O'Brien, both from Rathkeale, admitted importing eight antique horns worth nearly €500,000. It emerged in court that they had flown in from Portugal, but claimed they had been supplied the antiques by a dealer who had asked them to carry out work on them. It was suggested in court that the antiques would have trebled in value since being seized and would be worth €1.5 million on the black market supplying the Chinese medicine market. An antiques expert gave evidence at Ennis District Court that the seized rhino horns at Shannon Airport were 'worth more in weight than gold'. A defence lawyer for the O'Brien brothers said the two were antique dealers who travelled across Europe and had no previous convictions. It was added that they lived from time to time in caravan parks in France and Germany and 'were not in good circumstances'. They were both fined €500 by Judge Patrick Durcan, who described the case as 'intriguing'. The €500 fine was considerably less punishment than that received by Richard 'Kerry' O'Brien junior and Michael Hegarty, who had spent six months behind bars in Colorado. Members of the same O'Brien clan were those involved in selling dodgy electrical generators across Australia in 2008.

Sadly, the extra security measures taken by the staff at the Natural History Museum in Dublin didn't work. The exhibits had been taken off public display and moved to a storage facility in Swords, north County Dublin. There was no signage on the sprawling building to suggest that it was being used by the Museums Service. One night in April 2013 three men broke into the facility and tied up the security guard. They loaded four rhino heads into a van and drove away. Someone had clearly done their homework to pull off the robbery of those rhino horns, which were worth as much as €500,000 to the traditional Chinese medicine market.

The significance of the arrests, extraditions and in some cases convictions hasn't been lost on the Traveller traders from Rathkeale. Their escapades in Australia attracted plenty of media attention, but it was nothing compared to the interest in the bizarre multinational crime spree they inspired when it came to rhino horns. As a result it has become far harder for the criminal element among the Rathkeale Travellers to operate. During 2012, they were specifically targeted by Europol in Operation Oakleaf, which reportedly saw thirty arrests and €9 million in assets seized.

There are some Rathkealers who operate as legitimate traders, for instance selling goods at home and garden shows around the UK and Ireland. The question going into the future is whether more of the families will opt for a life within the rules and regulations of the wider community or whether they will prefer to stay operating in the black market and keeping themselves to themselves in a shadowy parallel world. More than a few Traveller traders have already shown no compunction when it comes to committing crimes to make money.

17

The Battle of Dale Farm

The Traveller traders never enjoy being in the limelight. Traveller camps are regularly a point of controversy with the wider community. Over the years the Rathkeale Travellers, among others, have played their part when the topic surfaces in the media. A sudden 'invasion' of several dozen caravans on parkland or a car park in a European city is bound to attract attention. In such cases, the Traveller traders sometimes play the cultural card with the police and media, which is usually enough to buy them three or four days before they are moved on. One case was the stand-off witnessed in Cologne in 2011, when Patrick Hegarty tragically died of a heart attack. In Easter 2012 it was the turn of Auvergne in France to play the role of reluctant host to four hundred uninvited Travellers for three days. The media coverage is usually split on ideological grounds, with one side arguing that Travellers aren't allowed to practise their cultural habits while the other sees their encampments as acts of aggression by wealthy traders who don't care what impact they have on their temporary neighbours.

Both those arguments surfaced during the long legal wrangle that occurred over a halting site in Essex much favoured by members of the Rathkeale clans. They had first begun to use the bays at the official halting site at Dale Farm in Basildon in 2001. Within a few years, one of the wealthy traders had bought up a number of the plots. According to some media reports, Dale Farm developed into the biggest concentration of Travellers anywhere in Europe. This wasn't a temporary halting site where the Rathkeale diaspora briefly came together for a wedding, a birthday party or the Easter holidays. It became a semi-permanent home from home, from which Traveller traders could travel to parts of northern Europe on short trips. It was the perfect 'come and go' place for traders on the move between the ferry ports in Ireland and those in the UK, linking to Belgium, Holland and France. Most of the traders would simply pass through, rarely pausing more than a few days. Others, who had become too old, or too sick, to follow the nomadic way of life, also stayed put to make use of the UK's medical system and social welfare support in their time of need.

The difficulties began when Travellers expanded the site without planning permission, taking over adjacent space and more than doubling the size of the settlement. What had once been a scrap yard next door was turned into a halting site where the occupiers put down paving, made connections to the electricity grid, built walls and gates and placed caravans or chalets. When the council began to enforce the planning regulations many individual Travellers applied for permission to retain those plots which they had bought and developed. They argued that local authorities had failed to provide enough places for Traveller families to live, and maintained that it was a civil-rights issue.

In the meantime, many of the Rathkeale traders and their families hadn't endeared themselves to the locals. The *Basildon Echo* reported how there were signs that some individuals were using Dale Farm as a base for cigarette smuggling. Then Trading Standards investigators got involved over the sale of soft furniture that didn't meet basic safety standards. Len Gridley, whose house backed on to the site, became a vocal opponent of the Travellers' occupation. He complained to the media and the council about antisocial behaviour at Dale Farm and how litter and rubbish was regularly dumped on his property. Gridley claimed he was the subject of persistent verbal abuse from Irish Travellers. He continued his opposition over the subsequent years, even after he had received death threats. On four occasions he chartered a helicopter to take aerial photographs to monitor how the site had been growing and developing while the legal wrangle continued. The pictures showed a long rectangular site, surrounded by countryside, into which dozens of chalets and caravans had been packed.

Like most controversies over Traveller sites, it had re-mained a local issue. That changed in 2010, when the legal battle to shut down the unauthorized part of Dale Farm began to turn in favour of the local authorities. It emerged that the council had earmarked £9.5 million for the policing costs to carry out evictions at the site. In total it was thought evictions at Dale Farm could cost the local authority as much as £18 million. As a result, Dale Farm became a national political issue, and Irish Travellers from Rathkeale were at the heart of it.

A number of the Travellers were also quite vocal in their resistance to being moved off the site by the council in spite of any legal rulings. 'We can't just vanish off the face of the earth, we're human, we just want what everybody else wants, a quiet peaceful life,' said Mary Anne McCarthy, in an interview on the BBC's *Big Fat Gypsy Eviction*. She told how she had been living at Dale Farm since 2002, and wanted to stay there after a tough early life living on the side of the road:

> I have now what I never had in my life, that's to press a
> button and I have electric light, water and toilets, and the
> best part of it was the children going to school and seeing
> they could learn to read and write. I can read now, the
> children learned me to read and write. Not good, but I
> can read a newspaper.

Her story suggested a hard Traveller's life on the road, enduring poverty and hostility.

There were others from the Traveller community at Dale Farm who stood up against what they saw as the local authority being blind to the needs of their unique culture. One of those was Richard Sheridan, who proved an eloquent spokesperson for the under-siege Travellers. He took over as chairman of the residents' association at Crays Hill – the village containing Dale Farm – in 2005 and also became a governor of a local primary school. Sheridan was president and a trustee of the UK's Gypsy Council, which in previous years had got funding from Comic Relief in recognition of its campaigning work. In his role as chairman, he lobbied Members of Parliament to let the residents at Dale Farm be allowed to keep their homes. He won awards for his campaigning work and had been invited to sit on government panels in relation to Traveller and Gypsy policy.

However, in Sheridan's background lay the same issues that had caused such a divide between the Travellers and their neighbours. It emerged that Sheridan was also known among Irish Travellers as Richard O'Brien. He represented a strong connection between Dale Farm and the multimillionaire traders from Rathkeale. His father, John, is a brother of Richard 'Kerry' O'Brien senior, one of Rathkeale's most successful Traveller traders, whose international business dealings have made him a wealthy man. He is also a cousin of Richard 'Kerry' O'Brien junior, jailed in Colorado for rhino-horn smuggling.

It was under the name Richard O'Brien that Richard Sheridan had been convicted of playing a leading role in a tobacco-smuggling operation. During the 2000s tobacco smuggling had become a staple earner for many Irish Traveller traders, as they exploited the low-tax regime in Belgium and France to bring products into the UK for resale. O'Brien was a key figure in a gang that set up a sophisticated enterprise to smuggle 67.6 million cigarettes into the UK in 2003, at a potential tax-loss to the UK exchequer of £9 million in lost duty.

On one occasion the contraband was hidden in furniture being imported into the country while another consignment was concealed in a load of fruit and vegetables destined for a legitimate Manchester firm. The first shipment was seized by customs and police in Hull in June 2003. A month later O'Brien was caught red-handed with other smugglers as they unloaded 640,000 cigarettes from a trailer. O'Brien used anonymous ready-to-go mobile phones in an attempt to cover his tracks, and an invoice made out to a Manchester fruit and veg trader to explain the consignment. The firm were unaware their name had been used in this way. One of his co-accused, Laurence Myers, was described as the gang's bookkeeper after police discovered details of tobacco dealers, eighteen different brands of cigarettes and price lists in his possession. Myers, a convicted welfare fraudster, with an address at Park Lane, Manchester, was caught with £826,000 of cigarettes while on bail for a previous seizure. He was ordered to pay the exchequer the significant sum of £4,447,927 after a confiscation hearing at Hull Crown Court. The figures suggest that this was no small-time operation, but a large-scale and well-resourced illegal business run by an organized crime gang.

In June 2006, O'Brien was jailed for a year for

fraudulently evading excise duty on the one million smuggled cigarettes which he had imported with his father, John, who was also jailed for his part in the scam. O'Brien hadn't let his criminal background get in the way of his work campaigning for Travellers' rights. It did, however, feed into the idea that many of those who used Dale Farm were in fact commercial traders who had enough resources not to be dependent on the services of the council. It was perfect fodder for those who wanted to suggest that many Travellers were only interested in exploiting the state and its services for what they could get, without any sense of civic loyalty in return.

There were other links, too, between Dale Farm and Rathkeale. During the early planning hearings one of those who turned up was antiques dealer Simon Quilligan. The millionaire trader, however, turned down a chance to explain his interest in Dale Farm when approached by *Basildon Echo* journalist Jon Austin, who charted the many links between Dale Farm and Rathkeale.

At the graveyard in Rathkeale, where burial plots are marked with fabulously ornate memorials, there is more evidence of a connection between the Rathkeale families and Dale Farm. Tragically, in 2005 Kathleen and Patrick McCarthy died when their caravan went on fire at the Essex site. They were brought home to County Limerick, where they were buried. Theirs is not the only gravestone to bear the words 'Dale Farm' inscribed in stone. Using details from the court proceedings in the UK, along with the electoral rolls and property registers in Ireland, Jon Austin highlighted how over a dozen individuals at Dale Farm had property interests or were registered as residents in Rathkeale. It ran contrary to the claims being made that all the Travellers facing eviction were without means and dependent on the local authorities. Among the families camped at Dale Farm were Sheridans, Flynns, O'Briens and Slatterys, all names familiar in Rathkeale.

The contradictions and complexities of the Dale Farm controversy were again emphasized when it also emerged that the council were paying rental subsidies for some Traveller families to their landlord, who was another Traveller with an address in Rathkeale. Such complexities were lost on many of the campaigners from the wider community who showed up in support of the Travellers at Dale Farm.

From August 2011, it looked as if there could be a violent confrontation if bailiffs and police went ahead with court-ordered evictions. No one was sure when the council would make their move. Parts of the site had been effectively fortified with fencing topped with barbed wire. Some residents claimed that booby traps had been set up that could injure anyone who came on to the site to force an eviction. By now, Dale Farm, Irish Travellers and Rathkeale were on the radar of not just the Irish and UK media, but also media from all over Europe and even Australia. A scaffold platform had been set up on Len Gridley's property for photographers and TV cameras. Sky News was on hand ready to provide live, rolling images from the site. In September, the Prime Minister, David Cameron, lent his support to the planned evictions, citing the need for 'fairness' in applying the law.

The end came in October 2011 when police finally moved on to Dale Farm. They avoided the gate where one activist had chained herself by her neck to prevent it being opened. Two officers used their Taser guns to subdue an individual, but otherwise the fears of violent resistance proved entirely unfounded. Most of the forty-two bays in the legal part of the site had been left unoccupied as the controversy drew more and more attention, and some families being evicted simply moved on to those vacant plots. One chalet had been taken off the site by a low-loader just days before, but otherwise many of the Irish Travellers had long since departed, leaving the activists from the wider community to face the police and bailiffs.

Although it didn't cost the entire allocated budget, it still proved an expensive exercise in enforcing planning law. A year later, the local authority billed the evicted families an average of £73,000 each for their part of the £4.3 million cost. Many Travellers had returned within a few weeks to park their caravans illegally on the road which leads to Dale Farm. They had been offered alternative pitches and accommodation in other areas, but most had turned these offers down. The illegal part of the site was effectively sealed off with large mounds of earth piled up by machinery to prevent the area being reoccupied. It created an eyesore, where pools of stagnant water stood amid the debris and rubbish that was dumped after the media and bailiffs had left. In February 2013 Basildon council approved a plan to create a hundred-bay Traveller halting site close to Dale Farm.

It had been a costly exercise for the sake of eight hundred metres and the creation of a fly-blown dump. Neither side can claim to be happy with the result. The residents of Crays Hill still have several Traveller families camped illegally in the area, along with a patch of land which has been turned into a wasteland by the bailiffs' bulldozers. The council spent millions of pounds of scarce resources to achieve very little, while the Travellers haven't gone anywhere. The episode afforded plenty of material for those members of the media who wanted either the local authority or the Travellers cast as the villains of the piece. Disputes between Travellers and the wider community are frequent, but the protracted wrangle at Dale Farm was the mother of all battles. It had also put the media focus on the hitherto mysterious Irish Traveller traders.

18

The Slavers

There was a lot of unwelcome attention and bad publicity for Irish Travellers in Britain as the long-running row between the council and residents at Dale Farm came to a head. Separately, the police had taken an interest in some of the Traveller traders doing driveway work around the UK, and the culmination of one investigation came in September 2011, just as the final battle lines were being drawn in Essex. The fact that the families accused were a completely separate entity to the Travellers in Dale Farm was a nuance lost in much of the media coverage. Suddenly, Irish Travellers were close to the top of Britain's news agenda for all the wrong reasons.

The latest controversy centred around the use of labourers from outside the Traveller community by wealthy traders involved in various types of construction work who took their workers under their wing to live with them on their halting sites. One family was accused of slavery, forcing vulnerable and destitute men to carry out back-breaking manual labour for little or no pay. The details of the quasi-medieval cruelty and psychological torture were shocking.

The case served to highlight how some Traveller families take in non-Travellers down on their luck, providing them with somewhere to stay in exchange for a portion of their dole money and doing odd jobs. There are anecdotes of how some Traveller families in Belfast effectively acted as an unofficial social service, providing accommodation, food and booze for destitute men, many of them chronic alcoholics, in return for their dole money. Whatever savings were made by the Travellers represented a profit. The practice was referred to as 'dosser farming'. One Traveller recalled how, as a youngster, he witnessed an exchange between two older men discussing how they would get some labouring work done. They both agreed they'd send their 'dossers' to do the job.

While some Traveller traders are choosing to operate their businesses in the legitimate world, others have become increasingly criminalized. They have effectively withdrawn further and further from the wider community. The dark fringes of the antiques trade, such as the sale and supply of rhino horns, are the preserve of a small minority of traders. Not everyone has the know-how or the contacts. For the rest, the mainstay of business revolves around home repairs, driveway paving, landscaping and small building jobs. It provides the opportunity to hoodwink householders and force them to pay way over the odds for botched work. A nomadic lifestyle is a distinct advantage, especially when looking for new business and for avoiding irate clients unhappy with substandard work. Yet the Traveller patriarchs and their favoured sons who choose the life of a cowboy builder still need to do a certain amount of hard labour. They have to produce a finished product of sorts that will last long enough until they have been paid and are back on the road. Just as is the practice among the Rathkeale tarmac crews, there are those families who take on labourers from the wider community to do the heavy work.

One such man taken in by a Traveller family was Philip

John Smith, an English drifter and occasional fairground worker. When he was hitchhiking near Kinnegad in County Westmeath in 1998, he was picked up by some members of a Traveller family driving home to a halting site in Athlone forty miles away. He ended up staying for a couple of months, handing over a portion of his welfare cash in return for the use of a tiny caravan on the site. He also did a bit of driving for family members who wanted to enjoy a few pints on a night out. It was a mutually beneficial arrangement.

Smith took off again in October 1998, but returned the following April for a family wedding. He was seen on a video of the wedding dancing with the girls and with his arms around a man celebrating. He didn't drink much, but his personal hygiene left a lot to be desired. He rarely washed or changed his clothes, according to those who spent time in his company. He enjoyed his food, polishing off a can of creamed rice after every meal. Smith seemed to be pretty much the regular 'dosser' that some Travellers kept around to do a little bit of work. He had led a nomadic life, taking casual jobs, and was even homeless for a while. Eventually, members of the Traveller family felt things didn't sit quite right. His habit of making remarks about the Traveller girls rubbed people up the wrong way. 'If they changed their top he'd tell them he preferred the top which showed more cleavage. Fellas just don't make remarks like that to Traveller girls, it's very unusual,' said one of the family. He left the halting site and wasn't heard of again until early 2001.

That was when police officers from the UK came to visit the family to ask questions about Smith. He had been arrested and charged with the murders of three women over ninety-six hours in Birmingham in November 2000. It turned out he was no ordinary dosser, and the uneasiness the family had felt had proved to be the right instinct.

Smith was convicted of the three murders in 2001 and is serving life in prison.

Up until the point where it emerged that Smith was a serial killer, his interaction with the Traveller family was typical for those who take in outsiders in such a way. He was a person living hand to mouth, on the fringes of society, dependent on social welfare, with nowhere to call home. He was just the type of person that wealthy Traveller trader Tommy 'Lyncham' Connors would have approached to offer work. Connors has a kind round face, with a mop of curly red hair, and he can be a real charmer. He grew up at his mother's side as she went door to door selling flowers. By the age of nine he was knocking on doors by himself.

An unemployed and homeless man who had just left a soup kitchen at Charing Cross, London, in 2009 couldn't believe his luck when one day Connors offered him £50 a day to work as a labourer. Not only that, he'd also get a place to stay, with meals thrown in for good measure. Little did the man know at this first meeting that he was about to go to work for one of the most prolific rogue traders the UK had ever seen. Connors, who has claimed to be a horse-dealer, previously featured in *The Outsiders*. That book detailed how he had become the first person subjected to an injunction that not only prevented him carrying out home-repair jobs, but even went as far as banning him from touting for work. If he knocked on a door, he would be in breach of the law.

It was a drastic solution, but Connors had plagued people in the greater London area and in the Home Counties. At a court hearing in March 2007, when he was convicted of making a false statement, his defence lawyer suggested that Connors was being singled out because he was a Traveller and therefore regarded with suspicion:

There are elements of the community that are a pain in the neck, but they are all tarred with the same brush, wrongly. And in some people's eyes there is only one thing worse than a gyppo, and that is a rich gyppo. Tommy Connors is a wealthy man and has been for decades, through inherited money, wise investments and hard work. He has probably not needed to work for many years, but it is in his blood. He does not need to con or bully people out of their money. He and his family would get up early and work from sun-up to sunset.

His lawyer also claimed that Tommy had always insisted on being paid in cash because he couldn't read and feared being ripped off if a cheque was used instead.

The reality is that Connors had left a long trail of botched jobs behind him. He had built gutters that diverted water back into a house, and laid a driveway so high that a householder's garage door couldn't be opened. If anyone didn't like the work and demurred when it came to payment, Connors and his sons would become abusive and aggressive. One householder in South Yorkshire told the court how Connors had turned nasty, telling him: 'We know you have a posh car, a caravan and where your kids go to school. We are going to firebomb your house and get your kids.' Yet there was another, possibly darker side to Connors that had yet to emerge.

Authorities in the UK had become increasingly aware that there existed unscrupulous gangers and foremen, who effectively forced vulnerable people to work for little or nothing. The callous nature of the black-market gang-masters was tragically highlighted in 2004, when twenty-one immigrant Chinese mussel pickers were left to die at Morecambe Bay in the UK. It later emerged that these workers got just £5 per bag collected compared to the £15 profit made by their two bosses. The gang-masters had ignored warnings about the fast-flowing tides and left their workers to die when they became cut off rather than alert the authorities to their plight.

In April 2010, a stand-alone offence was introduced under the Coroners and Justice Act 2009, to criminalize those who hold another person in slavery or servitude or require them to perform forced or compulsory labour. It was a very specific change in the law. Those convicted could face up to fourteen years behind bars, and it also allowed the Crown Prosecution Service to confiscate the slavers' money and assets. Very quickly, a number of cases were brought to court, many by the London Metropolitan Police's Anti-Trafficking Unit. Detective Inspector Kevin Hyland from the unit explained how the change in the law gave the police a legal framework within which they could go after the modern-day slavers:

> I wouldn't say there's been an increase [in trafficking], but what I would say is that everyone has got better at spotting it and identifying it. That's both the UK and internationally, because there's a lot of emphasis on it now from the EU and from Europol and Eurojust. If you are not looking at it you won't find it.

There were clear indications that Irish Traveller traders had become involved in using vulnerable men as unpaid labourers. A Swedish report into human trafficking, published in 2010, found twenty-six incidents of non-sexual trafficking. It stated: 'In particular, these concern British and Irish tarmac and paving layers in Sweden. The victims do not usually report personally that they have been the subject of human trafficking because they often have no confidence in the authorities that administer justice and are afraid of acts of reprisal.' During 2012, two scandalous court cases served to highlight just how far some of the rogue Traveller traders were willing to go in the pursuit of profit at the expense of others.

Among the first targets of the new law in the UK were Tommy 'Lyncham' Connors and his sons. They were living at Leighton Buzzard, Bedfordshire, just north-west of London. They had a parcel of land at Greenacres caravan park on which they had constructed neat yards complete with chalets. These perched on cobble-locked driveways surrounded by walls topped with ironwork. They had high-end cars and the site was kept immaculately clean, thanks to the hard work of the men they had hired to do the labouring. Tommy's chalet had a jukebox, and crystal-ware worth thousands was on display. From there, Tommy and his family ran their business across England, using their men to push leaflets through letter boxes and knocking on doors to drum up business.

On a Sunday morning, 11 September 2011, the police went back into Greenacres. This time they weren't after the Connorses' cash from botched jobs, they wanted to rescue their workforce. They found twenty-four men, some of whom, it was discovered, were suffering from malnutrition. One even had scurvy, a condition caused by having a poor diet that lacks any vitamin C. Some were also found to have untreated injuries and bone fractures.

The raid was the culmination of Operation Netwing, which had begun four months earlier when officers had put Greenacres and the Connors family under surveil-lance. They chose Sunday morning to launch the raid be-cause it was the only day of the week when the work crews weren't out on the road.

There was a huge media reaction to the story, in which people were reminded that it had been two hundred years since slavery had been abolished in the UK. Initially, four men and a woman were arrested by the police, although Tommy 'Lyncham' Connors was not among them. It quickly emerged that previous allegations had been made to the police by men who had left the site controlled by the Connors family. The change in the law had made the prosecution possible. Detective Chief Inspector Sean O'Neil, from the Bedfordshire and Hertfordshire Major Crimes Unit, said in an interview:

> The new legislation has allowed the investigation more scope, and takes into account emotional rather than physical harm. I am confident that while the investigation is in its early stages this is a family-run 'business' and is an organized crime group that has been broken up by the Netwing operation.

But the Connors clan weren't going to go down without a fight. One of the Traveller women blamed the raids on anti-Traveller prejudice and told reporters:

> The men who were taken were getting paid thirty pounds a day, they had somewhere to live, this is all a load of nonsense. Isn't it better that they have a roof over their head? What are they going to do now – when the police have finished with them they will be homeless? It's up to them how they kept their homes, but they could come and go whenever they pleased. It's complete lies and they are trying to make Travellers look bad. There are two sides to this story.

Within a few days it looked as if the woman had a point. Nine of the men who had been rescued said they didn't want any help from the authorities. One of them went even further, accusing the police of acting in a heavy-handed manner by raiding the Greenacres site.

David Radcliff was homeless during the mid-1990s and living on the streets when he met the Connors family, who he said offered him a job and accommodation. As far as he was concerned the police raid was unjustified and the officers had thrown him out of his home. He denied the allegations that he and the other men were unpaid slaves:

> Of course I got paid. When I tried to get back, two policewomen came up and said they would do me for breaking and entering for going into my own home. I said, 'How can I break into my own home?' They promised me a house or a flat, that they would get me a job. The police say I don't know best. I told them I know what's in my own best interests and want to stay with my family.

The 57-year-old denied that he suffered from 'Stockholm syndrome' or that he was institutionalized after spending so long under the influence of the Connors family.

By February, Tommy 'Lyncham' Connors had been charged with various counts of slavery and assault. Also charged were four of his sons: James, Tommy junior, Patrick and Johnny. His daughter Josie and her husband Big Jim Connors were also to face trial on similar charges. His wife Mary said that her husband would be proven innocent and that he was the victim of vindictive police, claiming that Greenacres had been raided twenty times. She also claimed that the authorities had given incentives to the men found on the site to testify. 'It's all a set-up. It's not fair. They took the children's savings boxes in the raid.' Mary said that her husband was only arrested because he was acquitted for running a tarmac racket just before the raid. 'It was only three days after the acquittal that he got arrested again,' she said in a *Sunday World* interview.

When the trial began in April 2012, the prosecution opened the case by entering into the record a number of statements from men who had worked for the Connorses. The stories outlined how Tommy 'Lyncham' Connors and

his son-in-law Big Jim operated their business. They recruited homeless men from all over the UK, luring them
to Greenacres with promises of work, food, accommodation and cash. But on arrival at the site new recruits went
through a process that effectively imposed the family's
control. Their heads were shaved, the supply of food was
limited and the workers were woken up in the early hours
of the morning and kept labouring until late at night. They
were too busy or too tired to contemplate walking out. The
threat of physical violence and verbal assault always hung
over the men. There were rumours, which were unfounded,
that one slave had been murdered and his remains buried
in a nearby field. For men who were already vulnerable,
suffering from chronic addiction, mental problems or
homelessness, there was no easy way out.

A number of the former workers were called to give
their testimony of life with the Connors clan. There were
sorry tales of humiliation, hard work, starvation and the
ever-present threat of physical violence. One man recalled
having his head shaved when he arrived at the site and
seeing other arrivals being treated in the same manner. A
Scottish man explained how he had met members of the
Connors family in Newcastle, where he had been living
on the streets at the time. He was also told to refer to
James Connors and his wife Krystal as 'Dad' and 'Mum'.
Although promised £50 a day, he was never paid.

Another man, who was in his late twenties, was picked
up by the Connors clan in north London in March 2009.
At the time the men were housed in a small caravan and
a horsebox which had been converted to sleep twelve
people. 'The caravan was a little dirty, scruffy. It was
liveable in, but small and very cramped. The horsebox
was not fit to live in. Everyone was always on top of each
other. It was difficult to keep the horsebox clean,' said the
man in his evidence. He recalled how his head had been

shaved and that his personal documents were burned when he first arrived at the site. The Travellers regularly referred to him as 'a good-for-nothing jackass' when he didn't perform to their standards. He was eventually able to leave when a probation officer gave him the train fare to Brighton.

Violence at the hands of the Connorses was a feature of life at the Leighton Buzzard site. A 54-year-old man went to work for them on a promise of £30 after being approached in a London park. Immediately on arrival his hair was cut and he was shaved. He was shown the horsebox and then the next morning at 5.30 a.m. began work. It was heavy labour and they were driven all over the UK to carry out jobs. He never saw any money and described his wages as being second-hand clothes, biscuits and crisps. He described how the workers could be randomly attacked by members of the Connors family. The worst incident he recalled was when a man from Liverpool was kicked in the head as he lay on the ground. Doing the heavy manual work left him exhausted and physically unable to escape. The workforce were left powerless in the face of the relentless workload and the close control over their day-to-day lives exerted by the Connors clan.

Big Jim Connors took to the stand to give a different version of events to the ones given by former slave-workers. He maintained that the workers had been free to leave if they had wanted to. Even after the damning testimony given in court, Big Jim showed no sign of any remorse and stuck to his denials. For Tommy Connors senior, the use of unpaid labourers he could bully and cajole into doing the hard work was part and parcel of life. When he took to the witness box in his own defence he said that it was an aspect of the Irish Traveller lifestyle that casual workers would come and go from their halting site. 'Some would leave and come back again and some would stay for longer, some for years. They were paid. If they wanted to leave we would let them leave. There was no need to force them to work,' he said under oath. Asked if he had exploited his workers he replied: 'No, not at any time.'

The jury also heard how Connors was born in Belfast to a seven-generation Traveller family, the youngest of nineteen children. He had never been to school and had never learned to read or write. His family travelled all around the country in a horse-drawn carriage and for many years he did tarmac driveways, before block paving came along. In recent years that type of work had become too hard for him and he mainly collected and sold scrap metal, bred horses and traded goods to make a living. He had to admit, however, that he had a number of convictions, including one for making false statements and another for false imprisonment in 1999. Like his son-in-law, Tommy flatly rejected any wrongdoing.

The jury heard the closing arguments from both sides and then a final statement from Judge Michael Kay. He warned that any prejudice towards Travellers should play no part in their deliberations. It proved to be a difficult case for the jury who were out for thirty-eight hours. Johnny Connors was acquitted of all charges, but they failed to reach verdicts on the charges against Tommy junior and James Connors. Big Jim and his wife Josie were convicted of two charges of forcing men to work, while he was also convicted on one charge of assault. Tommy Connors senior was found guilty on three charges, including one for assault and another for forcing men into servitude. His son Patrick was similarly convicted on three charges.

The reaction in the courtroom suggested that the Connors family had yet to comprehend how their actions could be interpreted as being criminal. Josie sobbed in the dock as the verdicts were read out, and embraced her husband as other members of the family began to weep in the public gallery. The next day Big Jim and Josie were brought back to Luton Crown Court to be sentenced for their crimes. Judge Kay said they had 'brutally manipulated and exploited' the slave-workers for financial gain. It was a deep shock to the family when Big Jim was sentenced to eleven years in jail and Josie was given four. Because the jury had been unable to reach a verdict on some charges Tommy senior and his sons Tommy, Patrick and James had to have a retrial and go through the process all over again.

It was another marathon court battle in early 2013 when Tommy and three of his sons were again before a jury. They all pleaded not guilty to three charges of conspiring to hold a person in servitude and three charges of conspiring to force a person to work. Many of the same witness statements were aired again in court while Tommy senior took to the stand to defend himself. There was another long session of deliberations by the jury during which they failed to reach a verdict and the trial collapsed. This time the Crown Prosecution Service said they would not be seeking a retrial. It meant Tommy junior and his brother James were free to go. For Tommy senior, however, and Patrick, who was twenty-one years old, it meant they could be sentenced on the three charges each had been convicted of after the first trial.

Passing sentence, Judge Kay said Tommy senior had targeted men who were homeless, addicted or isolated. 'It was a monstrous and callous deceit,' he said. The judge handed down an eight-year sentence to the Traveller patriarch. Patrick got five years in jail. Immediately after the hearing the Chief Crown Prosecutor in the case, Baljit Ubhey OBE, said that the convicted members of the Connors family were motivated by greed to mistreat their workers:

They failed to pay them for their work and took advantage
of their vulnerability and inability to protest in doing so.
The offences were financially motivated, allowing these
Connors family members to live in relative luxury while
many of their victims were provided with the most basic
and cramped living standards possible.

He added that they would also be chasing the money
made by the Connors clan on the backs of their slaves:
'The prosecution team have restrained in the region of
£1 million from these members of the Connors family and
identified a further £2 million of assets, and the court will
now consider questions of compensation and confiscation
arising from these convictions.'

The damage Lyncham has done to his own community
is huge. Connors used the traditions of the Traveller
community to hide his nasty criminality. He attempted to
portray the practice of forcing vulnerable men to work as
a charitable act, as if he was saving them from themselves
and life on the streets. By inviting the men to live with his
family he claimed he was giving them something valuable
that was missing from their lives. The truth, as the jury
found, was that he was a boorish bully, obsessed with
making money and possessed of a sadistic streak when
it came to his dealings with his enslaved workforce. The
fact that his story came out at a time when the Travellers
in Dale Farm were facing a forced eviction didn't help
further the argument that Irish Travellers were the victims
of a hostile society.

During 2011 it was to emerge that Lyncham and his family
were not the only members of the Traveller community
to engage in the practice of exploiting otherwise homeless
men as labourers. An Irish Traveller with the same
surname, Billy Connors, had also done well for himself in

Britain. Unlike his distant cousin, Billy hadn't developed a reputation as a complete cowboy when it came to paving work. The Connors family made their money by travelling across the country offering block paving and tarmacking services using a string of different company names such as Pro Groundworks Drives & Patios, Designer Drives & Patios, Oxfordshire Drives & Patios, Sofisicated (*sic*) Drives and Quality Driveways. To give the impression of a professional operation, they had glossy leaflets printed, which always had a landline phone number for customers to call.

As a police investigation would later uncover, the business had been rewarding for Billy and his family. They bought the Willows and the Beggars Roost sites on Bamfurlong Lane, and Willowdene in Staverton near Cheltenham for £375,000 and £170,000. They later snapped up adjacent plots of land when they came on the market, spending another £137,000. They owned a house nearby called 'Hayden Laurels', bought in July 2007 for £390,000. Billy's oldest son John Connors was the registered joint-owner of a house in nearby Uckington. Bought in March 2004 for £208,000, 'Ikiru' was fitted out with a hot tub and large flat-screen TV. There was another site in Leicestershire, a house called 'Twelve Oaks', as well as a house in Middlesex. The family's property portfolio was worth well in excess of a million pounds.

Billy's wife Mary, usually called Breda, helped handle the cash, while their youngest son James and their son-in-law Miles Connors were also involved in the paving and tarmacking work. Billy liked to dress well, as did Mary, and they also enjoyed plenty of foreign holidays, including an expensive trip to Dubai and a ten-day cruise around the Caribbean on the Cunard flagship liner *Queen Mary 2*. They also took breaks to Tenerife and Cancun in Mexico. Another indulgence of the Connors clan was their choice of cars, which included an A-Class Mercedes saloon, a Rolls-Royce, a red Mini convertible, a Toyota Hilux pickup, a Ford Ranger and a Mercedes van.

The Connors family were likely to have escaped the close attention of the police if it had not been for the discovery of a decomposed body in a garden shed at Beggars Roost in May 2008. Christopher Nicholls had been working for the family after a period of homelessness following the breakdown of his marriage. In October 2004 he had suffered serious head injuries after being hit by a car outside the halting site where he lived with the Connorses. As a result of his injuries and brain damage he was no longer able to do labouring work or even to knock on doors in search of new business. His skeletal remains were found under a tarpaulin in the shed.

Police believe he may have died during the winter of 2005, but it was impossible to determine the cause of his death – or even whether he had passed away in the shed or his body had been moved after he had died somewhere else. Either way, it was a shocking indictment of how little the Connors clan cared when it came to the most basic welfare of the men they had hired to carry out hard labour. Relatives of Nicholls later said that members of the Connors family had tried to get Christopher to seek compensation for the accident through a solicitor. They also expressed their concern that the exact circumstances surrounding the accident were never established.

The following year, a former worker went to the police with a story of how he had been lured to the site by promises of work and accommodation after being approached on the streets of Cheltenham. He said that on arrival his personal documents had been burned, that he had lived in a shed and rarely been fed or paid. He also claimed that workers who managed to leave were later rounded up by Billy Connors – who was familiar with their haunts – and brought back to Beggars Roost. When contacted by the police Billy Connors was adamant that the men were free to leave whenever they wanted and that his family were acting as good Samaritans in providing the men with food, work and a roof over their heads. But the introduction of the Coroners and Justice Act in April 2010 finally made it possible for the police to put Billy and his family under closer scrutiny.

In August 2010 the Gloucestershire Police set up hidden surveillance cameras in Willowdene to keep a watch on the Connors clan and the goings-on at the sites. By March 2011 they had more than enough grounds for suspicion and launched a series of dawn raids at the various properties occupied by the family. They found a workforce of twenty men living in squalid conditions at Beggars Roost. A grim picture of life with the Connorses soon emerged, in which men worked eighty hours a week of hard monotonous labour for no pay and little food. Some were ordered to carry out humiliating tasks such as emptying out buckets used by members of the Connors family as toilets.

At the time, the police raids passed off almost unnoticed by the media compared to the high-profile operation when it came to Tommy Connors and his family at Leighton Buzzard six months later. Five members of Billy Connors's family were eventually brought to trial, charged with conspiracy to hold a person in servitude and conspiracy to force a person to carry out labour. Those charged were Billy and his wife Mary, their sons John and James and their son-in-law Miles Connors. The case against them followed a similar narrative to what had happened at Leighton Buzzard. The slave-workers were deceived with promises of work and pay after being approached on the street. They had lived with the constant threat of physical violence, and sometimes been singled out for deliberate acts of humiliation designed to strengthen the Connorses' control over them. The Connors clan also doled out enough alcohol among the men to keep them from suffering withdrawal, but not so much that they wouldn't be able to work the next day.

The men were effectively used as a labour pool from which any family member could draw workers when a job needed to be done. The Connorses also collected the men's social welfare allowances, pocketing £96,000 over six years. The defence team for the Connorses argued that it was no coincidence that it was men who were already hard up who were prepared to give the Traveller lifestyle a go with all its hardships. The offer of work and accommodation, it was argued, was a shot at a second chance that no one else was prepared to give such men. It was claimed that the Connors family shared the same privations, including washing with a cold-water hose; and that their workers were annoyed by the police intervention and that one even cried at the prospect of losing his home. One former worker had said in their defence that the Connorses had effectively rescued him from being homeless and living on the streets.

After a trial that stretched over twelve weeks, the jury returned verdicts of guilty against the charges of conspiring to force people to carry out labour. Even though they weren't called to give evidence, the sense of injustice among the Connors family was apparent. Chaos broke out in the courtroom as the verdicts were delivered. Billy was the only one not to burst into tears, while his wife Mary pulled at her hair and screamed as the first verdict was read out: 'Oh, Daddy! Oh, Daddy! Mind the children, why are you doing this? I have never done anything to anyone in my whole life.' The half-dozen security guards needed the help of police witnesses to clear the public gallery, and other family members jumped to their feet. The wives of John and Miles Connors were physically carried from the court. Even as a jury found the Connors family guilty of forcing men to do hard labour the reaction was one of self-pitying despair.

There was another outpouring of emotion the following week, when the five were sentenced. As the head of the family Billy was sentenced to six and a half years while Mary was given twenty-seven months. Having already served over a year in prison while on remand, she was due for release not long afterwards. The Traveller boss kept his cool again, blowing kisses to relatives in the public gallery while Mary sobbed. John, then aged twenty-nine, got four years, while twenty-year-old James was sentenced to three years in a young offenders' institution. Miles also got three years behind bars. The Crown Prosecution Service decided to appeal the sentences on the grounds that they had been too lenient, considering that the new legislation allowed for jail terms up to fourteen years. The Appeal Court judges in March 2013 upheld the sentences, saying that though they were lenient the accused did not need to be given additional time.

During those years of recruiting and exploiting the vulnerable men who had made up his workforce Billy Connors hadn't thought that he was doing anything wrong. His defence lawyer told the judge in mitigation that Billy's 'naïve justification' was that if the men had been paid any more cash they would have bought alcohol and been unable to work. 'He has learnt a bitter, bitter lesson,' said the counsel. Likewise Tommy 'Lyncham' Connors and his sons and son-in-law saw using such workers as a normal part of life. If anything, in their view, the men were being saved, because they were incapable of looking after themselves and wider society no longer had an interest in them.

A third case involved two Travellers with the same surname, Connors, and came to court in January 2013.

This time a William Connors and his brother-in-law John Connors, both from Bulwell, near Nottingham, on the eve of a retrial, pleaded guilty to exploiting two homeless men over a five-month period. These men had been made to work for up to eighty hours a week, suffered the humiliation of having their heads shaved, and had been left to live in squalor compared to the luxury of the bosses' trailers. John Connors, who was described as the boss and used violence on occasion, was jailed for forty months, while William got thirty. The judge in this case also dismissed the argument that the Travellers had in fact been reaching out to help vulnerable men.

In less than seven months eleven members of the Traveller community had been jailed. Not only that, but the police were chasing their assets, and their flimsy arguments in defence had been swept aside. The clear message had gone out that so-called 'dosser farming' was no longer to be the lucrative enterprise it had once been.

Judging by the reaction in court from the families of the defendants convicted of slavery, there is little indication that any lesson had been learned by those engaged in hiring vulnerable men as workers. Perhaps, it could be argued, Tommy and Billy Connors, who were themselves victims of oppressive prejudice, were acting out their frustrations against a society that denied them an equal opportunity because of their background as Irish Travellers. As heads of their respective families, they bore greater responsibility than others. They clearly had the resources, as shown by the evidence of their assets in court, to have chosen a legitimate business model long before the police had shown an interest in their activities. They had made the hard, callous choice to operate as criminals, heads of their own organizations carefully tailored to make money. In the end, they were made to pay the price of that decision.

Epilogue

In the modern era of social media and instant communication, Irish Travellers are becoming more and more visible for both the right and wrong reasons. After the success of *Big Fat Gypsy Weddings* and Paddy Doherty's deserved victory on *Celebrity Big Brother* in 2010, Irish Travellers had been largely cast in a positive light. Whatever warm glow of affection there had been, it was steadily eroded during 2011 and 2012 thanks to the slavery cases and the sadistic cruelty meted out to the captive workforces. The debacle at Dale Farm, where wealthy Traveller traders had tried to hide behind the facade of being poor Gypsies, also added to the negative perception of a community hitherto unknown and even mysterious to most people in the UK.

Professional and amateur boxers have shown that being a Traveller is not an obstacle to success. The stories of Tyson Fury and Michael Armstrong, who battled through shocking personal tragedy to reach the top level of professional boxing, should be an inspiration to anyone. Willie 'Big Bang' Casey also defied the odds to compete with the best, while friends and relatives around him died. Francis Barrett provided the inspiration for his own people with his remarkable journey, which saw him become the first Irish Traveller to compete at the Olympic Games. While bare-knuckle boxers have sometimes added to the poor perception of Travellers, they have also helped to produce a growing cohort of boxers who are taking their place in the world of licensed fights. Boxing is one area where Travellers have shown they can integrate with the wider community and vice versa. Travellers have made a huge contribution to the sport, especially in Ireland, where the nation's best hopes of Olympic glory rest with the boxing team. John Joe Nevin is a household name, and Joe Ward will be too, very soon.

There is a wellspring of goodwill towards Travellers that exists in the wider community. The boxers are not the only people who have their fans, as Paddy Doherty demonstrated with *Celebrity Big Brother*. Shayne Ward in the UK won *The X Factor* in 2005, while in Ireland singer Kelly Mongan was the runner-up in the 2013 season of *The Voice of Ireland*.

The problem seems to be that there are too few positive role models who can show a way forward. Irish Travellers are a young community. As mentioned in the introduction to this book, more than half are aged just twenty or younger, a much higher proportion than in the wider community. Unfortunately, it is the likes of Tommy 'Lyncham' Connors in the UK or Christy 'Ditsy' Nevin in Ireland who have guided far too many young Travellers down the wrong path.

While only a minority have been engaged in active acts of feud violence, the tight-knit nature of the community means such violence has far deeper effects than it would in wider society. The likes of the Connors family, found guilty of slavery, or the tarmac gangs operating around the developed world, have enough resources and the ability to become legitimate traders. Many individuals are worth considerable sums of money, some well into the millions. Yet still, they chose to operate in the underworld, when they could have opted for a legitimate way of earning money and still maintained their Traveller identity.

The activities of the gang behind the theft of rhino horns from all over Europe has added to the perception of Irish Travellers as being enmeshed with organized crime. For many people in those countries, the first time they had heard of Irish Travellers was in connection with the criminal racket. Organized crime gangs based in ethnic minorities is a pattern repeated all over the world. Like a nascent Cosa Nostra, Irish Traveller gangsters are exploiting lucrative niches in the criminal underworld. While they are not the only ones doing such things, there can be few other social groups or ethnicities where such a high proportion of the population, even though a minority, are so actively involved in illicit practices.

Irish Travellers have been moving out from Ireland for decades. In an increasingly globalized world, where travel and communication is far more efficient, they are putting their skills to use all over the globe. As a result, police and enforcement agencies are becoming increasingly aware of the Irish Travellers who engage in illegal activity. In 2010, a detective in Germany delivered a paper to his colleagues on the activities of the '*teerkolonne*' who ripped off householders with botched tarmacadam jobs. In 2011, the Fair Trading commission in New South Wales set up a unit specifically to target Travellers carrying out home-repair scams in Australia. Europol, in their 2012 annual report, identified the Rathkeale Travellers involved in rhino-horn thefts and money laundering as one of Europe's 1,300 organized crime gangs. For a community with the population of a medium-sized town in Ireland or the UK, that is a very heavy cross to bear.

In the seven years since *The Outsiders: Exposing the Secretive World of Ireland's Travellers* was published, Irish Travellers have come to greater notice, thanks to the various TV shows and documentaries. More people from the wider community have become curious about Travellers, to whom so little attention was previously paid. The criminal gangs within the community have also been put under the spotlight. But even the negative publicity has had the advantage of highlighting how Irish Travellers are not a homogenous group, but a collection of families and individuals. Their elite boxers have continued to blaze the trail that Francis Barrett first began, bringing Irish Travellers to public attention for their feats as athletes. No doubt they will continue to do so. The question remains as to what way the various other elements of the Traveller community will go: whether more traders will opt for a legitimate way of life and whether feuding clans can leave the past alone. One way or another, whatever the future brings, it won't be dull.

Photo Acknowledgements

Page 1: Michael Faulkner photo © Dominic Walsh; Charlie McDonagh photo courtesy of the *Sunday World*; funeral procession © Liam O'Connor/*Sunday World*.

Pages 2–3: Ann Quilligan and her niece Joan photo © author/*Sunday World*; Julia Mongan © Conor McCaughley/*Sunday World;* Mongan brothers photo © Conor McCaughley/*Sunday World;* Smithfield Market photo © 2011 Barbara Lindberg; Wesley McDonagh photo © 2011 Barbara Lindberg; Dalton Park riot photo © Press Association; Christopher 'Ditsy' Nevin photo © Press Association.

Pages 4–5: Ainey McGinley and Dan Rooney, photo © Tom Conachy; Dan Rooney, the preacher, video grab courtesy of Life and Light Church; Barney 'The Gorilla' McGinley, photo © Conor McCaughley/*Sunday World*; Paddy 'Jaws' Ward fighting Barney 'The Gorilla' McGinley, video grab from YouTube; Big Joe Joyce, photo © Liam O'Connor/*Sunday World*.

Pages 6–7: James Quinn McDonagh, photo © Conor McCaughley/*Sunday World;* Tyson Fury with Paddy Doherty, photo © Colm Lenaghan/Pacemaker Press; Willie 'Big Bang' Casey with Guillermo Rigondeaux, photo © INPHO/Donall

Farmer; Rathkeale traders in Sydney, photo © New South Wales Fair Trading; generators being crushed, photo © New South Wales Fair Trading; tarmackers' work in Bergamo, photo © Liam O'Connor/*Sunday World*.

Page 8: Rhino horn, photo courtesy of *Sunday World;* Tommy Connors, photo © South Beds News Agency; high-rollers in Rathkeale, photo © Ernie Leslie/*Sunday World*.

Acknowledgements

Behind every book is a looming deadline and for their assistance in dealing with that I have to thank Ann-Marie, Robert and Jennifer as well as Mick and Mary.

There are many others who I can't thank in public, including members of the Travelling community who have given their time and patience to help me put *Gypsy Empire* together.

My colleagues at the *Sunday World* again have proven to be great sources of support and inspiration. Particular thanks go to editor Colm MacGinty who sent me down this road many years ago and to news editor John Donlon who has always been an encouraging influence both to me personally and to the reporters in the *Sunday World* newsroom.

I also want to thank Paula Mackin in the *Sunday World*'s Belfast office, Sean McGoldrick in our sports department and Donal MacIntyre whose interviews I have used in sections of the book.

Photographer Liam O'Connor was a solid colleague on many assignments, some of which were in difficult conditions, and I wish him all the best in his well-deserved retirement. Thanks are also due to Ernie Lesley and Conor McCaughley who remain on active service behind the lens.

I also would like to thank my crime desk colleagues Niamh O'Connor, Alan Sherry, Mick McCaffrey, Nicola Tallant and Niall Donald for their ebullient company and support and who will carefully analyse the order in which their names have appeared. Thanks also to managing editor Neil Leslie, whose enthusiasm and professionalism when it comes to letting journalists chase stories makes the *Sunday World* an easy place to work. Thanks are also due to Managing Director Gerry Lennon whose stewardship of the *Sunday World* means it will be around for years and years to come.

Other journalistic colleagues who cover court hearings all over Ireland deserve thanks for their work which I have relied on in sections of this book: Claire O'Brien in Tullamore, Barry Roche in Cork, Ciaran Murphy in Waterford, Ann Healy in Galway, Paul Deering in Sligo, Diarmuid McDermott at Ireland International, Jon Austin at the *Basildon Echo* and the people at South Beds News Agency in Luton. Thanks also to Teresa Mullan in the New South Wales Office of Fair Trading for her help.

I would also like to express my gratitude to the people at Transworld Ireland, including Eoin McHugh, Brian Langan and Lisa Horton as well as copy-editor Lucy Pinney for their patience and professionalism.

Eamon Dillon is a prize-winning journalist with the *Sunday World* newspaper in Dublin where he is Assistant Editor (Crime and Security). His first book, *The Outsiders: Exposing the Secretive World of Ireland's Travellers*, was a best-seller in Ireland and established him as an authority on Traveller-related issues. His second book was *The Fraudsters: How Con Artists Steal Your Money*. He has been a guest speaker at the Toronto Fraud Police annual conference as well as at Google HQ in Dublin on the topic of fraud and social engineering. In 2009 he received the Ruhama Award in Journalism for his investigative piece into the organized sex-trade in Ireland. Follow him on Twitter: @EamoD